Progress and Identity in the Plays of W. B. Yeats, 1892–1907

Major Literary Authors
Volume 25

Studies in Major Literary Authors

Outstanding Dissertations
Volume 25

Edited by
William Cain
Professor of English
Wellesley College

A Routledge Series

STUDIES IN MAJOR LITERARY AUTHORS
WILLIAM E. CAIN, *General Editor*

HENRY JAMES AS A BIOGRAPHER
A Self among Others
Cathy Moses

JOYCEAN FRAMES
Film and the Fiction of James Joyce
Thomas Burkdall

JOSEPH CONRAD AND THE ART OF SACRIFICE
The Evolution of the Scapegoat Theme in Joseph Conrad's Fiction
Andrew Mozina

TECHNIQUE AND SENSIBILITY IN THE FICTION AND POETRY OF RAYMOND CARVER
Arthur F. Bethea

SHELLEY'S TEXTUAL SEDUCTIONS
Plotting Utopia in the Erotic and Political Works
Samuel Lyndon Gladden

"ALL THE WORLD'S A STAGE"
Dramatic Sensibility in Mary Shelley's Novels
Charlene E. Bunnell

"THOUGHTS PAINFULLY INTENSE"
Hawthorne and the Invalid Author
James N. Mancall

SEX THEORIES AND THE SHAPING OF TWO MODERNS
Hemingway and H. D.
Deirdre Anne (McVicker) Pettipiece

WORD SIGHTINGS
Visual Apparatus and Verbal Reality in Stevens, Bishop and O'Hara
Sarah Riggs

DELICATE PURSUIT
Discretion in Henry James and Edith Wharton
Jessica Levine

GERTRUDE STEIN AND WALLACE STEVENS
The Performance of Modern Consciousness
Sara J. Ford

LOST CITY
Fitzgerald's New York
Lauraleigh O'Meara

SOCIAL DREAMING
Dickens and the Fairy Tale
Elaine Ostry

PATRIARCHY AND ITS DISCONTENTS
Sexual Politics in Selected Novels and Stories of Thomas Hardy
Joanna Devereux

A NEW MATRIX FOR MODERNISM
A Study of the Lives and Poetry of Charlotte Mew and Anna Wickham
Nelljean McConeghey Rice

WHO READS *ULYSSES*?
The Rhetoric of the Joyce Wars and the Common Reader
Julie Sloan Brannon

NAKED LIBERTY AND THE WORLD OF DESIRE
Elements of Anarchism in the Work of D. H. Lawrence
Simon Casey

THE MACHINE THAT SINGS
Modernism, Hart Crane, and the Culture of the Body
Gordon Tapper

T. S. ELIOT'S CIVILIZED SAVAGE
Religious Eroticism and Poetics
Laurie J. MacDiarmid

THE CARVER CHRONOTOPE
Inside the Life-World of Raymond Carver's Fiction
G. P. Lainsbury

THIS COMPOSITE VOICE
The Role of W. B. Yeats in James Merrill's Poetry
Mark Bauer

Progress and Identity in the Plays of W. B. Yeats, 1892–1907

Barbara A. Suess

Routledge
New York & London

Published in 2003 by
Routledge
29 West 35th Street
New York, NY 10001
www.routledge-ny.com

Published in Great Britain by
Routledge
11 New Fetter Lane
London EC4P 4EE
www.routledge.co.uk

Routledge is an imprint of the Taylor & Francis Group
Printed in the United States of America on acid-free paper.

Copyright © 2003 by Taylor & Francis Books, Inc.

All rights reserved. No part of this book may be reprinted or reproduced or utilized in any form or by any electronic, mechanical, or other means, now known or hereafter invented, including photocopying and recording, or in any information storage or retrieval system, without permission in writing from the publisher.

10 9 8 7 6 5 4 3 2 1

Library of Congress Cataloging-in-Publication Data
Suess, Barbara Ann.
   Progress and identity in the plays of W. B. Yeats, 1892–1907 / by Barbara A. Suess.
     p. cm. — (Studies in major literary authors ; v. 25)
   Includes bibliographical references and index
   ISBN 0-415-96654-X (alk. paper)
   1. Yeats, W. B. (William Butler), 1865–1939—Dramatic works. 2. Verse drama, English—History and criticism. 3. Identity (Psychology) in literature. 4. Progress in literature. I. Title: Progress and identity in the plays of W. B. Yeats, 1892–1907. II. Title III. Series.
PR5908.D7S84 2003
822'.8—dc21   2003003929

For my parents, with thanks

Contents

Acknowledgments	xi
Abbreviations	xiii
Introduction	xv

Chapter One
"[F]ull of personified averages": Progress in the Victorian and
Edwardian Eras   3

Chapter Two
Literatures of Progress   29

Chapter Three
Progress as Material Gain: The Bourgeois Peasant as Invented Tradition
in *The Countess Cathleen, Cathleen ni Houlihan,* and *The Land of
Heart's Desire*   57

Chapter Four
Recovering the Feminized Other: Psychological Androgyny in *The King's
Threshold, On Baile's Strand,* and *Deirdre*   91

Chapter Five
"[N]ice little playwrights, making pretty little plays": Yeats, Irish Identity,
and the Critical Response   129

NOTES	157
BIBLIOGRAPHY	173
INDEX	187

Acknowledgments

This book would not have been possible without the support of my dissertation director, Lee Jacobus, and my associate advisors, Brenda Murphy and Regina Barreca. I thank them for their intellectual and practical insights and their continued support. Formal and informal discussions at Yeats International Summer School (1999) enhanced my understanding of Yeats's life and his works, particularly in my courses with Declan Kiberd and Lyn Innes. Conversations with many friends and colleagues similarly helped enrich the ideas that went into this study, but Patrick Colm Hogan, Rachael Lynch, James Rogers, Thomas Dillon Redshaw, Scott Boltwood, Ellen O'Brien, Kristine Byron, and Tom Shea deserve particular recognition for their insightful commentary on my work. A special debt of gratitude goes to Marjorie Howes for her continuing guidance and encouragement.

Grateful acknowledgment is made to Michael Yeats for permission to reprint excerpts from manuscript material held at the National Library of Ireland, namely typescripts of *Deirdre*, a letter from Yeats to George Russell, and Yeats's Notebooks.

For this and for the use of the Abbey Theatre Papers and Cuttings I also thank the Council of Trustees and the staff of the National Library of Ireland. I would also like to acknowledge the Irish Theatre Archives and the Pearse Street Library for their kind attention to my inquiries.

Finally, I am grateful to my family for their support, especially Ernest and Isabelle Adamo, who endured many absences so that I could complete this book.

Abbreviations

AV	*A Vision.* New York: Macmillan, 1937.
CLI	*The Collected Letters of W. B. Yeats, Vol. I, 1865-1895.* Ed. John Kelly and Eric Domville. Oxford: Clarendon Press, 1986.
CLIII	*The Collected Letters of W. B. Yeats, Vol. III, 1901-1904.* Ed. John Kelly and Ronald Schuchard. Oxford: Clarendon Press, 1994.
CP	*The Collected Poems of W. B. Yeats.* New Ed. Ed. Richard J. Finneran. New York: Collier, 1989.
EI	*Essays and Introductions.* New York: Macmillan, 1961.
L	*The Letters of W. B. Yeats.* Ed. Allen Wade. New York: Macmillan, 1955.
UPI	*Uncollected Prose I: First Reviews and Articles, 1886-1896.* Coll. and Ed. John P. Frayne. New York: Columbia UP, 1970.
UPII	*Uncollected Prose II: Reviews, Articles, and Other Miscellaneous Prose 1897-1939.* Coll. and Ed. John P. Frayne and Colton Johnson. New York: Columbia UP, 1976.
VP	*Variorum Edition of the Plays of W. B. Yeats.* Ed. Russell K. Alspach. New York: Macmillan, 1966.

Introduction

*P*ROGRESS AND IDENTITY IN THE PLAYS OF W. B. YEATS, *1892–1907* TAKES as its point of departure the cultural milieu in which Victorian bourgeois and colonial definitions of class, gender, ethnicity, and subsequently Irish identity were cultivated. Examining Yeats's plays written and produced in the 1890s and early 1900s within the framework of modern dramatic history, I trace Yeats's evolution from a writer of popular nationalist drama to a writer of esoteric verse drama and read his plays against the standard line of criticism that denies his career a social agenda. When studied in a cultural and historical context, Yeats's plays become dramatizations of a crisis of social as well as individual identity. With characters continually struggling against narrowly defined definitions of success, Yeats's plays enact his struggle to redefine "self" and "other" in a colonial or, more appropriately, anti-colonial context.[1]

As my title indicates, progress and identity comprise the key components of this study. I am particularly concerned with progress as defined in its post-Enlightenment form, that is, as authorized by scientific and rationalist philosophies and as advancing a teleological vision of the world that, significantly, is rooted firmly in materialism. In its most basic definition as a set of behavioral characteristics by which an individual is recognized as a member of a group, the Victorian conception of identity cannot be understood separately from the notion of progress, the basis of which was the maintenance of the group identifications of class, gender, and race which were fostered by scientific, rationalist, and imperialist theories and practices.

My specific interest in these concepts, their relationship to one another, and their relationship to Yeats involves their effect on definitions of "self" and "other." I base my arguments about Yeats, progress, and identity on his conception of the self in Platonic or Romantic terms whereby, in its ideal form, the self is understood to be a unified whole. In Yeats's system, the achievement of full subjectivity, however, requires us to move toward blending with their opposites not gendered traits only but each of the intrinsically fragmentary characteristics that make up our individual personalities. The unfinished quality of our personalities derives from Yeats's "belief that ultimate reality, symbolised as the Sphere, falls in human consciousness . . . into a series of antinomies" (*AV* 187). Always seeking the opposite, the nature of which changes as we change, we continually augment our personalities with the inclusion of the other.

Another important element of this study concerns the ways in which the essentialist origin of Platonic and Romantic philosophical versions of the self was reinforced, in the Victorian era and following, by definitions of progress that entered the social domain in the form of fixed categories of identity, specifically those of class, gender, and race. In particular, I am interested in Yeats's aesthetic and political response to the social implementation of essentialist categories of identity. Moreover, my study provides a reevaluation of Yeats's own essentialist inclinations within the historical context in which progress and identity came to be seen as inseparable cultural constructs. At the foundation of this reevaluation is an exploration of the ways in which Yeats's philosophical system of opposites, or the doctrine of the mask, can, when enacted by actual individuals, provide these individuals with a method of changing what science, Platonism, and moralistic Victorian bourgeois ideologies claimed to be inescapable qualities of self. In this way, Yeats's precursors are less Platonic than Blakean-Romantic: Within Yeats's doctrine of the mask, repeated encounters between essentialized (biologically or, more often, socially defined) opposites such as masculine/feminine and English/Irish ultimately lead to progress. Or, as Blake maintains in *The Marriage of Heaven and Hell*, there is no "progression" without "Contraries."

Two ideologies that were heavily invested in this conception of progress in Victorian England and Ireland, those of the bourgeoisie and British imperialism, form the basis of my arguments about the construction of identity in the era. Whether their criteria were economic, biological (e.g., racist), or both, the bourgeois and imperialist hegemony evaluated individual success according to materialist measures. As used by imperialist apologists and advocates of bourgeois moralism and materialism, progress thus became the rationale for social, political, and economic reform efforts, both at home and abroad, in which normative, essentialist, and exclusive categorizations of class, gender, and ethnic identity came to be seen as fixed entities. Viewed from this angle, progress was not a minor constitutive element in social constructions of identity. Rather, identity in the Victorian era could be considered, to a large extent, a derivative of progress.

The trajectory of this study is, first, to trace the relationship between Yeats's definition of progress and those definitions that became standard in the Victorian and Edwardian eras, as well as the way these definitions informed and were informed by social constructions of class, gender, and ethnic identity. The second, more direct aim of this study is to explore Yeats's social critique of conventional constructions of progress and identity, as well as the ways in which he restructured the definition of progress and created a system in which alternative versions of progress and, therefore, identity could be achieved. Moreover, when considered within the context of Yeats's esoteric doctrine of the mask, the plays show the theories on which *A Vision* is based to have a strong heritage in social criticism as well as in the critically more well-established foundations of philosophy, history, and spirituality.

During the years that comprise the scope of this study, Yeats experienced some of the most significant personal and professional experiences of his life, experiences that served to alter his identity, making it increasingly multivalent. Just a few of the major evolutions Yeats underwent included that from student and poet to poet/playwright/theater manager/literary reviewer, from sexually inexperienced to sexually initiated, from theosophist to high-ranking member of the Order of the Golden Dawn, and, after the fall of Parnell, from political to cultural nationalist. Yeats's identity in this period also assimilated the effects of literary movements, from French Symbolism to theatrical innovations including verse-chanting and Gordon Craig's symbolist set designs to Irish Literary Revivalist versions of Irish mythology, fairy stories, and folklore. And, as Deirdre Toomey observes, from 1895 on, Yeats experienced the increasing inclusion of women—especially Maud Gonne, Lady Gregory, Florence Farr and Olivia Shakespear—in his circle of influence, which previously had been dominated by men, including his grandfather, his father, John O'Leary, Arthur Symons, Edward Martyn, and Lionel Johnson (xvii).[2] Having taken on a large range of roles or, in other words, put on a wide variety of personal, aesthetic, political, and cultural masks, Yeats underwent a rapid-pace construction and reconstruction of his own identity during this time period. Terence Brown reads Yeats's "youthful crises of identity" similarly, noting that "his early encounters in Dublin and London offered him a range of possible modes of life and challenged the shy, insecure youth to acts of social self-definition" (36). This, combined with the James Clarence Mangan's and Oscar Wilde's influence on Yeats's conception of the mask,[3] provides biographical support for my contention that Yeats was preoccupied largely with the concept of identity formation as a self-consciously evolutionary process at the turn of the century. It should be no surprise, therefore, to find identity as a central issue in the plays Yeats wrote during this time period.

But where does the notion of progress come into the picture for Yeats? A brief survey of Yeats's employment of the term provides an insightful introduction to the topic. Focused on "always-increasing wealth" (*EI* 499), progress, according to Yeats, must ever be envisioned as a "straight line" that is "impelled by moral enthusiasm," the "Patent Office," and the newspapers (*Explorations* 354, *AV* 262). The opposite of revelation (*EI* 171), progress also represents the modernizing impulse that "shut behind more successful races, when [it] plunged into material progress" (*UPII* 44).

Merely an "illusion of change" (*EI* 225) and "the sole religious myth of modern man" (*Explorations* 355), progress is nonetheless all pervasive, having, Yeats recalls, filled the minds and conversations of nearly everyone Yeats encountered as a boy (*Explorations* 392). And finally, as a Victorian imperialist construct, progress is also, as Yeats sees it, a primarily English-inspired convention (*EI* 206). Couched in terms of malediction rather than, as was typical in the era, commendation, Yeats's portrayal of progress consisted entirely of negative connotations.

The negative nature of Yeats's assessment of progress reflects his antipathy toward Victorian rationalists and what he would later call "their contempt for the past, their monopoly of the future" (*Autobiographies* 115). Always focused on some future moment, rationalist philosophers, scientists, Social Darwinian theorists, moralistic social reformers, authors of social reformist realist literature, and propagandistic Irish nationalists also had something else in common. They advocated essentialist definitions of identity as the sole, fixed, and immutable ideal to which everyone should attempt to obtain, but ironically which they believed many—that is, others in the form of women, the Irish, and the lower classes—were barred from obtaining by their so-called natures.

Yeats's counter-definition of progress, in terms of an individual's successful achievement of a unified—that is, multivalent—subjectivity, did not achieve maturity until well after 1917, when Yeats and his wife, Georgie Hyde-Lees Yeats, began to work out the complicated system of Unity of Being and the related doctrine of the mask in the Automatic Scripts that in 1925 became *A Vision*. However, early indications of Yeats's treatment of identity as a social crisis directly related to conventional definitions of progress appeared in Yeats's plays in his choice of theme, character formation, and dramatic form beginning with *The Countess Cathleen* and continuing through 1907, after which Yeats became increasingly focused on symbolic and ritualistic forms of drama. Yeats's later plays, beginning with *Plays for Dancers* (1921), evince the incorporation of the doctrine of the mask as an overt and, more importantly, increasingly spiritual element. I am interested in the early incarnation of Yeats's use of mask-related theories as they pertain to more specifically social constructions of progress and identity.

Yeats's perception of progress remains fairly constant throughout his career in its aspect of being neither steady nor fixed on a set course; instead, it "is miracle, and it is sudden" (*EI* 172). A revelatory moment of insight, Yeatsian progress occurs when an individual faces his or her mask, or his or her opposite personality. This act enables the individual to see with new eyes or to incorporate a different (or an other's) perspective into the perspective he or she previously held. Or, as Herbert Levine explains, "'[t]hrough the mask of an anti-self the poet comes to terms with everything that is outside the self, with everything that has long remained hidden from daily view, with everything that puts him in touch with a collective mind greater than his own'" (qtd. in Malone 253). Yeats's system of progress thus allows, even encourages, individuals to continually escape from the limits of any and all previous definitions of self, and especially those constructed by the social and moral directives legislated by those in power—that is, by a materialistic, philistine, moralistic, imperialistic bourgeoisie. Standard connotations of progress define strict boundaries for the constitutive achievement of the status of "middle class," "feminine," or "Irish." This sort of progress insists that individuals fit themselves into narrow and already established categories of identity, which only serves to create narrow-minded and homogeneous individuals. Within this essentialist system of progress in which, for instance, all males are X while all women are Y, a man who shows elements of Y is not considered to have achieved maleness. By partaking in the system of identity constitution fostered by the doctrine of the mask, on the other hand, individuals become increasingly diversified, continually moving out of one temporarily fixed position into another until they are ultimately "free from that circle." Therein lies the most important difference between the conventional and Yeats's view of progress. The former is exclusive, essentialist, and normative, while the latter is inclusive, flexible, and broad-minded.

Yeats's choice to dramatize this difference in the plays he wrote during his first twenty years of theater involvement reflects an interest in social critique not often attributed to him, in part because of his own pronouncements against literary propaganda and social didacticism. However, because the bulk of Yeats's plays in this period so clearly announce his stance against conventional notions of progress as a prominent theme, one must account for the element of social criticism in the plays. This is one of the central goals of my study. More specifically, I argue that Yeats, having newly discovered at the age of twenty-five the possibilities afforded authors by the theater world, recognized that, in a world in which the bardic voice no longer directly represented the public, it was the public ritual of theater, rather than the private refuge of poetry, which would allow him to voice his more public concerns.

The implications of this study, therefore, extend beyond the scope of Yeatsian scholarship. Although Yeats's philosophical system of masks, as depicted in its rudimentary form in the early plays, did not become a way of life for many people, Yeats's critique of Victorian and Edwardian configurations of progress and identity as socially and, more particularly, colonially constructed have a wider significance in the fields of Irish cultural criticism and identity theory. The early plays demonstrate his belief that the issue of identity need not be mired in the strictly dichotomous and hierarchical forms enforced during the colonial era but might, in the name of what contemporary cultural critics call hybridity or heterogeneity, come to transcend these limitations. Yeats's proposition thus not only provided a cultural critique of progress. More importantly, it furnished a point of departure from which his contemporaries could begin to question their identities as defined by the institutions of bourgeois moralism, materialism, and colonialism and, therefore, from which they could begin to take their first steps into postcolonial thought.

The book unfolds in a manner designed to first introduce the social and cultural milieu that provides the background necessary for understanding that which inspired Yeats to use peasant and mythic dramas to allegorically portray Irish society in crisis. Chapter one outlines the ways in which predominant discourses of progress, informed by the scientific rationalism of Darwin and Huxley and the cultural and race theories of Matthew Arnold and Ernest Renan, manifested themselves in cultural institutions. Yeats's vision of progress as fostering inclusivity and syncretistic hybridity, a positive version of hybridity defined by Patrick Colm Hogan, as opposed to exclusivity and essentializing, normative forms of identity comprises the subject for the second chapter. Using cultural materialist, gender, and postcolonial theories, the final three chapters of this book demonstrate the nature and progression of Yeats's social critique of English, colonial definitions of, respectively, class, gender, and ethnicity through close readings of a selection of his plays.

Yeats's earliest produced plays, *The Countess Cathleen*, *The Land of Heart's Desire*, and *Cathleen ni Houlihan* portray most clearly the anti-materialist dimension of Yeats's arguments about progress. Exhibiting Yeats's peasant characters to be motivated by bourgeois and, to a certain extent, English imperialist definitions of progress—in particular, progress as financial success—in chapter three, I explore Yeats's critique of progress from the perspective of class issues. In chapter four, I utilize standard and, in some cases, unpublished manuscript versions of *The King's Threshold*, *On Baile's Strand*, and *Deirdre* to outline Yeats's critical assessment of normative notions of gender using androgyny as a theoretical construct. The psychologically androgynous nature of Seanchan, Cuchulain, and Deirdre provide just one example of ways in which progress can and should, according to Yeats, be defined in inclusive terms. In chapter five, I address Yeats's arguments against stereotyping in general, and of the Irish in particular, and his concomitant advocacy of multivalent forms of identity which, as I display, was influenced not only by Victorian debates about racial hybridity (in its negative form) but which foresaw contemporary theories on the subject. Finally, examining the initial critical response to Yeats's plays, and focusing especially on *Where There Is Nothing*, I conclude with a discussion of the correlation between Yeats's relative failure to reach his contemporary audience and their relationship to conventional conceptions of progress and identity.

Progress and Identity in the Plays of W. B. Yeats, 1892–1907

Chapter One

"[F]ull of personified averages"
Progress in the Victorian and Edwardian Eras

ACCORDING TO WILLIAM BUTLER YEATS, THE IMPORTANCE OF "PROGRESS" TO the Victorian and Edwardian public, to its individuals and institutions alike, was the crux of the era's social, spiritual, and philosophical dysfunction. Yeats perceived as ironically destructive the communal belief that the empiricism of Locke (*EI* 401), the scientific and social theories of Darwin, Huxley, and Tyndall (*Autobiographies* 115, 168), and "mechanical theory" (*EI* 518) engender social, moral, spiritual, and intellectual progress. Yeats did not deny the possibility of progress in particular or in general, arguing most extensively in *A Vision* that individuals and nations should aspire to self-improvement in both of these ways. The differences between Yeats's views of progress and those of the typical Victorian lie in both process and goal.

    Victorian ideas about the advancement of society and civilization, of course, gained their philosophical pedigree from Enlightenment ideas about humankind's capacity for reason. For instance, in *Essay on Human Understanding,* John Locke countered the essentialist belief in knowledge as inborn with his theory that, in the process of obtaining knowledge, while mental faculties are innate, knowledge is acquired. The *tabula rasa* concept thus made learning an individual and social initiative, a responsibility as well as an opportunity. This sense of possibility paired with the burden of obligation, in turn, inspired the social and economic reform and innovations that blossomed in the nineteenth century. Like philosophers of the Enlightenment, Yeats believed in the transformative power of culture[1] as much as he loathed censorship and, as I will illustrate in this study, bourgeois forms of intolerance. However, he could not, as an Irish person and a critic of the widespread and markedly bourgeois deployment of reason, advocate progress in the Victorian form that emerged, in part, from Enlightenment ideas.

Institutionalized, popularized, and made gospel through the advent of scientific and rationalist philosophies, popular culture, and Christian compliance with secular goals, Progress relegated everyone, whether English or not, to his/her/its place. Bourgeois, Christian (or more specifically Protestant), and patriarchal ideals concerning gender, race, and class defined correct or normal behavior and reinforced them in ways that left little room for deviation. Furthermore, the seemingly preordained hierarchies of class, race, and gender—and the moralistic judgments that accompanied them—which had long been in place in Western society, earned the authorization of science and logic. The equation of progress with specifically English, patriarchal, Protestant, bourgeois ideals, which I shall discuss in detail in this chapter, seriously limited the definition of success or even social acceptability for individuals and nations, even as it purported to enhance these entities. As evinced in the social reformist agendas of the Church, education, the health reform movement, Social Darwinism, race theory, and other proponents of bourgeois morality, progress in the Victorian era had as its foundation two related convictions: that the world had always improved and would continue to improve, socially, morally, and biologically; and that the Victorian English were as close to perfection, in the Darwinian scheme of things, as any race-nation could be at that time. It follows, then, that they would attempt to make others fit their mold—or, if that were impossible or undesirable (as with the so-called naturally inferior Africans)—to make them take their scientifically or rationally "proven" place in the hierarchy of civilizations.[2]

Progress toward the Yeatsian goal, on the other hand, occurs along a circular path in which a given soul progresses not according to socially ordained dictates, but in an individualized process that occurs throughout and between lifetimes.[3] His theory of individual and historical consciousness, as depicted in his much later work *A Vision*,[4] thus imparts the following goal: "Neither between death and birth nor between birth and death can the soul find more than momentary happiness; its object is to pass rapidly round its circles and find freedom from that circle" (*AV* 236). The ultimate bliss of permanent escape from the circle of history, struggle, and conflict—Unity of Being—is foreshadowed during our lifetime in the momentary achievement of this freedom. We attain this state by facing up to and incorporating into our individual personalities all that is our opposite for, as Yeats's spiritual instructors explained to him, "all the gains of man come from conflict with the opposite of his true being" (*AV* 13). Thus, in Yeats's philosophy, the definition of progress differs from person to person and nation to nation, the only directive being to "identify consciousness with conflict, not with knowledge, substitute for subject and object and their attendant logic a struggle toward harmony, toward Unity of Being" (*AV* 214).

Unlike the standard Victorian view in which the formation of class, gender, and ethnicity is limited by essentialist theories of identity, Yeats celebrates the multifaceted nature of society by fostering difference and opposition, not conformity, as the quality most conducive to progress. He explains in *Per Amica Silentia Lunae*: "'If we cannot imagine ourselves as different from what we are, and try to assume that second self, we cannot impose a discipline upon ourselves though we may accept one from others" (*Mythologies* 334). He points to William Wordsworth as an exemplar of the problems inherent in "the passive acceptance of a code," and attributes his perception that Wordsworth's poetry fell "so often flat" (334) to his moral sense which, according to Yeats, was as "a mere obedience" because it was not self-created.[5] Similarly, in "The Theatre, the Pulpit, and the Newspapers," first published in *The United Irishman* in October 1903, Yeats laments that:

> [c]ertain generalisations are everywhere substituted for life. Instead of individual men and women and living virtues differing as one star differeth from another in glory, the public image is full of personified averages, partisan fictions, rules of life that would drill everybody into the one posture, habits that are like the pinafores of charity schoolchildren. The priest, trained to keep his mind on the strength of his Church and the weakness of his congregation would have all mankind painted with a halo or with horns. (*Explorations* 119)

In the passages above, Yeats condemns as weak both the people and systems that capitulate to and reinforce the strictly defined moral and social codes of the era. Instead, he advocates the transformative potential inherent in more inclusive processes of identity formation that admit a continuum of "virtues," "differing as one [individual] differeth from another." It is well documented that Yeats was no enthusiast of democracy and subscribed to a few unyielding hierarchies of his own, as can be seen most famously in his general disdain for the bourgeoisie, his faith in the Anglo-Irish Ascendancy's potential (in fact, the necessity for them) to act as exemplary leaders for other classes in Ireland, his fostering of an elite dramatic audience in later years, and his brush with Fascism.[6] However, with their direct and indirect arguments against the Victorian notion of progress, his early plays have the overall opposite effect of encouraging the acceptance of difference. Moreover, Yeats specifically disparages those who believe the pathway to truth and consciousness can be paved only by science and reason, and fosters instead a theory in which instinct, passion, and a relatively non-exclusionary version of faith gain equal footing with their more socially accepted counterparts. In this way, Yeats's works offer an alternative conception and, even more importantly, a strong indictment of Victorian definitions and modes of progress.

PROGRESS IN THEORY AND PRACTICE

The Victorian mantra of progress, taken up with fervor especially by followers of Darwin such as Huxley and Tyndall, who had admitted social and political agendas of their own, had its inception in the teleologically infused concept of natural selection.[7] *On the Origin of Species* (1859), in fact, culminates on a teleological note, comforting its readers with the consolation that, "as natural selection works solely by and for the good of each being, all corporeal and mental endowments will tend to progress toward perfection" (489; 428).[8] Gertrude Himmelfarb points out that Huxley later applauded the teleological bent in Darwin's implication that the world is the result of "'mutual interaction, according to definite laws'" (344). Similarly, idealists credit Darwin with reestablishing teleology "not, perhaps, in the cruder . . . sense that all organisms tend to the good of man, but that they tend to the good, the realization of themselves" (344). Thus, according to Darwin, progress is not simply a man-made moral imperative based on subjective feelings or blind faith, but an innate condition of biology. In effect, progress came to be viewed as a universal directive of nature.

Thomas Huxley famously followed in Darwin's steps, fashioning the theories of evolution and natural selection into a social program. From early in his career, Huxley strongly supported science and reason as the only viable moral and spiritual modes of instruction. In *On the Advisableness of Improving Natural Knowledge* (1866), he argues that "natural knowledge, seeking to satisfy natural wants, has found the ideas which can alone still spiritual cravings . . . [and] lay the foundations of a new morality" (40).[9] He goes on to commend the "man of science" who "has learned to believe in justification, not by faith, but by verification" (41). Similarly, in *Joseph Priestley* (1874), he associates moral progress with a social and philosophical climate in which "reason has asserted and exercised her primacy over all provinces of human activity . . . [and] the ecclesiastical authority has been relegated to its proper place" (181). As he acknowledges in *Controverted Question* (1892), Huxley promotes not religion but the sciences as "the foundations of right action" (120). It is this insistence on the association of morality with science and reason that inspired Yeats to consider Huxley a prototype for all that was wrong with Victorian values.

Because of his faith in the moral accomplishment of rational thinking, Huxley proposed a "liberal" education, which meant, for him, the relegation of our selves, our very souls, to the command of science. In *A Liberal Education; and Where to Find It* (1868), Huxley purports:

> That man, I think, has had a liberal education who has been so trained in youth that his body is the ready servant of his will, and does with ease and pleasure all the work that, as a mechanism, it is capable of; whose intellect is a clear, cold, logic engine, with all its parts of equal strength, and in smooth working order; ready, like a steam engine, to be turned to any kind of work, and spin the gossamers as well as forge the anchors of the mind; whose mind is stored with a knowledge of the great and fundamental truths of Nature and the laws of her operations; one who, no stunted ascetic, is full of life and fire, but whose passions are trained to come to heel by a vigorous will, the servant of a tender conscience. (193–94)

For Huxley, the well-educated person is predictable and stable, more well-oiled machine than mortal. Just as his body is a mechanistic "servant of his will," his mind is an "engine" whose gears work in a "smooth" and "orderly" fashion; "anchored" by natural "laws," his "cold" and "logical" mind has been "trained" to reign in his passions. By learning, and learning to submit to, the laws of nature, the belief went, there would be no reason why one could not live a successful—that is, efficient and productive—life. Yeats sees as misguided such individuals who, misprizing passion, "prefer the stalk to the flower, and believe that painting and poetry exist that there may be instruction, and love that there may be children, and theatres that busy men may rest, and holidays that busy men may go on being busy" (*EI* 251). Yeats further disparages those who believe that all actions must have a practical result with the accusation that such individuals have "so little belief that anything can be an end in itself that they cannot understand you if you say, 'All the most valuable things are useless'" (*EI* 251).

Huxley's ideal of human social progress, then, evolves only when our intellect, spirit, morality, and passions are smoothly integrated into and regulated by our "biology"—an important word for Huxley. In *On the Study of Biology* (1876) he declares, "we must include man and all his ways and works under the head of Biology; in which case we should find that psychology, politics, and political economy would be absorbed into the province of Biology" (39). Huxley's subordination to biology of all other fields of knowledge reflects a trend of the era shared by another of Yeats's nemeses, John Tyndall. In "On the Scientific Use of the Imagination" (1872), Tyndall's defense of imagination betrays its nonetheless provisional approval: "Bounded and conditioned by coöperant reason, imagination becomes the mightiest instrument of the physical discoverer" (250). Like Huxley, Tyndall advocates imagination as what he would term a less capable system of knowledge only under the proviso that it serve as a controlled "instrument" of science and reason. Furthermore, because, compared to traditional religious morality, biology provides clear and unequivocal guidelines for action, Huxley argues that it advances a theology of its own. With the advent of a social system that hailed Biology as its god, Huxley believed that the world would progress toward perfection. Indeed, in *Joseph Priestley* (1874), he admits, "as regards other than material welfare, although perfection is not yet in sight[,] . . . it is surely true that things are much better than they were" (180).

The faith in logic, reason, and science as indicative of and procreative of progress, which Yeats saw rooted in Huxley and like-minded scientists and social theorists, permeated Victorian culture. It played an especially big role in the everyday lives of the English and Irish, finding its way into theoretical and practical applications of education, health reform, and popular literature for children and adults. For example, J. A. Mangan notes that public school education in late Victorian and Edwardian England encouraged social Darwinist over Christian (turn the other cheek, do unto others) morality: "What frequently characterised the public schools of this period was an implicit, if not explicit, crude Darwinism encapsulated in simplistic aphorisms: life is conflict, strength comes through struggle and success is the prerogative of the strong" (142).

In its national schooling system, Ireland followed suit, fostering a "new system" of education after 1831 in which, according to John Logan, the "reading lessons would be used 'to convey information', . . . the writing lessons would be used for 'fixing instruction on the memory' and . . . arithmetic, instead of being taught by unexplained rules, would be the means of training the mind 'to accuracy of thinking and reasoning'" (45). As welcome as the new system was, it failed to earn the approval of Yeats, who was known to remark to one schoolmaster, "'I know you will defend the ordinary system of education by saying that it strengthens the will, but I am convinced that it only seems to do so because it weakens the impulses'" (*Autobiographies* 93). However, the weakening of impulses—an action deemed positive by the school system if not by Yeats—was, if fact, an important part of the plan. Taught to be rational thinking machines, students would learn related lessons in morality through readers depicting, positively, tales of hard-working, honest men supported by "thrifty and inventive" wives and, negatively, of "squalid, complaining cottier[s] whose downfall is hastened by the extravagances of a slovenly spouse" (Logan 45). Through such stories, the students were to learn to differentiate between proud "poverty" (or, if they could imagine themselves so lucky, prosperity) and morally culpable "pauperism." This lesson was echoed elsewhere in Victorian culture. The middle-class, English readers of *Leisure Hour*, for instance, were tutored by writer Thomas Walker in the differences between poverty and pauperism because, according to the popular periodical and its Victorian obsession with categorizing, it is "of the utmost importance" to distinguish accurately between the two. Whereas poverty "strives to cure itself," and, therefore, is a good example for individuals struggling to be economically fit, pauperism "contaminate[s] others" (80). Here lies evidence that even those struggling for mere subsistence could not escape the moralistic hierarchizing of the middle class.

Although progressivist Victorian beliefs flourished in nineteenth-century Irish schools, students also met with a competing, more traditionally religious point-of-view in readers that, somewhat contradictorily, "maintained the didactic tradition of the voluntary societies and the religious congregations and conveyed a world view that emphasised respectful deference to hierarchy, the justness of a divinely sanctioned social structure and the appropriateness of the modest rewards that accrued to honest labour" (Logan 45). Thus, students of nineteenth-century Ireland learned both to submissively submit to a preordained social hierarchy and to work toward individual economic success, both to do what their so-called betters told them to do and to be individualistic rational thinkers. The inconsistent philosophies of nineteenth-century Irish education find their origin, in part, in the fact that, unlike in

English public school education, religious instruction in one's own belief was compulsory (Logan 44). Not only do Catholic and Protestant beliefs conflict with those of many scientific and rationalist philosophies; the religious compulsion flies in the face of even the most basic of the stated hopes for Irish education: that every Irish person "would follow a standardised curriculum and emerge bearing the marks of a common culture" (Logan 36). With Protestantism taught to some, Catholicism to others, and "accuracy of thinking and reasoning" to all, common culture had little hope of coming to fruition. Students were caught between what Homi Bhabha calls "the shreds and patches of cultural signification and the certainties of the nationalist pedagogy" (294). John Logan might be said to concur with this view when he points out that, "despite the apparent promise that [national school reform] would weaken the barriers deriving from class, religion or race, it became instead an instrument that promoted a knowledge of the immutability of those forces" (49). School lessons, therefore, presented Irish students with a murkier, more complicated path to progress than their English public school counterparts.

Both within schools and without, Victorian society latched onto another movement that embraced individual and national progress: health reform. Conveyed through school readers, scouting manuals,[10] popular literature, and a penchant for group and individual sports, the health reform movement, as Roberta J. Park recognizes, grounded itself in an "optimistic belief" in improvement. She goes on to explain: "Millennialism placed the responsibility for attaining perfection on the individual; therefore, . . . physical degeneration was seen as a spiritual as well as a medical and physiological problem" (8). The notion of individual responsibility, clearly Darwinian, was extended quickly, then, into the social Darwinian notion that the physically fit ("survivors") are also morally sound. The benefits of individual health and self-improvement extended even further: those who believed that strengthening the body strengthened the will also thought that taking responsibility for self-improvement led to a stronger and healthier community (Park 9)—and, subsequently, to a more economically powerful nation. As Gerald Early explains, "sports, imitating the rampant industrialism of the day, became a highly, if arbitrarily, rationalized system"; in following, "business culture . . . began to assimilate the values of sports" (18).

Victorians of widely diverse philosophical backgrounds associated athletic ability with implied moral worth. For example, as Patricia Anderson reminds us, Clergyman Charles Kingsley "allied the morality of the playing field to the honor of the true Christian gentleman" (54). Based on contemporary notions of physical fitness which valued bulging muscles, physical vigor, and endurance in men (Anderson 50, 54), the importance of playing literal games and sports also reflected the more general belief in the values of productivity and self-control—values that had a direct effect on the socioeconomic health of the nation. Sportsmen, after all, ostensibly learn the importance of winning and of besting their last efforts; they learn to abide by the sport's—or society's—rules; and they strive to triumph over others, whether the others are football players, economic competitors, or another nation or "race." Huxley supported the health reform movement as well. He asserts in *Address on Behalf of the National Association for the Promotion of Technical Education* (1887):

> You may develop the intellectual side of people as far as you like, and you may confer upon them all the skill that training and instruction can give; but, if there is not, underneath all that outside form and superficial polish, *the firm fibre of healthy manhood* and earnest desire to do well, your labour is absolutely in vain. (219–20, emphasis added)

According to the principles of health reform, a nation such as England, which is healthy in its people and therefore sound in its possessions and (more or less) comfortable with its moral right to colonize, could feel quite good about itself.

Sport's lessons in competition were reinforced by classist and racist theories of sexuality. According to Michel Foucault in *The History of Sexuality*, the bourgeoisie responded early and often to all Victorian scientific theories, particularly those dealing with sexuality.[11] By being the first to submit itself to the "direction of consciences, self-examination, the entire long elaboration of the transgressions of the flesh, and the scrupulous detection of concupiscence" (120), the middle class displayed its faith in the new religion of scientific rationalism. Yet it did not leave the moral structure of traditional religion behind. Rather, the medical, psychiatric, biological, and geological sciences were "subordinated in the main to the imperatives of a morality whose divisions it reiterated under the guise of the medical [and psychiatric, biological, and geological] norm[s]. Claiming to speak the truth, [they] stirred up people's fears" (53).

In the Victorian and Edwardian era, discourses on or, in Foucault's terms, the "deployment" of sexuality—scientific, evaluative, creating hierarchies of normal and abnormal, at times Darwinian—flourished. Absorbing the categorization and resultant values system, and feeling obliged to "preserve a healthy line of descent for [their] . . . social class" (121), the bourgeoisie, according to Foucault, "staked its life and death on sex by making it responsible for its future welfare; it placed its hopes for the future in sex by imagining it to have ineluctable effects on generations to come; it subordinated its soul to sex by conceiving of it as what constituted the soul's most secret and determinant part" (124). Foucault defends this attitude, claiming it "has to be seen as the self-affirmation of one class rather than the enslavement of another: a defense, a protection, a strengthening, and an exaltation that were eventually extended to others—at the cost of different transformations—as a means of social control and political subjugation" (123). However, I maintain that the bourgeoisie's affirmation of self comes at a high cost to the other, because implicit in the affirmation of one group is the denigration of the next. In the Darwinian scheme of things, the "protection," "strength," and "exaltation" of members of the middle class emerge from their struggle with others for the best exploitation of their environment. Those who lose the struggle in the sociopolitical arena are not inherently weak, but rather defined by society as weak. By constructing "white," "European" (and more specifically "English"), "middle-class," "male," "Protestant," and "heterosexual" as the norm, Victorian society cast non-whites, non-Westerners (and in the context of my argument "Irish"), the working class, women, Catholics, and homosexuals/bisexuals as other—as abnormal and inferior.

PROGRESS AND THE GENDERED BODY AND MIND

The two forms of the other that provide the central focus of this study, gender and ethnicity,[12] have been shown to be inextricably linked to one another by means of their Victorian and Edwardian codification.[13] In a time when masculinity ruled not only by patriarchal precept but by means of scientific and rational theories of "natural" dominance, femininity became allied specifically with weakness, passivity, and emotion. In England and Ireland, therefore, both men and England, seeing themselves as the world's primary movers and shakers (they were the ones, the argument went, who successfully conquered the planet) came to represent all that is admirable in a dog-eat-dog world: strength, aggression, authority, and rationality. Essayists including the oft-quoted Matthew Arnold and Ernest Renan, both of whom greatly influenced Yeats, helped to fulfill this worldview by developing a comparison between England and Ireland. In designating Ireland, like women, as essentially feminine, Victorian society had a ready-made scapegoat in both Ireland and femininity: Using science and reason to justify the sovereignty of masculinity (and Englishness), it demonized femininity (and Irishness) as an enemy to progress while bolstering itself.

The concept of femininity-as-deficiency and the corresponding superiority of masculinity gained visibility through many venues, from political economics to medicine to popular literature. As Foucault has pointed out, professional discourse on sexuality flourished in the eighteenth and nineteenth centuries. Medical, psychiatric, and criminal justice theories appeared, "undertaking to protect, separate, and forewarn, signaling perils everywhere, awakening people's attention, calling for diagnoses, piling up reports, organizing therapies" (*History* 30–31). Sexuality had become fodder for science and reason; gender roles could not be isolated from this contagion. Around the turn of the century in particular, the construction of gender roles was influenced by a crisis of identity in which two opposing forces worked: the traditional and the modern. People clung to the traditional (as they thought, divine) division of Western society into separate spheres of the public/masculine and private/feminine in order to ground themselves in a quickly changing modern world.

In 1890s England, a morally disapproving society had to contend with such publicly gender-bending figures as Oscar Wilde and his colleagues in Decadence who all but erased the borders that heretofore had, for the most part, kept gender roles in their assigned places. Similarly, the fin de siècle heralded the age of the New Woman who might choose to cut her hair short or to be sexually active outside the context of marriage, as did Yeats's good friend Florence Farr (Brown 40, 41). She might work instead of or in addition to marrying. Or she might use her own mind and her own voice, previously more often than not silent (or silenced), to advocate women's suffrage, temperance, or their right to higher education. In *Yeats's Nations*, Marjorie Howes explains that fin-de-siècle conceptions of the Decadent and the New Woman allied them with one another as well as with social deviance: "Sexual pathology and effeminacy were central to contemporary descriptions of decadence, as were the decadent's similarities to the perceived depravities of the New Woman" (24). As one of the few who chose to stand by Wilde during his trial and as an enthusiastic admirer of strong women—Maud Gonne, Lady Gregory, the independent-minded female university students he met during his travels in the States, just to name a few—Yeats did not share the mainstream aversion to the Decadent and the New Woman.

Another widely debated topic in the second half of the nineteenth century, that of women in the workplace, in fact revolved around the doctrine of separate spheres. On one side, traditionalists such as Charles Kingsley and William Neilson Hancock argued for the maintenance of a social order in which women do not, as they saw it, waste time or energy on duties other than those of home and family. Others, most famously Arthur Houston, a professor of political economy at Trinity College Dublin, vociferously supported women as individuals with the right to work outside the home as required or if they so chose. However, as liberal and modern as his views were (and as was true of most people in the Victorian era), he did not divest himself completely of the ideology of separate spheres. T. P. Foley points out that although Houston advocated women working in a wide range of fields, he nevertheless presumed that "it was not in the least likely that women 'would be at all satisfied to sacrifice their own natural tastes and feeling so far as to become barristers or surgeons'" (29).[14] Clearly, by contemporary standards, liberal, feminist women still had a long way to go, even where their supporters were concerned. Nonetheless, where changes had not already occurred, the threat of change was imminent. With aberrations lurking, society, and the middle classes in particular, felt the need to "take sex 'into account,' to pronounce a discourse on sex that would not derive from morality alone but from rationality as well" (Foucault, *History* 24). If the spheres could not remain separate, then another form of social and moral legislation would have to be put in place.

Whether directly or indirectly, the combination of rationality and morality permeated almost every discourse, diagnosis, rule, and belief. With the advent of scientific rationalism, men and women were locked into a given place by their respective genders. Anne Digby explains part of the ethical reckoning behind such beliefs:

> Liberal assumptions of the Enlightenment required that evidence was needed to justify an inegalitarian denial of social and political rights to women. The constructs of eighteenth-century anatomist and nineteenth-century craniotomists *appeared* to show that fundamental gender differences were not due to nurture but to nature, and that women were permanently below men in the hierarchy of species. (214)

In their introduction to *Sexuality and Subordination*, Susan Mendus and Jane Rendall point to two nineteenth-century philosophical arguments characteristic in their depiction of women: the dualistic scientific rationalism of the Royal Society and John Stuart Mill's notion of "natural kinds." The Royal Society's dualism associated "mind" or rationality with men and "matter" with women, the "essential inertness" of which/whom allowed it/them to be controlled by the mind/men. They explain that:

> the belief that matter was inert itself provided the philosophical underpinning for the image of women as passive, innocent, sexually inactive, and malleable. *Just as* matter, woman was possessed of these qualities. *Just as* body, she was inert, incapable of activity until influenced by male motion. The ground was thus laid for those representations of innocence and passivity which so dominated the Victorian era. (8–9)

Scientific rationalism thus depicts woman as naturally innocent and, by extension, morally upright. According to this reasoning, furthermore, the natural passivity of woman allotted her the role of follower to more rational man's leader: Only under his direction would she be likely to think and act appropriately—that is, according to the dictates of reason.

Mill's "natural kinds" concept in *System of Logic* reiterated the notion that rational faculties separate man ("mind") from beast ("matter"). However, whereas Mill defined both men and women as rational, the Victorian bourgeoisie took this theory one step further to claim that women (and other races and classes) are closer to the base animal and therefore more "prone to weak rationality and strong sexual appetite" (9). Left to their base nature, the theory suggests, women have the potential to unleash "threatening and morally damaging . . . animal instincts of the most base sort" (Mendus and Rendall 10), which poses a social menace. By extension, Mill's notion of natural kinds and the Royal Society's scientific rationalism led to the following contradiction: "Despite the fact that the perfect Victorian lady was construed as passionless, the 'low and vulgar' Victorian woman was perceived as retaining the animal's sexual voraciousness" (9). Therefore, Mendus and Rendall explain, "the image of woman as sexually innocent and passionless became not a truth of nature but a social and moral necessity" (10), as did the image of men as authoritative, rational, and in control of their minds and bodies at all times.

Medical and psychiatric practitioners similarly were invested in creating normative, as well as aberrant, images of men and women, which gradually filtered out to the general populace. Digby notes, for instance, that medical doctors such as Clouston, Maudsley, Playfair, and Thorburn, who were involved in the debate over women in higher education, published their thinking in both medical and popular journals (208). In addition, around the time that Havelock Ellis scientifically and morally categorized sexual norms in *Man and Woman* (1893) and *Sexual Inversion* (1897), British groups such as the Society for Psychical Research—of which Yeats was a member—began discussing Freud (Anderson 23).[15]

Women garnered special attention during this scientific/rational/moral blitzkrieg, figuring prominently in medical theories of weakness, illness and abnormality. These classifications, created by medical practitioners, also soon were used in social tracts. Social Darwinist Herbert Spencer argues in *The Study of Sociology*, for example, that women are less evolved because all their energy is and must be conducted toward reproductive, not rational, faculties. In the heated debate over women's place in higher education, American Edwin H. Clarke drew on Darwin's law of conservation of energy to argue in *Sex and Education* against middle-class women squandering their energy in school when they should use it for procreative purposes in order to ensure the continuation of their class. Englishman Henry Maudsley followed in Clarke's footsteps in 1874 with "Sex and Mind in Education," agreeing that women should not be involved in higher education because their menstrual periods would interrupt the steady pursuit of their studies (Digby 209). Instead, these theorists endorsed the concentration of all women's efforts on reproduction and motherhood. In an 1850 discussion of Charlotte Brontë's *Shirley*, George H. Lewes provides another such argument:

> The grand function of woman, it must always be recollected, is, and ever must be, *Maternity*: and this we regard not only as her distinctive characteristic, and most endearing charm, but as a high and holy office—the prolific source, not only of the best affections and virtues of which our nature is capable, but also of the wisest thoughtfulness, and most useful habits of observation, by which that nature can be elevated and adorned. But with all this, we think it impossible to deny that it must essentially interfere both with that steady and unbroken application, without which no proud eminence in science can be gained—and with the discharge of all official and professional functions that do not admit of long or frequent postponement. (161)

Lewes's assertions, like those elaborated by Spencer and Maudsley, turn the biological fact of motherhood into women's sole reason for existence and make full attention to the role a moral and social imperative, thus devising another rationale for separate spheres.

Burgeoning psychiatric practice and scholarship likewise situated women apart from men in a separate, and inferior, sphere. In a study of the Connaught District

Lunatic Asylum, the first public institution in the west of Ireland, Oonagh Walsh found the causes of mental illness to have two main categories: moral (e.g., stress-related illnesses) and physical (mental handicap and damage to the brain). As could be expected, many more women than men were admitted for "moral" reasons. In 1861, for instance, seventy percent of the hospital's female patients were judged morally insane (161). Digby points out comparable practices in Victorian England, where the "evolution of medical views on physical and psychological nature created an image of women as frail and unstable" (193). Because women were seen as inseparable from their biological functions, most forms of female insanity were ineluctably linked to menstruation, pregnancy, childbirth, lactation, or menopause (Digby 201). Thus, according to nineteenth-century psychiatry, women's physical makeup predisposed them to hysteria. With a large portion of society having been apprised of this posited fact, women had little hope, and no acceptably scientific methods, of proving otherwise.

Although some doctors began to recognize that men also suffer from hysterical symptoms, by the late Victorian era, the equation of hysteria with femininity had been firmly implanted in the minds of the professional and general public alike. Yeats discloses a similar prejudice in an April, 1904 letter to George Russell in which he complains of the need for his writing to evolve along a more masculine track. In particular, he wants to escape the "region of brooding emotions full of fleshly waters and vapours which kill the spirit and the will" that rouses him "to a kind of frenzied hatred which is quite out of [his] control" (*Letters* 434). I will save a detailed analysis of the passage from which this is an excerpt for chapter four. However, it is clear from these few lines that, at this point in his life, Yeats concedes at least in part to the communal and negative equation of hysteria with femininity. What is more, as Digby points out, "there was no reluctance to make general inferences from [such beliefs], and so derive misleading 'insights' into female personality" (215).

Not left out of the social (or Social Darwinist) construction of gender roles, men garnered the attention of another, related field: health reform. Proponents of progress, health reform activists focused primarily on the physical fitness of boys and men. Victorian and Edwardian males were encouraged to "reform" their bodies—and, consequently, their minds and morals—in school, as scouts, and as adults, both for their benefit and for that of society. The physical and moral lesson taught by example in English public schools could be phrased as J. A. Mangan does here: "life is conflict, strength comes through struggle and success is the prerogative of the strong" (142). In these hallowed halls, in which boys were often cold and hungry and, if smaller or weaker, bullied (142), the physically and emotionally stronger served to either toughen up or weed out the "weaker" members of the community, thereby fortifying the whole.

The assessment of sports and the sportsman as heroic also speaks to the high esteem in which strength and physical fitness were held in schools and in Victorian and Edwardian society in general. As Patricia Anderson explains, masculinity in some measure consisted of "strength of character, physical toughness, a capacity for action, and endurance even in the harshest of outdoor conditions. At the heart of this model of masculinity was sport, especially open-air team sports such as cricket, rowing, and football (soccer)" (54). Equal to the praise that the sportsman earned was society's scorn for the man unable or unwilling to compete. Fostering this bias, individuals like the original scoutmaster, Baden-Powell, aided in the cultivation of a manliness defined by good health, anti-intellectualism, a belief in action over reflection, and the espousal of frontier life over that to be had in the debilitating and materialist city (Allen 199–200). Charles Kingsley's "muscular" or "manly Christianity"[16] offered a similar path toward progress. A muscular Christian fears and appreciates God and his gifts, notably nature, but also excels at sports. Religious fervor and strength provide the raw materials for the medieval chivalric life the muscular Christian lives: He must train his body and bring it into subjection for use in the protection of the weak, the advancement of good causes, and the glory of God (Mangan 137)—and, perhaps more importantly in the eyes of the general public, the glory of England.

Although no theory or practice confined itself entirely to only one gender, to a certain extent, even those that played a powerful role in defining masculinity and femininity seemed to divide themselves according to gender, with psychiatry focusing on women (and, in particular, their "biological" femininity) and health reform on men. According to psychiatry, women suffer from being "women"; and health reform requires a man to be more "manly." Then again, are these so-called problems not similar and, therefore, do they not require similar solutions? That is, as defined by medicine, psychiatry, and health reform, both men's and women's infirmities have to do with femaleness or femininity. Although, for women, the "condition" of femaleness was seen to be innate, the solution offered was not so different from advice given to Victorian men. Women were told to curb their (feminine) weakness and hysteria with (male) strength and reason. For men it was more of the same, in that the stronger and more rational you were, the further from femininity and, therefore, the better man. Both genders, then, could feel confident that, by following the dictates of science and reason, they would help civilization progress to a higher level. It is interesting to conjecture whether female hysteria and the penchant for a reflective, city life would have been "diagnosed" in a society uninterested in categorizing, hierarchizing, and taking over the world. Furthermore, nineteenth-century science made it possible to blame women's biological nature for their socially defined problems, thus disallowing any viable solutions. And only scientific rationalism (via social Darwinism) could justify a so-called factual interpretation of men as more evolved, thus burdening them with the duty of hypermasculinity.

With such essentialist philosophies in the air, gender roles became, in some ways, even more solidified than they ever had been before. This is not to say that no one challenged the borderlines. However, moralistic scientism acknowledged only two options: either to act within the strict boundaries of one's gender identification, or to act like the other gender. And there could be no mistaking the ideal man for the ideal woman. Even if you were completely unaware of the theories of Freud or of the social Darwinists, gender characteristics hailed themselves loudly and clearly in the advertisements, articles, and fiction in magazines and newspapers of the Victorian and Edwardian eras. Similarly, with the popularity of stories about and pictures of their lives, actresses, dancers, and music hall entertainers loomed large in the public mind, helping to fix the growing standardization of feminine beauty which came into being by the 1890s (P. Anderson 34, 46). For instance, common depictions of women in beauty advertisements included the, for the most part, decidedly feminine characteristics of "a delicate hand, white teeth, luxuriant hair, . . . 'speaking eyes,' . . . and a shapely figure" (P. Anderson 28). Portrayals such as "delicate," "white," and "speaking eyes" convey the image of women as frail, pure, brimming with emotion, and, consequently, in need of masculine protection. A telling example can be found in the pages of *The Leisure Hour* (circa 1890)[17] in an article entitled "Some Women's Manners and Ways." In this piece, which takes the form of a discussion between two women, the author allows the voice of Pleasance, a New Woman,[18] to have her say; however, the discussion ends on a much more traditional note. The essay's literal and metaphorical last words depict the more popular view of woman, whose duty it is to acquire "humility, patience, and firmness, and [to discover] her need for the best of all culture, physical, mental, and moral." Upon discharging these obligations, the essay concludes, the woman will "fulfil the grand ideal" of the lines that close the piece and which follow here:

> "Every woman is, or ought to be, a cathedral
> Built on the ancient plan — a cathedral pure and perfect —
> Built by that only law, that Use be suggester of Beauty.
> Nothing concealed that is done, but all things done to adornment;
> Meanest utilities seized as occasions to grace and embellish." (261)

In other words, the woman who quietly fulfills her duties of humility and patience and whose beauty reflects an inner purity exemplifies "true womanhood" (261).

Popular depictions of men, on the other hand, relayed images of hardness and hardiness, vigor and emotional firmness. Anderson points out, for instance, that sportswriters chose terms such as "'so steady, so sturdy,' 'perennially vigorous,' [and] 'sound and solid'" for those famous Victorian and Edwardian heroes, sportsmen (54). Popular literature provides countless similar depictions. In one serialized novel, "The Caves of Kildoran," we see that the guests who have made a hostess's competitive party invitation list include a Sir Vincent Mowbray and Edward Orme. The appearance of the "straight" and "broad-shouldered" Sir Vincent "suggested great strength and power, and, at the same time, a lazy indifference." Strong and powerful, Mowbray's "lazy indifference" adds to his masculine cast, for too much emotion would belie a certain level of effeminacy. Furthermore, we are told, "So far, he had drifted along his life smoothly and pleasantly, and nothing had roused or interested him sufficiently to stir the *latent force* of his character or to make his apparent indolence give way to his *real energy and strong will*" (9, emphasis added). Indeed, beneath the completely socially acceptable masculine nonchalance (as opposed to the feminine emotion), Sir Mowbray has stores of even more vital, bestial masculinity: He is a real man.

Similarly, his "old college friend" Orme not only possesses a well-balanced, rational mind depicted by a "clear black eye [which] expresses shrewdness and intellect, with a good deal of determination and humour"; he also has the benefit of having had to fight "his own way in the battle of life" (9). Like a public school boy, a footballer, or a war veteran, Mr. Orme has struggled, survived, and emerged victorious. And one need glance only briefly at one of the pictures that accompanies the serialized story to recognize the gendered subtext. Subtitled "'A burly, forbidding-looking ruffian was struggling with a slight female form," the picture and caption reinforce traditional gender coding. Both men in the picture, rogue and hero alike, wear dark suits that reinforce their weight and power. The man who strides forcefully across the road to save the "slight female form"—she's merely a form, not even a person—has wide shoulders and a moustache, consistent with the Victorian ideal of masculine refinement. The woman, dressed in the color of virtue, fends off the ruffian as much as her delicate consistency allows as she waits to be saved. The picture replicates precisely an image Anderson designates as typical in popular Victorian literature: "While bosomy heroines heaved, sighed, and palpitated, their masculine counterparts flexed, flailed, and thrust" (50).

PROGRESS AS IMPERIALIST IMPERATIVE

As with its justification of the sovereignty of masculinity, that which defined women and femininity as inferior, Victorian society used science, reason, and progress to sanction England's imperial policies and racist attitudes, which created the hierarchies of "nation" and "race." Women and the Irish, of course, were victims of differential treatment long before the nineteenth century. However, the Victorian and Edwardian eras brought with them logically thought out systems of rationale by/for those in power. As Ashis Nandy explains in *The Intimate Enemy: Loss and Recovery of Self Under Colonialism*, with English imperialism, "ancient forces of human greed and violence . . . ha[d] merely found a new legitimacy in anthropocentric doctrines of secular salvation, in the ideologies of progress, normality and hyper-masculinity, and in theories of cumulative growth of science and technology" (x). The ideology of progress also evinced itself in the Victorian and Edwardian era's collection and categorization of nations and races. Just as psychiatry and medicine defined norms for women's, men's, and children's sexuality, for health, and for gender classifications, the colonial enterprise acted, in Edward Said's terms, from "an undeterred and unrelenting Eurocentrism" that "accumulated experiences, territories, peoples, [and] histories" and, furthermore, "studied them, classified them, verified them; but above all, it subordinated them to the culture and indeed the very ideal of white Christian Europe" (72).

Nineteenth-century Ireland, Christian and white but primarily Catholic and designated ethnically Celtic, nonetheless suffered under the English rule that had been hoisted upon it hundreds of years earlier and which, in Victorian times, treated the Irish, like Indians or Africans, as an other to be studied, classified, and verified. Victims of the English "enthusiasm for . . . sheer bloodthirsty dominance over innumerable niggers, bog dwellers, babus, and wogs" (Said 73), the Irish remind us of the "uniformly retrograde" (Said 72) treatment of the other which flew under the flag of progress. Here, Said follows in the footsteps of Aimé Césaire who, in *Discourse on Colonialism*, condemns the imperialist corruption of the Victorian doctrine of progress. Where colonizers talk about "progress, about 'achievements,' about diseases cured, improved standards of living," Césaire sees "societies drained of their essence, cultures trampled underfoot, institutions undermined, lands confiscated, religions smashed, magnificent artistic creations destroyed, extraordinary *possibilities* wiped out" (21). Césaire's condemnation of progress includes in its scope the "subjective good faith" of colonizers (34). Obvious examples in Ireland include intrusions ranging from the Cromwellian era expropriation of Catholic landowners, which put the land into what the conquerors considered worthier and more able English and Protestant hands, to Matthew Arnold's condescending view, two hundred years later, that the Irish could improve themselves by being more like the English. These are the sorts of good intentions that Césaire would inevitably define, in negative terms, as "entirely irrelevant to the objective social implications of the evil work [performed by] watchdogs of colonialism" (34).

The "drive for mastery over men," according to Nandy, belies "a world view which believes in the absolute superiority of the human over the nonhuman and the subhuman, the masculine over the feminine, the adult over the child, the historical over the ahistorical, and the modern or progressive over the traditional or the savage" (x). Built into the colonial system, then, is a hierarchy that, although socially constructed, disguises itself as divine or—moreso in the late nineteenth and early twentieth century—innate by decree of science and reason. The result, as Albert Memmi notes in *The Colonizer and the Colonized*, is the following: "Ethical or sociological, aesthetic or geographic comparisons, whether explicit and insulting or allusive and discreet, are always in favor of the mother country and the colonialist. This place, the people here, the customs of this country are always inferior—by virtue of an inevitable and pre-established order" (67–68). According to these rationalizations, what are, in actuality, socially scripted differences between cultures become "standards of absolute fact" (Memmi 71).

The stage had been set for the scripting of the "inevitable" rightness of English rule of the "inferior" Irish by some of the main proponents of Victorian progressivism. Darwin, a self-professed liberal, somewhat ironically offered prime material for racist motives in his *On the Origin of Species*. Although, as Himmelfarb points out, the work has been read as anti-racist by virtue of the fact that the theory of evolution traces us all back to the same origin (414), it also might be seen to provide ballast for the other side. Perhaps the most obvious, if arguably misguided, evidence of racism can be found in the full title of the work, *On the Origin of Species by Means of Natural Selection, or the Preservation of Favoured Races in the Struggle for Life*. Although Darwin did not intend for the title to be used for the vindication of racial cleansing or the imperialistic control of one race or nation by another, the phrase "preservation of favoured races" enabled it to be appropriated in this fashion. Contributing additional weight to such arguments is Darwin's contention that "the struggle almost invariably will be most severe between the individuals of the same species, for they frequent the same districts, require the same food, and are exposed to the same dangers. In the case of varieties of the same species [elsewhere equated by Darwin with "races" (15; 12)], the struggle will generally be almost equally severe" (75; 59). In comparison to other peoples colonized by the English, the Irish have traditionally frequented practically "the same districts" as their oppressors and, by the mid-nineteenth century, were struggling to recover the land and rights (and, more literally during the famine, food sent to England), which, as the Darwinian argument could go, and the English argument went, they lost through their lesser "fitness."

During the Victorian era, Darwin's arguments made perfect sense in the sociopolitical arena of English-Irish relations, in that they were made to serve as a scientistic rationale for the racist beliefs of the English about the Irish. Having conquered Ireland centuries before, England could now assuage any residual guilt with the unalterable because scientifically proven fact that the struggle was inevitable—as inevitable as that between different varieties of wheat which, having been sown together, fight for dominance through the process of re-seeding. Some of the more racist of the English might even have hoped that, in the battle between the strong English and weak Irish seedlings, "some of the varieties which best suit the [social, political, and religious] . . . climate . . . w[ould] beat the others and so yield more seed, and w[ould] consequently in a few years quite supplant the other varieties" (75; 59). Although I do not suggest here that the English and Irish actually did battle on this eugenic level, the ease with which the metaphor may be transferred to the sociopolitical arena is obvious, especially for minds so predisposed.

That Darwin did not deny differences between races or between species and even encouraged hierarchical judgments about the differences also made his work fodder for racist beliefs. At the conclusion of *Origin*, he rejoices in the differences between those fit and less fit, noting that the "consequences" of Natural Selection include "divergence of character and the extinction of less-improved forms. Thus, from the war of nature, from famine and death, the most exalted object which we are capable of conceiving, namely, the production of higher animals, directly follows" (490; 428). The leap from war of "nature" to that of human society is not a big one, and Darwin himself recognized the applicability of his theories of natural selection and survival of the fittest to the interpretation and improvement of Western civilization. In an 1881 letter, Darwin applauds the' role natural selection has played in the "progress" of civilization, making his case as follows:

> Remember what risk the nations of Europe ran, not so many centuries ago of being overwhelmed by the Turks, and how ridiculous such an idea now is! The more civilized Caucasian races have beaten the Turkish hollow in the struggle for existence. Looking to the world at no very distant date, what an endless number of the lower races will have been eliminated by the higher civilized races throughout the world. (*Life and Letters I* 316).

Here, having not only admitted to a belief in racial difference but reveled in the defeat of the "lower" by the "higher civilized" races, Darwin does not surprise us by sanctioning theories in favor of racial purity. More specifically, he recommends that the mixture of races should occur only under emergency circumstances, such as the need for preservation or betterment of a given race (Himmelfarb 415). Again, although Darwin's theories were confined to plant and animal species other than that of the human, *On the Origin of Species* nevertheless betrays a predilection for racial purity that could be construed as applicable to humans as well as to other species. For instance, the following passage reveals Darwin's squeamishness about the wisdom of one race sharing its naturally selected characteristics with another: "the possibility of making distinct races by crossing has been greatly exaggerated. There can be no doubt that a race can be modified by occasional crosses, if aided by the careful selection of those individual[s] . . . which present any desired character" (20; 15). Thus, according to Darwin, if it is to be done at all, crossing races should be done carefully and with supervision. Such notions provided a breeding ground for theories as seemingly different as the eugenics which rose in popularity in the late Victorian and Edwardian eras (and which influenced Yeats[19]) to the somewhat less destructive but nonetheless racist theories of Matthew Arnold, who foresaw the improvement of both races occurring through a marriage of the feminine Celt to the masculine Anglo-Saxon. The tie that binds them is the scientism utilized to reinforce racial domination and/or betterment, essentially through prescribed breeding practices.

However, it is Social Darwinists who have been most popularly (and deservedly) credited with taking what Himmelfarb calls the "short step" from the "preservation of favoured individuals, classes, or nations" to the "glorification" of the same. As she explains, "exalting competition, power, and violence over convention, ethics, and religion," Social Darwinism informed "nationalism, imperialism, militarism, and dictatorship, . . . [and] the cults of the hero, the superman, and the master race" (416). Indeed, in his 1871 treatise, *On Some Fixed Points of British Ethnology*, Thomas Huxley comments specifically on the race-related discourse concerning England and Ireland which was evolving at the time. However, in this instance, he denounces the notion of racial definition. Writing about Ireland after the conquest of Henry II, after which the English "made their footing in the eastern half of the island, as the Saxons and Danes made good theirs in England," he acknowledges the British attempt to extirpate "the Gaelic-speaking Irish." He then asks:

> What, then, is the value of the ethnological difference between the Englishman of the western half of England and the Irishman of the eastern half of Ireland? For what reason does the one deserve the name of a "Celt", and not the other? And further, if we turn to the inhabitants of the western half of Ireland, why should the term "Celt" be applied to them more than to the inhabitants of Cornwall? And if the name is applicable to the one as justly as to the other, why should not intelligence, perseverance, thrift, industry, sobriety, respect for law, be admitted to be Celtic virtues? And why should we not seek for the cause of their absence in something else than the idle pretext of "Celtic blood"? (153–54)

Here, Huxley calls into question the validity of allegedly biological determinants of personality, naming the Victorian trend an "idle pretext." In this case, however, Huxley is more anomaly than average.

Ernest Renan and Matthew Arnold, two major proponents of Victorian racial/racist theories of the Irish, and whose ideas Yeats more or less espouses in "The Celtic Element in Literature," proffered the sorts of arguments against which Huxley bristled. Renan's *The Poetry of the Celtic Races* (1854; translated from the French in 1893) and Arnold's *On the Study of Celtic Literature* (1867) both reflect and magnify common Victorian treatments of the Celt as a proponent of "foolish interference with the natural progress of civilisation and prosperity" (Arnold xiii).[20] Here Arnold excerpts the *Times* in order to display the popular view of the Celts, a depiction with which Renan concurs. Renan foresees the Celts having difficulty maintaining their natural ways in the "presence of the ever-encroaching progress of a civilisation which is of no country, and can receive no name, other than that of modern or European" (59). Arnold, on the other hand, at first seems more defender than critic of the Celts. With the suggestion that *not only* the Celts but the English could benefit from a mutual understanding and incorporation of certain of one another's traits, Arnold appears to place both sides on equal ground. However, before long, we see that he favors the "Germanic" as opposed to "Celtic" side of the English personality and genius for reasons heavily imbued with Victorian notions of progress.

"Science" is a key concept in *On the Study of Celtic Literature*. To Arnold, science is a "real, legitimate force" and one he equates with "modern civilisation" (9). Unstoppable, it "march[es]" along according to the "bent of [Victorian] times," with the mandate to "[know] things as they are" (17, 12). Here, Arnold characterizes the world in essentialist terms: "things" exist "as they are"—including, he will go on to show, the racial characteristics of the English and the Celts. Moreover, he advocates science as useful for all studies including that of the Celt and Celtic literature because it provides stability (57) to the conclusions of those who depend on it. Thus, according to Arnold, an application of the steady hand of science is all it takes to reveal what *is*.

Like Yeats, Arnold admits that science tends to focus on differences and to divide or separate (60). In this he continues a critique of science and reason that extends (at least) back to William Blake, whose ideas on the topic Yeats saw fit to record in his 1897 essay, "William Blake and the Imagination." In this piece, Yeats paraphrases Blake as follows: "The reason, and by the reason he meant deductions from observations of the senses, binds us to mortality because it binds us to the senses, and divides us from each other by showing us clashing interests" (*EI* 112). One example of the divisive nature of science can be seen in the race-based theories advocated by linguists, philologists, and craniologists that served to create an opposition and tension between the English and Irish. Judgments about the evolutionary stage of each race according to the derivation of their respective language or head size, for instance, revealed the supposed distinctions between the two. However, Arnold perceived the possibility for science to come to other conclusions as well. "[T]rue science," he writes, recognizes "a law of ultimate fusion, of conciliation" (60). He intends, moreover, for his essay on Celtic literature be one of the (rational) stepping-stones toward the inevitable "fusion of all the inhabitants of [the British isles] into one, homogeneous, English-speaking whole, the breaking down of separate provincial nationalities" (9). However, in spite of his goal, Arnold fails to extricate his views from those of the divisive forms of science, for the very essence of his study depends upon the perceived opposition between the Germanic and the Celtic personalities. In this way, Arnold partakes in what Memmi later depicts as an imperialist tactic: the stressing of differences between colonized and colonizer, a purposeful distancing which denies the possibility of community (71) and therefore a sharing of power. The imperialist's, and Arnold's, insistence on defining differences between colonizer and colonized makes racism, as Memmi puts it, "not . . . an incidental detail, but . . . a consubstantial part of colonialism" (74)—and, again not incidentally, of Arnold's study.

As with other colonialist ventures, then, Arnold's message is twofold. In his attempt to defend and help the Irish, he presents the "subjective good faith" of Césaire's equation, but not without the "evil" "objective social implication" of reinforcing the same racist notions that were the problem in the first place. Furthermore, the specifics of Arnold's depictions of the English and Irish reinforce the imperialist hierarchy. As Memmi explains in a passage that might describe Arnold, "Custodian of the values of civilization and history, he accomplishes a mission; he had the immense merit of bringing light to the colonized's ignominious darkness" (75). Arnold may not fit David Cairns's and Shaun Richards's estimation of the colonizer who "attempt[s] to convince the colonized themselves of their irremovable deficiencies and the subsequent naturalness and permanence of their subordination" (8). His concerned condescension, however, likens Arnold to the "paternalist" who, according to Memmi, takes "racism and inequality [even] further" by practicing "if you like, a charitable racism—which is not thereby less skillful nor less profitable" (76).

In comparing the Germanic to the Celtic sides of the English race, Arnold clearly favors the Germanic, the blood of which he observes to be the dominant strain in English veins. He does not fail to proffer several positive traits of the Celt; for example, he suggests that the Celtic "essence is to aspire ardently after life, light, and emotion, to be expansive, adventurous, and gay" (76). However, he ultimately finds the Celt a disappointment. In a world in which "the skilful and resolute appliance of means to end . . . is needed both to make progress in material civilisation, and also to form powerful states," Arnold asserts, the Celt has been "lamed" in spiritual and political matters by his "rebellion against fact" (79). Arnold builds his argument on Henri Martin's assertion that the Celt is "*always ready to act against the despotism of fact*" (77), a sentiment also voiced by Renan. In *The Poetry of the Celtic Races*, Renan asserts that the Celtic race is "endowed with too little initiative," having "worn itself out in resistance to its time, and in the defence of desperate causes . . . [I]t does not appear that the peoples which form it are by themselves susceptible of progress. To them life appears as a fixed condition, which man has not power to alter" (7). Arnold and Renan both color the Celts as not only biologically, racially, and intellectually incapable of progress but downright hostile to it. As Seamus Deane likewise attests in *Strange Country*, "the Irish community is consistently portrayed as one that it is impossible to recruit into the nineteenth-century normalizing narrative of progress and economic development" (146). The Germanic portion of the English heritage, then, legitimizes English authority in a modern world that considers fact to be hero, not despot. Representatives of "*steadiness with honesty*," the English are governed by their "Germanic genius," which leads them along the following path: "excellence of a national spirit thus composed is freedom from whim, flightiness, perverseness; patient fidelity to Nature,—in a word, *science*,—leading it at last, though slowly, and not by the most brilliant road, out of the bondage of the humdrum and common, into the better life" (74). Although the Germanic genius lacks verve, it nonetheless gets the job done. It succeeds in the modern world by virtue of "the idea of science governing all departments of human activity" (74).

Whereas "science" defines the Germanic genius, the Celt is associated with "sentiment," a word that, in Arnold's Victorian eyes, allies the Celt with the feminine. Sentimental, the Celt is composed of an "organisation quick to feel impressions, and feeling them very strongly; a lively personality therefore, keenly sensitive to joy and to sorrow" (76). Likewise, it is in the Celt's nature to be "sociable" and "hospitable" as well as "sensual; but it is not so much the vulgar satisfactions of sense that attract him as emotion and excitement" (77). Arnold finally gets down to business when he concludes, "no doubt the sensibility of the Celtic nature, its nervous exaltation, have something feminine in them, and the Celt is thus peculiarly disposed to feel the spell of the feminine idiosyncrasy; he has an affinity to it; he is not far from its secret" (82). Renan similarly insists:

> If it be permitted us to assign sex to nations as to individuals, we should have to say without hesitance that the Celtic race . . . is an essentially feminine race. No human family, I believe, has carried so much mystery into love. No other has conceived with more delicacy the ideal of woman, or been more fully dominated by it. It is a sort of intoxication, a madness, a vertigo. (8)

Moreover, he sees the Celts as "before all else a domestic race, fitted for family life and fireside joys. In no other race has the bond of blood been stronger, or has it created more duties, or attached man to his fellow with so much breadth and depth. Every social institution of the Celtic peoples was in the beginning only an extension of the family" (5–6).

If we return for a moment to Victorian standards of femininity, we see that Arnold's and Renan's Celt fulfills many traditional definitions that also define women as weaker, less stable, and not fit for the public sphere. Social, hospitable, and domestic, the Arnold-Renan version of the Celt is tied to the private sphere of home, family, and the provision of comfort. The impression that the Celt finds satisfaction through love and is dominated by the notion of the ideal woman—both of which are family-oriented (private), not business (public) concerns—similarly relegates him to the domestic circle. Arnold's depiction of the relationship between the Irish and English as a marriage of the respectively feminine and masculine secures the domestic positioning of the Irish. According to Renan and Arnold, the Celt also suffers from symptoms much like those of the psychiatrically-defined and female-coded hysteric: "nervous exaltation," emotional vertigo, madness, and the likelihood of losing control at any moment—all negatively-valued in the hypermasculine Victorian ethos.[21] Finally, the Celt's sensuality allies him, like women, with the more base, animalistic part of our natures as elaborated by J. S. Mill's theory of natural kinds and the Royal Society's dualism which associated women with matter—that is, with inert materials which need the guidance of "mind" (men or, in this instance, the English) in order to achieve anything. Following in Arnold's footsteps, Otto Weininger reiterates this paternalistic form of imperialism, in *Sex and Character*, allying the colonized with women according to their mutual need for supervision and protection.[22]

Arnold and Renan diminish the Irish not only through an alliance with the feminine; they also condescend to them by playing the role of (English) parent to (Irish) child—a move that inserts the Irish into the well-known negative equation of primitives, women, and children.[23] Renan, for instance, comments on the fitness of the Irish for submissive, sixth-century monastic life when he argues, "[c]redulous as a child, timid, indolent, inclined to submit and obey, the Irishman alone was capable of lending himself to that complete self-abdication in the hands of the abbot" (49–50). Elsewhere he remarks that Celts, "too much inclined to look upon themselves as minors and in tutelage, . . . are quick to believe in destiny and resign themselves to it" (7). Arnold similarly asserts that although the Celt is "undisciplinable, anarchical, and turbulent by nature"—the bestial nature rearing its ugly head again—"out of affection and admiration [he] giv[es] himself body and soul to some leader" (82). Interestingly, many liberal nineteenth-century philosophers and political theorists praised the first half of this assertion. Marjorie Howes notes, for instance, that Marx and Engels saw the anarchic nature of the Celts as an indication of "revolutionary potential," as an opportunity for "political effectiveness" (23), not weakness. However, the supposed association of the Irish with the savage was more often calumnious, as in the common depiction of ape-like or drunken and disorderly Irish men and women in English and American popular culture of the era.[24] Arnold, especially, reveals the more typical Victorian bias in his paternalistic belief that as economic world leaders, rational/scientific thinkers, and anything but credulous, the English are naturally (biologically/racially) suited to tell the Irish how to run their lives. This is an example of Memmi's observation that those in power create negative depictions of the colonized such as a supposed "lack of desires" or "ineptitude for comfort, science, [and] progress" in order to make the colonized unfit and in need of protection (82). The submissive nature of the Irish is another such fiction.

The Victorian evaluation of the Irish as feminine, submissive, closer to nature (i.e., bestial), and family-oriented exposes the importance of progress, science, and reason in the constitution of nineteenth-century English-Irish relationships. In an essay written more than a century after Renan's and Arnold's pronouncements, Terry Eagleton provides important socio-historical insight into the ways in which Irish traditions of "custom, lineage, and kinship" (73) contributed to this phenomenon. Eagleton opens his essay by giving a moment's credence to the question incited by his predecessors' race theories when he asks, "Can it be that Gaels are more affectionate, more genial and intuitive, than the emotionally inhibited English?" (68). His insightful teasing out of the question comprises the essay "The Good-Natured Gael," from *Crazy John and the Bishop*, in which Eagleton warns, "Stereotypes are not to be confused with reality; . . . but they may occasionally provide clues to specific social conditions" (68). Making reference to one of these social conditions early in his essay, Eagleton portrays the Celt[25] in ways that are similar to, though more sympathetic than, Renan's depiction. More specifically, he elucidates the historical reality behind the relationship between the Celt's dislike for "the ideologues of unfeeling Reason" (72), their reputation for sentimentality, and the nature of the traditional social and family order in Ireland. Eagleton addresses the same stereotype Renan elaborates:

> It is not, then, a question of the convivial yet melancholic Celt with a song on his lips and a tear in his eye, one hand wrapped around the ale-jug and the other thrust out in affable welcome to the stranger. It is a question of the ways in which, in family-based agrarian communities, personal and social relationships are less easily separable than they are in the market-places or political institutions of modernity. (73)

He goes on to argue that the Gaelic peasantry was "every bit as anti-Romantic as Jane Austen" and, in fact, that the "a-rational sanctions and pieties" representative of traditional Gaelic communities "are quite as systematic and authoritative as any more modern brand of instrumental reason" (73).

However, Enlightenment privileging of reason over sentiment widely influenced Victorian thought. As a result, Victorian depictions of the Irish exhibited an essentialist belief in racial characteristics, a faith in hierarchy, and a paternalistic assessment in the inability of the Irish to rule themselves in a modern (read: scientific, rational) world. Taking one more step back, we see that these Victorian convictions were fed by what Aimé Césaire calls "thingification" (21).

According to Césaire's theory, in order to be defined as feminine or barbaric, the Celtic race first had to be perceived as other. The very definition of the Irish or Celts as a race helped in its path to otherness.[26] As Memmi explains, viewing the colonized as a race leads not only to their depersonalization but also to their pluralizaton as a "they" (85). Reduced to object status (Memmi 86) through this same process, the individual personalities that make up the group recede into the background to make way for a simpler, easier delineation, and one that fits the ideological power structure of the ruling classes. In other words, by denigrating the Irish and demonstrating their own merits, the English reinforce their own potency, with the result that "the more the usurped is downtrodden, the more the usurper triumphs" (Memmi 52–53). In his introduction to Memmi's *The Colonizer and the Colonized*, Jean-Paul Sartre reiterates this, pointing out the colonial tendency to establish privilege by "debasing the colonized to exalt themselves, denying the title of humanity to the natives, and defining them as simply absences of qualities—animals not humans" (xxvi). Thus, the Irish, like other colonized groups, are defined as other, or as other than rational, scientific, thinking human beings.

The preeminence of science and reason infused Victorian and Edwardian culture in England and Ireland with a wholehearted belief in a particular mode of progress. Progress, in turn, defined nineteenth- and early twentieth-century views of the self and other, both by confirming old hierarchies and creating new, scientifically justified forms of the other. Of particular importance to the study of Yeats's early plays is the authentication, more substantial than divine decree because reinforced by the science-directed and reason-infused principle of progress, of hierarchized theories of gender and race that played a vital role in the relationships between England and Ireland and the public and private spheres. Living in the midst of all this, Yeats came to despise the Victorian, bourgeois notion of progress for what it was: an interloper in the social domain. He recognized that science and reason had been pushed beyond their limits for discovering empirical truths and, instead, were being utilized by progressivist moral, economic, social, and religious theorists to create man-made truths about men and women, England and Ireland. Desiring to break out of these strictures, I argue, Yeats aimed to show, in the words of contemporary postcolonial and feminist critics Himani Bannerji, Shahrzad Mojab, and Judith Whitehead, that "gender, 'difference,' [and] 'nation' . . . are not essentialist entities, but coexist as social practices in a continuous process of interaction and potential transformation" (25).

This theme reverberates loudly throughout Yeats's dramatic canon, especially in the last decade of the 1890s and the first decade of the 1900s, during which Yeats struggled most vehemently with issues of gender and ethnic identity on personal, social, political, and aesthetic levels. While Yeats's dramatic career evinces the many changes in political, social, spiritual, and artistic beliefs he experienced throughout his lifetime, within the canon exists at least one constant: the critique of progress. In *Strange Country*, Seamus Deane articulates a similar thought when he writes about Yeats's work as a "reply to the internationalized theories of cosmopolitanism and progress that seemed to him to be depriving the world of its imaginative order" (155). However, Deane diminishes the scope of Yeats's response when he argues that it is "a national literature, indeed a national ideology" that comprises the "reply" that "brings to a more intense pitch the division between universal reason, understood as such in relation to an Enlightenment model of science and of a progressive humanity" (155). As I will explain in chapter two and following, I see Yeats's reply in this regard to extend well beyond the limits of nationalist ideology.

Chapter Two
Literatures of Progress

> The movement of thought which has made the good citizen, or has been made by him, has surrounded us with comfort and safety, and with vulgarity and insincerity. One finds alike its energy and its weariness in churches which have substituted a system of morals for spiritual ardour; in pictures which have substituted conventionally pretty faces for the disquieting revelations of sincerity; in poets who have set the praises of those things good citizens think praiseworthy above a dangerous delight in beauty for the sake of beauty.
> —William Butler Yeats

> Beer, bible, and the seven deadly virtues have made England what she is.
> —Oscar Wilde[1]

YEATS'S VISION OF PROGRESS

YEATS'S CONTEMPT FOR THE MORALISM AND MATERIALISM INHERENT IN THE theories and practices of Victorian and Edwardian progressivists deepened when he considered their effect on the arts. That he did not abide by the "Anglo-Saxon" conception of "progress," which, "impelled by moral enthusiasm and the Patent Office, seem[ed] a perpetual straight line" (*Explorations* 354), is plain. Less obvious but more significant is Yeats's response to the narrowness of conventional definitions of progress, the selfsame moral enthusiasm of which prompted him to re-define progress in ways that not only permit but encourage deviation from that "straight line." For Yeats, human progress could not be counted or numbered or classified as one would trees in a botanical study or diseases in a medical experiment. He outlines this conclusion in a 1908 address to the British Association for the Advancement of Science, in which he recalls an insight that came to him during a train ride:

> A picture arose before my mind's eye: I saw Adam numbering the creatures of Eden; soft and terrible, foul and fair, they all went before him. That, I thought, is the man of science, naming and numbering, for our understanding, everything in the world. But then I thought, we writers, do we not also number and describe, though with a difference? You are chiefly busy with the exterior world, and we with the interior. (*UPII* 36)

Yeats continues, describing writers as social scientists, as "Adams of a different Eden, a more terrible Eden perhaps, for we must name and number the passions and motives of men. There, too, everything must be known, everything understood, everything expressed" (*UPII* 369–70).

Here Yeats reveals a rare alliance with the Victorian frame of mind Foucault describes as an obsession with creating a "careful analytical discourse" within which they could "take [the world] 'into account'" (23, 24). Two related instances of Yeats's advocacy of scientific cataloging are worth brief mention here. John Wilson Foster points out that in the 1880s and 1890s Yeats "classified fairies and fairy tales in an almost Linnean fashion" and even "lectured to the Belfast Naturalists' Field Club . . . , during which he made claim for the 'scientific utility' of the study of fairy belief" (129). Examples of this tendency can be found among Yeats's many manuscript notebooks housed at the National Library of Ireland, one of which contains autoscript notes on Irish gods and legends. (Although the notebooks are undated, those I reference most likely hail from the late 1800s, the time during which Yeats most closely studied Irish mythology and fairy lore.) He lists several gods and displays the relationships between them not only by connecting them with hand-drawn lines but also by including the categorizations allotted them by Ernest Rhys. In a second book, an address book actually, Yeats created another classification system in which he lists each god or mythical item under the letter he sees as most relevant to its meaning. For instance, he entered "Ogam" [sic] under "O" along with an inventory of the ogham alphabet and its symbolic meanings. Under "P" he enumerates "sacred places" including Knockany in Co. Limerick and Lough Foyle (POS 13,574). This scientific cataloging, undoubtedly inspired by his father, whose some time admiration of Darwin and Mill (Alldritt 14), as we have seen, influenced him in his earliest years, was, however, soon abandoned by Yeats for a fairly consistent anti-scientism.[2]

Moreover, while his cataloguing took a form similar to that of scientists, Yeats's "naming and numbering" eventuates a vastly different worldview than that of natural science, in part because he made literature, mythology, and spirituality his subject matter. Declan Kiberd's description of the "ecstatic lists of native placenames"

Yeats often employed in his poetry corresponds with the above examples as well. Kiberd writes that Yeats's lists invoke "the Adam-like incantations of writers, rediscovering the exhilaration with which the first persons in Ireland . . . named their own place and, in that sense, shaped it" (118). Thus, even when Yeats takes "into account" the external—for instance, Irish fairy tales, gods, or place names—their significance lay not in their existence as empirical facts or objects but in their symbolic or internal meaning.

More generally, Yeats saw the naming and numbering performed by writers and artists as an entirely different sort of process from that carried out by scientists, with the artistic process more closely reflecting his train-ride epiphany than the logical formulation of rationalists. Yeats believed in a spiritual, psychological, and intellectual progress through revelation, not a materialist/moralistic progress through deduction. Using images from William Blake, Yeats argues against reason, that darling of the progressivists, depicting rational man as "a drawer of the straight line, the maker of the arbitrary and impermanent." "Sanctity has its straight line also," he explains, "darting from the centre, and with these arrows the many-coloured serpent, theme of all our poetry, is maimed and hunted." Yeats replaces Blake's concept of the damaging "straight line" of sanctimonious reason with its unpredictable opposite, instinct, which "creates the recurring and the beautiful, all the winding of the serpent" (*EI* 288). According to Yeats, it is only through the immeasurable, immaterial, amoral entities of instinct and miracle that progress is possible. He illustrates this point in an essay, "The Irish Literary Theatre":

> New races understand instinctively, because the future cries in their ears, that the old revelations are insufficient, and that all life is revelation beginning in miracle and enthusiasm and dying out as it unfolds in what we have mistaken for progress. It is one of our illusions, as I think, that education, the softening of manners, the perfecting of law—countless images of a fading light—can create nobleness and beauty, and that life moves slowly and evenly toward some perfection. Progress is miracle, and it is sudden, because miracles are the work of an all-powerful energy. (*UPII* 199)

Yeats perceives himself—and his contemporary Irish citizens, if only they would heed his warning—as a member of one of the new races who can hear the future crying in his ears. The central message of this passage is Yeats's denouncement of the hegemonic belief in progress as a mistaken teleology. Though he does not deny the possibility of perfection, a spiritual condition we can achieve momentarily through facing our masks, Yeats describes both perfection and progress as possible only through the sudden, individual perception of an instinctual truth. That which his contemporaries called progress Yeats perceived as the self-aggrandizing pabulum of those in power, whose pre-ordination of themselves as models of the highest form of civilization had poisoned the major forms of social communication such as education, popular literature, advertising, and the arts. That form of progress, writes Yeats, is "the sole religious myth of modern man" (*Explorations* 355). Yet it is as a writer that Yeats was most concerned with the ways in which the arts, in particular, reiterated the progressivist, moralist, and materialist beliefs he perceived as dangerous. In "Certain Noble Plays of Japan," for instance, Yeats maintains:

> In literature also we have had the illusion of change and progress, the art of Shakespeare passing into that of Dryden, and so into the prose drama, by what has seemed when studied in its details unbroken progress. . . . Only our lyric poetry has kept its Asiatic habit and renewed itself at its own youth, putting off perpetually what has been called its progress in a series of violent revolutions. (*EI* 225–26).

Ultimately, Yeats concluded that neither in literature nor in life could one work diligently and logically toward perfecting one's form, be it poetic or human. In a world in which to be "civilised" meant to believe "in progress, in a warless future, in always-increasing wealth" (*EI* 499), Yeats found himself applauding anarchy. For instance, undoubtedly inspired by his subject matter, he writes in an 1897 review of Maeterlinck: "We are in the midst of a great revolution of thought, which is touching literature and speculation alike; an insurrection against everything which assumes that the external and material are the only fixed things, the only standards of reality" (*UPII* 45). In another review written that same year, he earnestly concludes that the "revolt against the manifold, the impersonal, the luxuriant, and the external" is "perhaps the great movement of our time, and of more even than literary importance" (*UPII* 42). And his own work shows the influence of anarchist thought, conspicuously in the unmistakably Nietzschean hero Paul Ruttledge in *Where There Is Nothing* and more subtly in his positive depictions of a-stereotypically gendered characters in *The King's Threshold*, *On Baile's Strand*, and *Deirdre*.[3] Thus, in a literary world in which realism and propagandistic social reform had become the norm, Yeats chose anti-realist and mythical themes; but he did not, as I will illustrate, abandon social critique so much as revise the standard message about progress.

Yeats's definition of progress cannot be fully delineated without a discussion of his cyclical view of history, the spiritual process of attaining Unity of Being, and the related doctrine of the mask. The concept of Unity of Being is itself most fully explored in *A Vision*, the philosophical, historical, and spiritual treatise first published in 1925 and which had its origins in the Automatic Script writings of Yeats's wife, Georgie Hyde-Lees Yeats, who began sharing her mystical talents with Yeats in 1917. The fact that even the first automatic writing scripts post-date the plays that comprise the focus of my study by several years does not discount *A Vision*'s relevance here. In fact, showing what the plays written around the turn of the century have in common with the later work—or even how they inform it—sheds light on an important dynamic of Unity of Being. That is, the plays' themes and characterizations reveal the social as well as spiritual and historical significance of Unity of Being. More specifically, my explication of Yeats's treatment of the social construction of identity in his early plays help us understand Unity of Being as, in contemporary feminist and postcolonial terms, a form of syncretistic gender and ethnic hybridity which, moreover, has as its emphasis the revision of conventional notions of progress.[4]

Yeats believed that every society experiences incarnations of time, place, nation, and individual, each of which, as he notes in *A Vision*, is "sealed at birth with a character derived from the whole" (253). The whole obtains its preordained, though not fixed, nature through Yeats's theory of history which he bases on traditions dating back to Anaximander, Empedocles, and Heraclitus (*AV* 246) and which include the doctrines of the Eternal Return (*AV* 248) and the Great Year (*AV* 251).[5] Briefly, Yeats contends that history evolves in 2000–year cycles that oppose each other "in perpetual alternation" (*AV* 247), the "primary tincture" opposed by the "antithetical." Individuals and nations that exist in the most recent cycle, which includes the history of Christianity, derive their personalities from the antithetical tincture (for secular life) and primary tincture (for religious life). In other words, history has colored Yeats's (and our) era with an emphasis on reason, logic, morality, and objectivity (*AV* 72–73). According to Yeats's theory of history, then, the predominance of historical progressivism during the Victorian era, in a sense, was pre-destined.

More specifically, Yeats's theory of history tells us that "[a]t the birth of Christ took place, and at the coming *antithetical* influx will take place, a change equivalent to the *interchange of the tinctures*. . . . Before the birth of Christ religion and vitality were polytheistic, *antithetical*, and to this the philosophers opposed their *primary*, secular thought" (*AV* 262–63). Thus, according to Yeats, in our historical cycle, the primary religious dispensation, which is "dogmatic, levelling, unifying, feminine, [and] humane, [with] peace its means and end," is opposed by an antithetical dispensation, which "obeys imminent power, is expressive, hierarchical, multiple, masculine, harsh, [and] surgical" (*AV* 263). In this description of the antithetical tincture we see an echo, a preordination really, of the progressivist tendencies that Yeats despises in his own culture's hierarchical, patriarchal, scientific leanings. But preordination does not necessarily imply unwilling submission on our parts. In fact, resistance, as described below, is the key to (Yeats's version of) progress within this system.

If society does and must exist according to the values of progressivism, then, according to Yeats's initially dualistic system, the only response to this problem is opposition. This Yeats learned from his spiritual instructors, Michael Robartes and Owen Ahearne, who taught him to "identify consciousness with conflict, not with knowledge, [and to] substitute for subject and object and their attendant logic a struggle toward harmony, toward a Unity of Being" (*AV* 214). Unity of Being, an ultimate state of consciousness, is reached only after continually facing and incorporating one's opposite personality or "mask." Yet, as Yeats's spiritual guides explain, one can neither approach consciousness/Unity of Being nor fight against the reign of progressivism with logic or knowledge, the tools of the enemy. Instead, the goal has to be reached through conflict, by a face-off between logic, as agent of progress, and passion/instinct. For instance, in order to attain Unity of Being, a society overwhelmed with the dictates of science and reason and therefore concerned with the material should "face," or in rough layman's terms try on or empathize with, its "mask," a society concerned primarily with the spiritual. By understanding its opposite—that is, the ways of thinking that inform the other—the society would widen its perspective, thereby gaining in overall strength. And it is in this way, by becoming a multiple subject, that one emerges from the inescapably dualistic structure of the *process* into a product, as it were, that is both something more and something less than the dualistic structure that produced it. That is, one emerges as a version of Patrick Colm Hogan's syncretistic hybrid, in which a synthesis of opposites creates a new personality which is "ideally superior to both precedents—or, if not superior, at least better suited to [the person who has] internalized aspects of both [precedents]" (16).

Recently, both Janis Tedesco Haswell and Terence Brown have similarly theorized about the role of Yeats's spiritual beliefs in forming Yeats's concept of self as a multiple entity. Haswell, via James Hillman, argues that, for Yeats, the self is "composed of multiple personae, none of which is more or less real than another" (10). In her useful analysis of the gender structure of Yeats's masks, moreover, Haswell highlights his representation of the self as "protean in nature," and his "interpretation of human identity" as "transcending any static or monolithic state" (11). Finally, although Yeats sees the self, as Haswell tells us, as an "'entire being,'" (11), his use of the mask, she argues, "does not express the authentic self but captures part of the poet at a particular moment" (12)—a moment that, by nature, is ever-changing. Brown focuses on Yeats's belief in reincarnation, or the "doctrine of many lives," which "allowed that the self was not an absolute but a site of possibility" and, he contends, might have stimulated Yeats's theory of the mask. "For in both conceptions," he argues, "the self is denied singularity, is subject to change and reconstitution" (36). More important to the focus of this study is the fact that Yeats's idealization of Unity of Being (or syncretistic hybridity or the protean self) before *A Vision* is evident in the dramatic works I discuss herein, which take this process of becoming, or more specifically the social process of identity formation, as a central theme. Yeats's cyclical theories also emerged, in part, from what he saw as the failure of Western religious traditions to oppose the forms of progress he despised. He frequently disclosed battle wounds, obtained from the contest between logic and passion/intuition, which were notable for their place within the established Western religions of the time. For instance, in "If I Were Four and Twenty," Yeats laments, "Logic is loose again, as once in Calvin and Knox, or in the hysterical rhetoric of

Savonarola, or in Christianity itself in its first raw centuries, and because it must always draw its deductions from what every dolt can understand, the wild beast cannot but destroy mysterious life" (*Explorations* 277). Having destroyed mysterious life, rationalism spreads in its stead a system of ethics that, according to Yeats, makes the churches not only infected by but partners in the crime of progressivism. The church, having "substituted a system of morals for spiritual ardour" (*UPII* 193–94), advocates a simplistic and, Yeats would argue, dangerous moralism in which "the priest, trained to keep his mind on the strength of his Church and the weakness of his congregation, would have all mankind painted with a halo or with horns" (*Explorations* 119).

Yeats was not alone in his perception that the Christian church had not escaped infection by progressivism. Mircea Eliade, for instance, points out that Judeo-Christianity, in its belief that history is determined by God and therefore leads, ultimately, to Salvation or the "end" of history, takes part in fostering the progressivist view of history. Similarly, Jung diagnosed the early twentieth century Western world as suffering from a "one-sided attention or awareness" influenced by the "Western concept of causality" ("Abegg" 655). In a time when even religions "shared the heavily extraverted [*sic*] values" of the West (Zabriskie 62), people began to become caught up in the rational, the scientific, the technological and, consequently, to doubt the traditional forms of religion. If Judeo-Christianity could not escape from and, in fact, celebrated the linearity of history, what could it do for those trying to escape the horrific historical moment? Rather than continue to rely on a religion that could seemingly do nothing to stop the social, political, and economic chaos surrounding them, many individuals, Jung points out, began to view the church as obsolete ("Spiritual Problem" 239). Critical of the state of Western religions, Jung thus echoes Yeats's call for forms of spirituality that did not authorize the tenets of progress, materialism, or a narrow, socially defined moralism.

Reading the effects of progress, as defined by science and reason, in the spiritual history of Ireland, Yeats became a strong critic of both moralism and materialism. Echoing Marx, Yeats proclaimed in 1918, "Science, separated from philosophy, is the opium of the suburbs" (*Explorations* 340). That is, without the tempering agent of another, more inclusive point of view, science creates a society of "sentimentalists"—a negative word in Yeats's vocabulary, whether referring to artists, nationalists, or the bourgeoisie. He explains:

> The sentimentalists are practical men who believe in money, in position, in a marriage bell, and whose understanding of happiness is to be so busy whether at work or at play that all is forgotten but the momentary gain. They find their pleasure in a cup that is filled from Lethe's wharf, and for the awakening, for the vision, for the revelation of reality, tradition offers us a different word—ecstasy. (*Mythologies* 331)

Elsewhere, Yeats depicts the progress-loving public not as drugged into complacency but, rather, dangerously enthusiastic. For instance, in 1895, he argues, "this zealous public loves vehement assertion better than quiet beauty and partisan caricature better than a revelation of reality and peace." He goes on to lament that even, or especially, "our educated classes are themselves full of a different, but none the less noisy, political passion" (*UPI* 383). Yeats sees these individuals—those who reinforce the idea that to be a man one must be physically, emotionally, and fiscally vigorous or that the Irish are innately incapable of achieving their own agency—as perhaps even more of a social threat than the scientifically opiated in that they enthusiastically help spread the contagion of progress. Describing their zeal as one of the most lethal forms of ignorance, he complains in a 1903 piece on the Irish National Theatre that "the worst passions must of necessity be the most conspicuous" (*UPII* 306). That this is echoed in the famous lines of Yeats's 1920 poem, "The Second Coming"—"The best lack all conviction, while the worst / Are full of passionate intensity"—suggests that Yeats held strong views on this matter.

Kiberd hints at the psychological impetus behind many of the "conspicuous" Irish zealots when he writes about their literary passions: "Those Irish who wrote literature in English were not great buyers of books and so Irish artists wrote with one eye cocked on the English audience. They were, for the most part, painfully imitative of English literary modes, which they practised with the kind of excess possible only to the insecure" (115). Like Yeats, Kiberd traces the problematic excess that results from insecurity to its source in imperialism. He explains that

> [c]ultural colonies are much more susceptible to the literature of the parent country than are the inhabitants of that country itself, since plays and novels of manners have always been exemplary instruments in the civilizing of the subject. A colonized people soon comes to believe that approved fictions are to be imitated in life. (115)

Luke Gibbons also speaks to this point when he argues, "Cultural identity . . . does not pre-exist its representations or material expressions, but is in fact generated and transformed by them" (10).

That Yeats would agree with Kiberd's assessment of the dangers inherent in the imperialist program of "civilizing the subject" is evident in his quarrel with sanctimony. Yeats found neither science nor logic pernicious in and of itself. Rather, he opposed the use of scientific or logical principles in a moralistic or otherwise socially controlling fashion. He argues, for instance, that the "antagonist of [imagination] in Ireland is not a habit of scientific observation but our interest in matters of opinion" (*Explorations* 197). Here, Yeats places the impetus for the negative sort of passionate intensity on the fact that people insist on self-imposed compliance with a socially defined norm. More specifically, by transforming "the habit of scientific observation" into an opinion, and especially a moral opinion, one misuses science.

Yeats advises that we should instead "ascend out of common interests, the thoughts of the newspapers, of the market-place, of men of science, but only so far as we can carry the normal, passionate, reasoning self, the personality as a whole. We must find some place upon the Tree of Life for the phoenix' nest, for . . . passion" (*EI* 272). Ascending out of common interests, moreover, included rebelling against the presence in Ireland of "a puritanism which is not the less an English invention for being a pretended hatred of vice and a real hatred of intellect" (*Explorations* 132).

VICTORIAN LITERATURES OF PROGRESS

Yeats's criticism of English philistinism developed in part through his recognition of what he saw as the limitations of nineteenth-century English literature. As with the general philosophical trends of the time, literature of the Romantic and especially Victorian era reveals a scientistic and rationalistic bias both in form (the oratorical, rhetorical) and content (the moralistic). Yeats calls to task Swinburne, Browning, and Tennyson for having, albeit in different ways, "filled their work with what [he] called 'impurities', curiosities about politics, about science, about history, about religion" (*Autobiographies* 167). He argues, similarly, in a 1936 radio broadcast that "Swinburne, Tennyson, Arnold, Browning, had admitted so much psychology, science, moral fervour," that their work suffered from "impurity" (*EI* 495). Referring to the general literary history of the nineteenth century, Yeats maintains that the literature, particularly poetry, of 1840s and 1850s had been ruined by the presence of the "impurities" mentioned above, especially because they were expressed "with moral purpose and educational fervour—abstractions all" (*Autobiographies* 204). He laments that change in England had lagged behind that in France, preferring later poets such as Rossetti to the works of writers, including those listed above as well as early Shelley, which "tried to absorb into itself the science and politics, the philosophy and morality of its time" (*EI* 190).

The fact that literature's content was brought to bear upon life in a rhetorical fashion completed the reasons for Yeats's dislike of most Victorian writers. As John P. Frayne explains, "[r]hetoric was for Yeats defined by its function, didactic, rather than its techniques, which he freely used in his own poetry and prose; rhetoric tried to convince rather than reveal" (*UPI* 63). Yeats found the effort to "convince" particularly loathsome because of what he saw as its tendency to advance a distinct and limited message, which he outlines in an 1899 article titled "The Literary Movement in Ireland":

> The writers who made [nineteenth-century] literature or who shaped its ideals, [especially those who wrote] in the years before the great famine, lived at the moment when the middle class had brought to perfection its ideal of the good citizen, and of a politics and a philosophy and a literature which would help him upon his way; and they made a literature full of the civic virtues and, in all but its unbounded patriotism, without convenient ardours. (*UPII* 185)

Such self-righteous rhetoric, according to Yeats, resulted in a widespread, generational antipathy toward moralistic and rhetorical literature: "My generation, because it disliked Victorian rhetorical moral fervour, came to dislike all rhetoric" (*EI* 497). However, aversion to rhetoric was not limited to Yeats's colleagues who were close in age; nor were these individuals the only influential factor for Yeats in this regard. As Yeats recalls in *Autobiographies*, his father, too, "disliked the Victorian poetry of ideas" (66). Although Yeats found fault with the "irrelevant descriptions of nature, the scientific and moral discursiveness of *In Memoriam* . . . , the political eloquence of Swinburne, the psychological curiosity of Browning, and the poetical diction of everybody" (*Oxford Book of Modern Verse* ix), he recognized, amongst his contemporaries, motions toward the reclamation of literature from the restrictions of morality. He reveals this optimism in an 1897 review of Arthur Symons's *Armoris Victima*:

> It seems to me that the poetry which found its greatest expression in Tennyson and Browning pushed its limits as far as possible, tried to absorb itself into the science and philosophy and morality of its time, and to speak through the mouths of as many as might be of the great persons of history; and that there has been a revolt—a gradual, half-perceptible revolt, as is the fashion of English as contrasted with French revolts—and that poetry had been for two generations slowly contracting its limits and becoming more and more purely personal and lyrical in its spirit. (*UPII* 39–40)

Although most of the preceding examples of rhetorical fervor come from Yeats's discussions of poetry, his "dislike [of] all rhetoric" extends to other genres as well.

Discussion about the improvement of self, country, and others was not limited to theorists or to the "high" art of poetry. Throughout the Victorian and Edwardian eras, the doctrine of progress was ubiquitous, having insinuated itself not only into the pages of serious reform tracts but of literature and popular magazines as well. And, as Terence Brown notes, it was this culture—that of "English-language newspapers, of an Irish-accented version of English-language middle-brow fiction, of the Dublin music halls and of the touring grand opera company"—that most influenced the typical Irishmen and women (130). Just a quick perusal through some of the magazines and literature popular in Dublin and London during Victorian and Edwardian times displays the extent to which progressivist notions infiltrated everyday living. With the rise in the mid-Victorian era of magazine and book publications for children, indoctrination could begin early. The most popular of the book series for boys, begun in 1857, offered as its hero Tom Brown, whom critics admired for his skill at sport, courage, and manly vigor (Mangan 137). His ability to fight for the best spot in his environment undoubtedly tutored school-aged male readers in the lesson of the survival of the fittest.

Similarly, later in the nineteenth century, children's books by W. H. G. Kingston, R. M. Ballantyne, and Captain Mayne Reid conveyed images of "guileless, noble, self-reliant" individuals, filled with imperialist self-righteousness, "killing to survive and to spread civilisation, illustrating at every turn the mastery that was wrought of technical advance, environmental knowledge, and moral worth" (MacKenzie 190). These stories portrayed wars, hunts, and quests as valid, necessary, and economically and morally profitable. They taught children to revere people who, like Kipling's Kim, "do their duty to the King and their countrymen and who form part of a heroic national tradition stretching back to the knights of King Arthur" (Warren 201).[6]

Stories of the heroic national tradition of Ireland awakened similar chivalric urges, thanks to the Irish Literary Revival and the Gaelic League, which aimed to instill in both children and adults national pride and a sense of Irish identity. As Maire West notes, many praised the Irish myths precisely for their Irishness. Fr. Stephen Brown lamented the dearth of school boy stories that took place outside of English, Protestant schools and subsequently praised the epic Irish literature emerging through the many nineteenth-century translations of Old Irish texts (166–67). In spite of Fr. Brown's preferences and the specific political aims of such organizations as the Gaelic League, however, many of the depictions of Irish mythological figures, the most popular of whom were Cuchulain and Fionn Mac Cumhaill, convey chivalric, moralistic tones quite similar to those in *Tom Brown* and other English popular boys' fiction.

Standish O'Grady, James Stephens, Patrick Pearse,[7] and others wrote stories and plays for children and adolescents, nineteenth-century revisions of ancient Irish stories. Replete with ideals their contemporary Victorian and Edwardian audiences would find familiar and could admire, Irish children's literature recounted chivalric heroes, brave and strong, noble and intelligent, who fight bloody battles for king, sometimes queen, and country. Nor did the moral quality of these stories fall on deaf ears. In his preface to *Cuchulain of Muirthemne*, for instance, Yeats praises Lady Gregory's stories for their revelation of the "great moral realities" (12). This is not to say that Yeats subscribed to a bourgeois Victorian morality. Rather, he admired mythological heroes for the same reason he did those of any ancient civilization: "They had imaginative passions because they did not live within our own strait limits, and were nearer to ancient chaos, every man's desire, and had immortal models about them" (*EI* 178).

Even more specifically, Yeats viewed Irish mythology as a tonic for the age. He comments on the reinvigorated interest in the subject during the late nineteenth century in "The Celtic Element in Literature," avowing that the interest "comes at a time when the imagination of the world is as ready as it was at the coming of the tales of Arthur and of the Grail for a new intoxication." Along with "the symbolic movement," the new interest in mythology, Yeats argues, comprised a needed "reaction against the rationalism of the eighteenth century [which] has mingled with a reaction against the materialism of the nineteenth century" (*EI* 187). Thus, Yeats's idealized version of ancient Ireland falls under the rubric of essentialist and history-blind cultural nationalism, the intellectual limits of which have been identified and discussed in the last decade or so by multiple critics. Seamus Deane, for example, notes that such essentialism produced "repetitive, typifying narratives" which lent the "national character" an air of "petrifaction" (*Strange Country* 157). Likewise, David Lloyd refers to the "obsessive rituals of repetition by which nation states assure the legitimacy of their foundations and maintain their equilibrium" (70). However, it is also true that Yeats's intended use of the mythology does attend to the problems of a specific time and place (his own) and, in that way, the "key to the intellectual strategy of [Yeats's] Celticism" is decidedly not, as George Watson suggests, "the annulment, elision or denial of history" ("Celticism" 223).

Like Lady Gregory, Pearse employed an ethical motive in his mythic plays written for children. According to West, Pearse considered Cuchulain the ideal hero and Fionn mac Cumhaill an exemplar of morality and, thus, perfect role models for Irish boys (181). Working to maintain or, when possible, expand their ancient empires, heroes like Fionn and Cuchulain are, in this way, indistinguishable from the Tom Browns and Kims of the world. This is not, of course, to say that young people's literature in the form of Irish mythology provides exact moral and social parallels to literature found in popular English periodicals. However, for the purposes of my argument, the similarities deserve singular notice. Most of the popular and epic children's literature in Victorian England and Ireland depicted progress as a chivalric duty—for boys, at any rate.[8]

Two prime examples in this regard are Standish O'Grady's *Finn and His Companions* (1892) and "The Boyhood of Fionn" section of James Stephens's *Irish Fairy Tales* (1920). Consciously constructed as boyhood adventure tales, the works function, to a large extent, as *bildungsroman*. As in *Tom Brown's School Days*, we learn of Fionn's initial forays into nature, his first fight against the neighborhood boys, and other details of his social education that suggest a shared heritage (and future) for both Tom Brown and Fionn mac Cumhaill. A crucial moment in both tales is the hero's escape from the demasculinizing influence of his early female tutelage. Although Stephens's Fionn received his "first training" (about nature and boyish feats) from women (37), his entry into civilization necessitates a stay with a group of men who teach him "[a]ll the things that he should have known as by nature: the look, the movement, the feel of crowds; the shouldering and intercourse of man with man; the clustering of houses and how people bore themselves in and about them; . . . [and] tales of births, and marriages and deaths" (53). Especially in this last, rather Lacanian analysis of a child's achievement of personal and social identity—Fionn is seen as evolving from the feminine, Imaginary Order into the patriarchal Symbolic Order—we are reminded of the more general codification of Western society as masculine and of the didactic nature of both works.

Victorian and Edwardian tales, O'Grady's and Stephens's stories also overflow with gender stereotyping. We are told by Stephens's narrator that Fionn's mother Muirne's fear of the Mornas—the clan that killed her husband, necessitated that she give up her newborn son to the care of others (for his safety), and usurped Fenian rule—is due to her innate femininity: "women have strange loves, strange fears, and these are so bound up in one another that the thing which is presented to us is not often the thing that is to be seen" (38). The narrator assumes a similarly lofty attitude toward the women in the following passage: "There was nothing in wells or nettles, only women dreaded them. One patronised women and instructed them and comforted them, for they were afraid about one" (41)—this condescending advice from six-year-old Fionn!

Nor do O'Grady and Stephens neglect the important social duty of making boys into men—a process that, in adventure tales, is almost unremittingly directed toward empire building. As Lance Salway explains, adventure stories frequently "demonstrate the advantages of imperialism, the invincible superiority of the British colonial ideal, and the immaculate virtue and remarkable heroism of young British manhood" (369). An example can be found in the opening of O'Grady's piece, which consists of the morally bracing scene of "pious Britons work[ing] industriously [with St. Patrick to build a church], making the most of what daylight still remained" (3). Moreover, the fact that the book was published in the T. Fisher Unwin's "Children's Library" leaves no doubt as to its inclusion in the category of instruction and edification of the country's youth. Included in the list of works advertised in the first edition of the O'Grady book are: *Dick's Holidays and What He Did with Them*, a book that shows how to spend your holidays in a *useful* manner, and *Daddy Jake the Runaway and Other Stories* by Joel Chandler Harris. The latter text, which the *Observer* hailed as "'A fresh and delightful addition to those quaint and laughable tales which have made the author of "Uncle Remus" loved and fancied wherever the English tongue is spoken,'" no doubt served as a reminder to its English readers of their so-called white supremacy and justified imperialism. The "Lives Worth Living" Series provides three more titles of this ilk with *Leaders of Man*, *Master Missionaries*, and *Labour and Victory*.

The gender coding of the Victorian and Edwardian Fionn myths, then, shows O'Grady's and Stephens's Fionn to be as much British empire builder or usurper of other cultures as he is independent, home-turf-defending Irish hero. In this way, the stories reflect Seamus Heaney's notion of "reimagining," which Robert Dunbar explains as the use of "the old stories as the starting point for new fictions, where the fantasy of old worlds and the reality of the new worlds meet" (316). However, gender conventions are not the only new world reality which meets the ancient Irish myths, for the racial stereotyping of the Irish as savage and the British as evolved/cultured also plays a key role in the new myths. In his Victorian incarnation, O'Grady's Fionn must, like Tom Brown, capitulate to a society in which "animal life in its fullest measure, good nature and honest impulses" are typically depicted as an "excess of boyishness" (Hughes 143) and therefore something to be expunged with the learning of more refined pursuits that benefit home, health, and nation—though, in other versions of the myth, these are the very qualities to which the hunter, lover, and epicure Fionn aspires. Similarly, when Stephens's narrator portrays Fionn's enemies, the Morna, as "wild Connachtmen all, as untameable, as unaccountable as their own . . . countryside" (45), we must interpret the condescending tone with which the Fenians are placed above their Irish neighbors as reminiscent of English colonial representations of the Irish.

    Recalling for a moment the centuries-long English depiction of the Irish as savage and in need of taming, we might ask: To what extent do O'Grady and Stephens buy into this stereotype? I do not suggest that the Unionist O'Grady and the nationalist Stephens advocate in these tales the complete abandonment of "Irish" for "English" ways. However, when understood within the context of O'Grady's and Stephens' repackaging of the Fionn myth as adventure tales, these passages become suspicious. J. S. Bratton describes the adventure tale heroes as "devoted to notions of duty, power and responsibility which are the values of an aristo-military caste: they define themselves by birth, by the profession of arms, by the practice of certain sports and games, notably hunting, and by adherence to a set of rules of personal behaviour which can loosely be designated chivalric" (81). So far, so good: Fionn, too, represents an aristo-military class, albeit an Irish one, with its concomitant chivalric code of behavior. However, because both public school stories and adventure tales typically focused on English empire-building, the definition of hero was often extended to include what Salway calls "that innate sense of superiority which was the prime requisite for future [British] colonial administrators" (369). And here is where the conflict in identity formation is located. As ancient Irish warrior-king, Fionn is charged with the defense of his country from the "'bad race'" (O'Grady 73) that threatens continued "tyranny" and has, in the past, caused the nation to suffer from "famine" (O'Grady 127–28): images which are blatantly anti-Imperialistic if, indeed, not direct references to British imperialism. Clearly, the idea of Fionn as British colonial administrator is absurd. Yet, by making these myths into parables of proper (English) behavior for modern children, O'Grady and Stephens confront their juvenile Irish audiences with just this paradox of identity.

    The lesson in progress differed for girls. The domestic tale, the social and literary equivalent of the boys' adventure stories, assuredly did not propose vigor, bravery, and strength as the correct virtues for either little girls or young women. Instead, as Martha Vicinus points out, as in boarding school and romance stories, in domestic narratives, heroines with diverse degrees of moxie were invariably chastened "either by circumstances or by marriage" (53). Authors of domestic fiction such as Charlotte Yonge, Rosa Cavey, and Louisa May Alcott[9] allowed their heroines only so much independence. More often than not, society tempered any heroine's movement toward independent thinking or action by the end of the story (think of Alcott's tomboy, Jo). Aimed at lower middle-class girls, periodicals such as *Girl's Own Paper*, *Monthly Packet*, and *Girl's Realm* reinforced this message, with social and moral narratives devised, as Sally Mitchell explains, to provide "healthful alternatives to the romantic novelettes and blood-and-crime 'penny dreadfuls' that were the most easily available and cheap reading matter" ("Girls' Culture" 246). Domestic fiction encouraged girls to train for their proper role in the domestic sphere, where the lesson to be learned was immobility. When their future husbands were off cutting a path through the jungles of Africa or, more likely, through economic provinces, the women were to be (or were expected to be) content in the physically and intellectually limiting world of home and family.

Alternatives to domestic fiction did exist, Martha Vicinus explains, in the biographies of "noble women," which found enthusiastic audiences in the late nineteenth century. In series such as *Noble Heroines* (a companion to *Noble Heroes*), girls had the opportunity to read about real women like Florence Nightingale, who had fought her way through various forms of difficulty early in her life but who had, importantly, obtained a high level of personal and professional success. Equally important was the fact that most of the "noble heroines did not suffer excessively from their nonconformity, as did their domestic tale counterparts" (Vicinus 54). In this way, the biographies encouraged girls to fear neither their individuality nor their potentially unconventional life goals.

As liberal as the biographies prove to be in comparison to the domestic tales, they still retain much of the conservative language of progress and reason. For instance, the notion of moral duty or, as Vicinus calls it, "Protestant activism" (53), relays itself in the following biographical titles: *Pioneer Women in Victoria's Reign*, *Women Who Win*, and *Twelve Notable Good Women of the Nineteenth Century*. Moreover, although the biographical format did not enforce the conventional compulsion of "humbl[ing] by circumstances," the heroines nevertheless were suppressed in a particularly Victorian way. The biographies impart the overarching lesson that through learning to "control and channel her assertiveness," a heroine (or reader) learned to "control her world" (54). Whereas such sentiments appear to allow a woman the power of self-mastery, they also reflect the somewhat inhibitory strains of Huxley's social Darwinism, which consents only to "passions" that have been "trained to come to heel by a vigorous will" (*Essence* 194). In other words, Victorian ideals of formal and informal education permit no one a great deal of leeway where individual desires are concerned.

Another perhaps unconsciously telling part of Vicinus's definition lies in the use of the phrase, "her world," as opposed to "the world." This usage subtly points to the reality of any given woman's situation: "her" world is considerably narrower than "his." It is important, too, to note that, although I applaud with Vicinus the biographies' capacity to awaken in girl readers "an imaginative affinity with active, public heroines" (55), the more traditional, progressivist goals of Victorian society remain as, I would argue, more than traces. I point to two examples. First, the biographies always push what Vicinus calls that "most Victorian" of merits: "the *progress* they bring to some part of the public world" (55, emphasis added). Such a message imparts to the books' impressionable readers a regard for the underlying assumption of English superiority. Second, the biographers' insistence on the need for girls in the reading audience to understand that they must "[fulfill] home duties before venturing into new fields" (55) might check any burgeoning hero. Thus, whereas popular literature for girls played some part in weakening the division between the public and private spheres, in the end, the girls still did not have much room in which to move. Moreover, the public sphere's values of scientific, economic, and moral progress dominate both space and action for both genders.[10]

From Christian publications to entertainment magazines, progressivism also pervaded the popular press for adults.[11] For instance, the lead article in *The Dublin Review* of October, 1885 by Joseph Rickaby, S.J., combatively deals with the question, "What has the church to do with science?" He begins with a bit of sarcastic analogy.

> There was no room for them in the inns at Bethlehem; that is how the Saviour of the world came to be born in a stable. Wherever His mother and foster-father went they found that they had come to the wrong place. In newspaper phrase, "they were warned off the premises." The lot of the Holy Family that winter evening has been the lot of the Church ever since. By lawyer and statesman, by king and by demagogue, by astronomer, biologist, metaphysician, historian, antiquarian, linguist, the Church is being continually warned off the premises. (243)

Although Rickaby's view could be dismissed as the resentment of a Christian writer in a Christian-oriented, London paper, in fact, it provides a quite accurate representation of the—for some destructive, for some victorious—stranglehold in which science and reason held the age. "Warned off the premises" was not only Christianity but any conflicting belief system that fostered intuition, faith, spirituality, and anything "not to be felt and seen and put down in figures," to borrow a phrase from "The Yellow Wallpaper," the 1890s American short story that similarly criticizes the overly rational (Gilman 1).

Whether or not they fostered specifically Christian ideals, most popular Victorian magazines and journals offered their reading public serialized, popular fiction of the type that nonetheless clearly reinforced conventional notions of gender, race, marriage, childhood, romance, and adventure. Yeats despised this sort of literature that, like the novels made popular in Ireland by Gerald Griffin and Charles J. Kickham, celebrated middle-class sentimentality and conventionality (*Explorations* 187). The stories found in *Every Week: Journal of Entertaining Literature* echo the sentimental and conventional nature of popular novels of the day. More specifically, they iterate progressivist ideologies, their plots and characterization often reflecting a narrowing movement toward the creation of a social Darwinian utopia in which "there would emerge an ideal man, the epitome of perfection and happiness, in complete harmony with his environment and unaffected by struggle or competition" (Himmelfarb 420). Aware of the unattainability of such a goal at the time, some authors nonetheless evoked a teleological ideal of progress in their work, as in "The Caves of Kildoran." In the story's opening, published June 25, 1884, Mrs. Vivian finds herself back at her country home at the close of the London season, joyously having had all the invitations to her next party replied to in the positive. The author goes on to explain the hostess's understanding of the world that, in microcosmic form, she controls:

> Mrs. Vivian understood to perfection the art of well assorting her guests, and no social advantage of rank, wealth, or distinction secured to their possessors the *entrée* to her country house unless they also had the will and power of making themselves useful, agreeable, or ornamental, so as to blend the different elements into one harmonious whole. (9)

The above passage, though short, reveals many assumptions about individual responsibility and competition, as well as about the possibility and methods of achieving a sound, healthy society or "one harmonious whole." In short, Mrs. Vivian's worldview manifests its source in Darwinian and social Darwinian thought. As someone who "understood to perfection" the art of social ordering, Mrs. Vivian may be seen as a master-planner—or, as Huxley's defense of Darwin's Paley-influenced teleology would have it, as the "power at the centre" of "mechanical dispositions fixed beforehand by intelligent appointment and kept in action" by that power (*Life and Letters II* 201).

"The Caves of Kildoran," of course, is not a Christian piece. Mrs. Vivian neither represents god, nor has complete control over or receives all the credit for the resultant "harmonious whole" of her party. Rather, the guests must use their "will and power" to help create the correct environment as well as their own places within it. As in Darwin's theory, in which organisms struggle against one other in order to best exploit their environment, Mrs. Vivian's guests must display their most desirable talents in order to obtain a place on the invitation list. Using whichever social acumen/survival tactic (usefulness, agreeableness, or ornamentation) he or she has mastered, the successful guest will be the one who survives the list and is allowed to attend the party, which is a microcosm of the Social Darwinian utopia described above in which "complete harmony" reigns. In addition to suggesting the potential achievement of complete harmony "unaffected by struggle or competition" (Himmelfarb 420), "The Caves of Kildoran" represents the possibility of a social ordering that works itself out through individual skill and competition.

Furthermore, the emphasis on individual accomplishment ("will and power") as opposed to possessions acquired by group status ("rank, wealth, or distinction") is not only an unusual requirement in conventional depictions of the upper-class guest lists; in this, too, the otherwise mundane example of serialized popular fiction manifests a quite specifically Darwinian view of evolution. For an emphasis on the struggle between individuals, not groups, is that which differentiated Darwin from his evolutionary theory predecessor, Lamarck (Himmelfarb 317).

As in popular literary and Christian-oriented magazines, secular non-fiction in Victorian and Edwardian publications evinced a similarly scientific and rationalistic bent. The composition of the "Varieties" section of *Leisure Hour*—which is much like contemporary television news in that it includes snippets of current events, historical events, advice, and human interest stories—discloses an almost obsessive desire to identify, categorize, and evaluate the other in ways that always display the bourgeois English reader to advantage. A random survey of two publications, one from 1876 and one from 1890, uncovers a series of statistical reports of the authoritatively termed and imperiously toned "inquiries into" factory children, smugglers, criminals, London fogs, and wars. For instance, having informed its readers of the horrid working conditions for working-class factory employees, the *Leisure Hour* of 1 April 1876 suggests that factories "would be better from [more] supervision, . . . to prevent overcrowding of rooms, long detention in over-heated rooms, and the use of deleterious and poisonous substances in manufacture" (224). This passage implies that the factory workers would benefit greatly from the intervention of the bourgeoisie's clear-headed thinking and organization because they cannot run the factories well or safely of their own accord—that is, without "supervision." In the same issue, readers were afforded the opportunity for self-congratulation with a reminder of the "vast power at [their] disposal, and for which [they] are responsible" as citizens of an Empire that occupies "upwards of 6,000,000 square miles." The author is quick to note, however, that this figure excludes colonies in Africa "which the white race can never properly colonize" (224)—read: which is not capable of progress in even the most limited (bourgeois) sense.

Attitudes appear to have changed little in the later years of *Leisure Hour*. For instance, as upright citizens of England, the bourgeoisie reading an 1890 "Varieties" column could feel proud of its indirect participation in "the extraordinary improvements in the military resources of European nations" and of the "probable influence of these appliances in future wars" (285). In other words, even though "Varieties" purported to be and was a random collection of facts and figures, it could escape neither the grasp of a society that felt the need to categorize and evaluate nor a belief in the inevitability of hierarchy, which is inherent in a social Darwinian theory of social and economic progress. Needless to say, this theory hails the bourgeoisie—and even more specifically white, Protestant, English men—as the most advanced of beings, thereby granting them the responsibility, really power, of "supervising" other, supposedly less evolved beings.

Detractors of Darwinism and its sociopolitical shock waves have pointed out as variously ironic or merely fitting that Darwin's theory of natural selection can be perceived as a defense not only of imperialism and racism but also of "extreme individualism, of laissez-faire in economics and government" (Himmelfarb 418). In this way, the theory endorses one of the strongest and most typical of nineteenth-century English beliefs. Himmelfarb outlines this argument in the following way: "only laissez-faire England provided the atomistic, egotistic mentality necessary to its conception. Only there could Darwin have blandly assumed that the basic unit was the individual, the basic instinct self-interest, and the basic activity struggle" (418). One of the reasons Darwin and his social theorist followers found such a responsive audience, then, was that they had already been well-indoctrinated with some of its related elements such as the primacy of the individual, the inevitability of hierarchy, and a do-for-yourself economic system—all of which, not in the least bit coincidentally, put the English at the top of the heap. To be sure, the bourgeois portion of society chose to embrace the tautology, and the literature that bespoke it, that "survivors, having survived, are thence judged to be the fittest" (Himmelfarb 316).

COMMERCIALISM AND REALISM

Yeats's apprehension about the future of literature will reveal itself further through an investigation of his attitudes toward realism and commercialism. His observation of literature at the turn of the century led Yeats to understand commercialism and realism as existing hand-in-hand. The realist forms and bourgeois themes and characters represented by most of the popular fiction published in magazines and in English and European theater, having whet the public appetite for socially realistic and middle-class-themed, self-referent works, continued to feed on and to feed the growing audience. Yeats perceived this so-called blight on literary enterprise as having not only a commercial but also, or especially, an English commercial origin. In a 1904 *Samhain* essay on the Irish dramatic movement, he goes so far as to connect anti-commercialism and anti-realism with the Irish antipathy toward imperialist England, even imbuing the hatred with "nob[ility]," if only "we turn it now and again into hatred of the vulgarity of commercial syndicates, of all that commercial finish and pseudo-art she has done so much to cherish" (*Explorations* 129). Yeats, then, bases commercialism's alliance with realism not only on the fact that realism sold the most tickets or books. More importantly, Yeats believed, both lay claim to success via a focus on material details. As Yeats saw it, commercial attention to money making creates not art but the pretense of art; it is merely a "finish" or "pseudo-art." His description of realism using similar imagery—as when he characterizes it as "an art which smothers . . . with bad painting, with innumerable garish colours, with continual restless *mimicries of the surface of life*" (*Explorations* 110, emphasis added)—further reveals Yeats's identification of realism with commercialism and accuses both of superficiality.

The symbolic significance of being "finished" or of having a "finish" did not occur to Yeats alone. Interestingly, in *Inventing Ireland*, Declan Kiberd also uses the symbolism of having a "finish" in his discussion of the Irish perception of the self—a discussion that provides further insight into Yeats's arguments about realism, commercialism, and Ireland. Kiberd writes:

> The republican ideal was the achieved individual, the person with the courage to become his or her full self. The imperialists were not to be thought of as different, so much as aborted or incomplete individuals. By a weird paradox, their incompleteness was evidenced by their polished surface, their premature, self-closure which left them at once incomplete and *finished*. The glossy, confident surface indicated a person immune to self-doubt and therefore incapable of development. The Irish self, by contrast, was a *project*: and its characteristic text was a process, unfinished, fragmenting. It invited the reader to become a co-creator with the author and it refused to exact a merely passive admiration for the completed work of art. (119–20)

According to this view, that which the Victorian, middle-class English (imperialists) perceived as their crowning glory, their perceived finish or achievement of the highest level of culture, was conceived by outsiders, here the Irish, as a limitation. As with Yeats's depiction of realism, in which any authentic value has been crusted over and trapped beneath the tyranny of surface details, the imperialists are depicted as ironically unable to bear fruit. The Irish, typically defined by the imperialists as very much in need of "finish" or refinement, are, in this alternative definition, understood to possess the only potential for progress. Indeed, Luke Gibbons turns a similar negative into a positive (albeit not entirely unconditionally), when he points out that because "the attrition of Irish history has the effect of removing any semblance of order and harmony from the passage of time," "disintegration and fragmentation were already part of its history so that, in a crucial but not always welcome sense, Irish culture experienced modernity" before the rest of Europe (6). Likewise, these descriptions of the fragmentary or unfinished nature of Irish self and Irish history as positive reflects Yeats's conception of progress, as well as his ever-changing literary "project," both of which are spiritual and not commercial in origin, and which are, therefore, *ideally* "a process, unfinished, fragmenting."[12]

At this point, it is important to recall the milieu of the typical late Victorian and Edwardian audience, which had been taught by centuries of dominant rationalism and, more recently, scientism, to perceive the world according to its observable and classifiable features or, more specifically, the Darwinian belief that "'definite laws'" govern the existence of the world (Himmelfarb 344). It followed that such "laws" not only might but should be used for purposes such as that fostered by Ernest Renan who "assign[ed] sex to nations as well as individuals" (8).

Classifications like Renan's were, of course, more dangerous and enduring than their seemingly innocent impetus to "[know] things as they are," which Matthew Arnold defined in *On the Study of Celtic Literature* as the "bent of the times" (12). But the directive to "know things as they are" is easily dispossessed of its innocence, for the rational and scientific modes of knowledge, as chapter one evinces, defined gender and race so rigidly as to be dictatorial. Jürgen Habermas further delineates these social imperatives as moralistic in *The Transformation of the Public Sphere*. In his critique of rationalism, he explains: "intrinsic to the idea of a public opinion born of the power of the better argument was the claim to that morally pretentious rationality that strove to discover what was at once just and right" (54). Moreover, and of prime importance to Yeats as a writer, the moralism and socially defined hierarchization implicit in the understanding of the world as defined by "definite laws" largely informed the literature that aimed to portray "things as they are"—that is, realism.

"Realism," Yeats scathingly declared, "is the delight to-day of all those whose minds, educated alone by schoolmasters and newspapers, are without the memory of beauty and emotional subtlety" (*EI* 227). Here we see that Yeats perceives realism's popularity as a socially bred preference, inspired by institutions such as secondary and higher education and the mass media which reinforced the dominance of rationalist and scientistic beliefs. He reiterates this notion, though somewhat more optimistically, in 1898 in "The Autumn of the Body":

> I understand now that writers are struggling all over Europe, though not often with a philosophic understanding of their struggle, against that picturesque and declamatory way of writing, against that "externality" which a time of scientific and political thought has brought into literature. This struggle has been going on for some years, but it has only just become strong enough to draw within itself the little inner world which alone seeks more than amusement in the arts. (*EI* 189)

Part of Yeats's argument with realism, then, was with its "externality"—seen in terms of form, in the detailed design of theatrical costumes and sets and, in terms of theme, in social realism's attempt to show life not in an ideal light but as it really is. Even more so, Yeats disliked realism's lack of attention to the less tangible but, for him, more important "inner world" of imagination. For Yeats, realism seemed to have drained art, spiritually and artistically, of its value. In *Explorations*, Yeats laments, "Has not the long decline of the arts been but the shadow of declining faith in an unseen reality?" (170). Furthermore, he contends, "every change toward realism coincided with a decline in dramatic energy" (172). Indeed, Yeats seems to have grown tired of those artists who, in their work as in their lives, chose externalities over the inner world of vision and imagination. A few lines from his poem, "Ego Dominus Tuus," from *Per Amica Silentia Lunae* (1917) illustrate this point:

> For those that love the world serve it in action
> Grow rich, popular and full of influence,
> And should they paint or write, still it is action:
> The struggle of the fly in marmalade.
> The rhetorician would deceive his neighbors,
> The sentimentalist himself; while art
> Is but a vision of reality. (*Mythologies* 322–23)

Not surprisingly, Yeats preferred art which did not mimic the mundane details of everyday life but which revealed a vision. He came to this understanding, he says, when watching a performance of *Phèdre* with Sarah Bernhardt and De Max: "It was the most beautiful thing I had ever seen upon the stage, and made me understand, in a new way, that saying of Goethe's which is understood everywhere but in England, 'Art is art because it is not nature'" (*Explorations* 87–88). Yeats's espousal of Goethe's adage reflects his sometime identification with the Decadents' art for art's sake movement. Though their plays differ greatly in style, Yeats's and Wilde's themes oftentimes reflect a correspondent critique expressed here in a Wildean epigram reproduced and clearly esteemed by Yeats: "'Beer, bible, and the seven deadly virtues have made England what she is'" (*UPI* 203). Declan Kiberd's depiction of Wilde as "a man who saw England as a holy place to be conquered by force of intellect and imagination" (32) also speaks to a partial political affinity between the two authors. However, Yeats's deep involvement with the spiritual aspects of art shows us an important difference between their approaches. In his 1891 review of Oscar Wilde's *Lord Arthur Savile's Crime and Other Stories* for *United Ireland*, Yeats explains his sense of the author: "Mr. Oscar Wilde . . . does not care what strange opinions he defends or what time-honoured virtue he makes laughter of, provided he does it cleverly" (*UPI* 203). Although Yeats means this as a compliment—in the larger context of the essay he is comparing Wilde favorably with eighteenth-century duelists who also "tried to really live, and not merely exist" (*UPI* 202)[13]—his depiction of Wilde's promotion of wit over all else dislodges any strict correlation between the execution of, if not the purposes behind, the two authors' literary agendas. For above all else Yeats idealizes the "imaginative" writer who, significantly, "identifies himself . . . with the soul of the world, and frees himself from all that is impermanent in that soul, an ascetic not of women and wine, but of the newspapers" (*EI* 286).

Yeats provides us with perhaps his most detailed discourse on the value of imaginative literature in the famous "moods" passage from 1895, from which I will quote here at length:

> Literature differs from explanatory and scientific writing in being wrought about a mood, or a community of moods, as the body is wrought about an invisible soul; and if it uses argument, theory, erudition, observation, and seems to grow hot in assertion or denial, it does so merely to make us partakers at the banquet of the moods.

> ... [A]rgument, theory, erudition, observation, are merely what Blake called "little devils who fight for themselves," illusions of our visible passing life, who must be made to serve the moods, or we have no part in eternity. Everything that can be seen, touched, measured, explained, understood, argued over, is to the imaginative artist nothing more than a means, for he belongs to the invisible life, and delivers its ever new and ever ancient revelation. We hear much of his need of the restraints of reason, but the only restraint he can obey is the mysterious instinct that has made him an artist, and that teaches him to discover immortal moods in mortal desires, an undecaying hope in our trivial ambitions, a divine love in sexual passion. (*EI* 195)

Yeats's moods passage argues explicitly against realism, especially social realism, which raises "argument, theory, erudition [and] observation" above "revelation." Implicit in the realist agenda lies the effort to gain control, an endeavor encouraged by the notion that humans and, more specifically, artists can master reality by formulating arguments and assertions and observations. Yeats's portrayal of realist artists as neither enabled nor informed but restrained by reason displays his identification of rationalist/scientist doctrines with the aims of realism and, moreover, of the rationalist program of progress and social realism. Elsewhere Yeats notably concludes that the "great sin against art" is "the sin of rationalism" (*UPI* 187).

In the moods passage, Yeats uses William Blake to pointedly denigrate literature that argues and observes as the product of "'little devils who fight for themselves,' illusions of our visible passing life." This passage criticizes propagandistic realists as self-seeking and self-deluding. In other words, Yeats sees this type of realist as too busy trying to convince others of his or her point-of-view to achieve access to "the invisible life" where is to be found "ever ancient revelation." By focusing on surface details of costumes and props rather than inner (spiritual or emotional) issues, and by aiming to persuade rather than to reveal, Yeats argues, realists are mired in "mortal desires" and "trivial ambitions" without the benefit of a discovery of "immortal moods" or the provision of "an undecaying hope."

Yeats, on the other hand, had a long-standing faith in the primacy of imagination, a belief he acquired, in part, from the Romantics. What I want to focus on here is Yeats's conception, via Blake, of imagination as communication with God. John P. Frayne explains in his introduction to *Uncollected Prose I*:

> According to [Yeats's] view of the imagination, the images formed by our minds have a reality as messengers from the beyond, and we have no moral right to assume that the reality of our imagination is inferior in importance to the palpable world apprehended by the senses. Since the world of sense denied the world of spirit, Yeats did not merely assert the equal importance of both but raised the world of spirit to a far higher plane of value than the mere world of things. (67)

Echoing his unknowing mentor, Blake, Yeats phrases his reading of imagination thus: "Imagination is God in the world of art, and may well desire to have us come to an issue with the atheists who would make us naught but 'realists,' 'naturalists,' or the like" (*UPI* 284).

Yeats's avowal of imagination (and disavowal of realism) quickly merged with his belief in symbolism to become the only hope for art's future. Frayne explains that Yeats "rejected the Victorians because their poetry was too full of the merely laudable and praiseworthy, too concerned with social causes and irrelevant psychologizing. By his continual announcements of the coming of symbolic art, he meant to remove all matters from poetry except emotion and passion" (*UPI* 73). Again, taking his cue from Blake, Yeats commends allegory and especially symbolism as "a natural language by which the soul when entranced, or even in ordinary sleep, communes with God and with angels" (*EI* 368). Yeats's interest in the coming of symbolic art, as Frayne notes, "reached messianic intensity" around 1897 and remained for the rest of the century (*UPI* 73). Of course, Yeats never lost interest in symbolism. As Terence Brown explains, he "shared certainly the French Symbolist sense of poetry as an art form that could induce transcendental consciousness, but for Yeats, increasingly, that transformation was to have significance in the human world" (72). Yeats nonetheless perceived the limitations of symbolic art as having real influence on real people, as he admits when he writes, "All symbolic art should arise out of a real belief, and that it cannot do so in this age proves that this age is a road and not a resting-place for the imaginative arts" (*EI* 294). Here Yeats again reminds us of his conviction that both society and art suffer from a belief in the material over the spiritual.

YEATS'S PLAYS AND THE SOCIAL EXPERIENCE OF DRAMA

Although they are most commonly interpreted as evidence of Yeats's involvement with Irish nationalism and/or mythology, Yeats's earliest plays can also be seen to evince his interest in the social conventions of the Victorian and Edwardian eras.[14] In the plays written between 1892 and 1907, Yeats makes motions toward the "retheatricalization" of theater in which his choices in terms of dramatic forms, themes, and characterizations are meant to provoke the spectator into a new understanding. More specifically, Yeats appears to want his audience to leave the theater with an understanding of the dangerous ways in which identity is socially constructed under the direction of conventional definitions of class, gender, and ethnicity. This goal speaks to Yeats's understanding of the social as well as psychic function of the theatrical experience.

As literary pieces written to be performed in a public arena before a group of individuals whose eyes and attentions are fixed upon the same spectacle, plays furnish for the audience a communal experience not as readily available to the solitary reader of a text. Harkening back to ancient Irish mythology or to a historic rural past, most of the plays Yeats wrote in the 1890s and early 1900s either taught or reminded the primarily middle-class audience of their shared and noble Irish roots and thus partook in the centripetal motion of race identity formation. Characters like Seanchan, Cuchulain, and Deirdre represent the respective Irish hero-martyr types of bard, soldier, and lover willing to fight and to die for the respective and honored traditions of the imaginative arts, love of country, and love itself. Resounding with hale and hearty examples of Irish heroism, the plays could not have failed to represent to Yeats's contemporary audiences a call to Irishness, even if they were not perceived, as was his most overtly propagandistic nationalist play *Cathleen ni Houlihan*, a call to arms.

It is important to note that the plays discussed herein were written and produced in the years leading up to and around that pivotal moment, the 1906–1907 Abbey season, during which Yeats was greatly influenced by the production of Synge's *The Playboy of the Western World*, which changed Yeats's view of what peasant plays, and Irish theater, could and should be—that is, "mocking, eloquent and heroic, turn by bewildering turn" (Foster, *W. B. Yeats* 358). The plays written during the period on which I have chosen to focus, therefore, represent Yeats's purposeful move from Irish peasant, legendary, and historical plays like *The Land of Heart's Desire* to plays like *Deirdre*, "larger, tragic pieces" that Yeats characterized as "'represent[ing] a higher phase of life, in which may be found something truly characteristic of Ireland'" (Foster, *W. B. Yeats* 353).

Although the plays' individual and collective impetus toward fostering an Irish community is significant, I find the opposing thematic construct, Yeats's treatment of the individual subject, even more important for the purposes of my argument.[15] I will address Yeats's thematic treatment of individualism, when relevant, within the context of each play in later chapters. At this point, I would like to explore the concept as it relates to the relationship between spectator and stage, to explore the ways in which Yeats's thematic emphasis on individual identity or the subject is forwarded by his formal dramatic choices. It is the consensus of many early twentieth-century theater critics that the typical bourgeois realist theater of the nineteenth and early twentieth century promoted and sustained the spectator-as-blank-wall, uninvolved in the theatrical event's creation of meaning. In 1918, for instance, Platon Kershentsev laments the "'passivity of the spectator,'" a theatrical commonplace that emerged from and was "'typically characteristic of the bourgeois order'" in which "'politics are controlled and ruled by a small group of politicians while the great masses of the people remain passive'" (qtd. in Fischer-Lichte 42).

Early twentieth-century avant-garde drama theorists like Filippo Tommaso Marinetti, Georg Fuchs, and Vsevolod Meyerhold contended that the only way to resolve the passivity problem was to literally move and/or metaphorically shock the audience into participation, to "provok[e] the spectators into activity and thereby transform them into . . . 'new' beings" (Fischer-Lichte 45). As a practitioner of a revised form of Noh theater, Yeats was, later in his career, an avid (if not conscious) proponent of Georg Fuchs's notion of "retheatricalization,"[16] a form of theater "which did not imitate a reality which actually existed but which created its own reality; a theatre which . . . developed new forms of communication" between spectator and stage (Fischer-Lichte 115). When, for performances of his Noh plays, Yeats enforced smaller, more intimate audiences and stagings, invoked the ritual elements of theater with the use of music, masks, verse language, and monotone speaking patterns, and experimented, with the help of Gordon Craig and Hilda Crop, with new theatrical technologies, he displayed many of the elements of "retheatricalization" that Fuchs had in mind.

Contemporary Yeats critic James W. Flannery goes so far as to claim for Yeats's theatrical experimentation a success that exceeds even that of more famous practitioners like Max Reinhardt because, he argues, Yeats was "striving always to make the arts and technology of the theatre serve his personal vision as a poet" (*Idea* 365). While it is true Yeats did succeed in shocking his audiences, as the earliest critical reviews of his plays display, the audience was not always favorably impressed. The mid to late productions of Yeats's plays show the audience had difficulty learning to accept new forms, such as that of Noh drama. In 1917, for instance, Joseph Holloway records the following commentary: "Mac and O'Casey saw *At the Hawk's Well*; the latter couldn't understand it, he candidly expressed." The December 1919 production of *The Player Queen*, likewise "baffled" Holloway: "while its unfolding is set in so picturesque an environment that it charmed the eye . . . it didn't wholly satisfy the mind" (206). Although only short excerpts from the pen of one reviewer, these comments reflect the typical response of Yeats's contemporaries to his plays and, moreover, reveal the biases of an audience which expects to "understand" plays, to a great extent, on an intellectual or logical, as opposed to spiritual or philosophical, level.[17]

However, as my study will make evident, even in the pre-Noh plays, Yeats had as one of his primary goals the provocation and, subsequently, the making new of the spectator. Breaking free from the bourgeois realist format to make use of the ancient/new verse and mythological formats, Yeats presented Irish plays that differed even from those of many of his Irish Literary Renaissance colleagues, such as Lady Gregory and J. M. Synge, whose invocation of Irishness had a purposefully realistic construction in terms of plot structure, speech patterns, and costume—though, of course, spectators and critics disagreed widely about the extent to which plays like *The Rising of the Moon* and *The Playboy of the Western World* actually represented the "real" Irish. But Yeats's plays, especially after 1900, faced their own brand of prejudice in the form of audiences unprepared, as they would be again with the Noh plays, for the making-new in which Yeats attempted to partake. The September 1903 audience of *The King's Threshold*, for instance, showed apparent distaste for the chanting speech patterns used by the Abbey actors. Further evidence that the bourgeois audience was not quite prepared for the advent of "retheatricalization" can also be found in the "nightly decreasing audiences" (Holloway 77) for the December 1906 productions of *Deirdre*. When Lady Gregory lamented this fact to Holloway, he suggested the probability that the verse drama format was at fault. Gregory replied, "'Then we must teach them to like [verse drama]!'" (76): further evidence that Yeats and his Abbey compatriots expected plays to partake in the education—in this case, the cultural education—of their middle-class audiences.

It is in his choice to diverge from formal convention and in his ability to surprise the audiences and thereby provoke their attentions in a new and different way that Yeats partook in the "retheatricalization" of theater. But he participated in "retheatricalization" on an even deeper level, with the use of poetic/mythic structures of meaning meant to appeal to the individual on a psychological and even spiritual level, as opposed to the generally intellectual and social appeal of social realism. This is not to deny the emotional appeal of realist theater; rather I would like to emphasize the potential Yeats (and many others) believed mythic, verse, and ritual dramas to have in terms of evoking a psychic renewal of the individual, as opposed to a social renewal of the community. Although Yeats's early plays appeal on a communal level, even more importantly, they serve to draw from the individual spectator his or her own personal response.

One of the topics on which Yeats's plays were meant to speak to the audience on both the personal and communal (or social) level is that of identity formation. Yeats's thoughts on realistic drama reveal as much about Victorian constructions of gender and ethnic identity as they do about the aesthetic and political reasons behind his preferred symbolic and/or mythic choice of dramatic form. His avowal that the "meagre language" of realistic plays forces "action" to be "crushed into the narrow limits of possibility" and merely serves to fill "one's soul with a sense of commonness as with dust" (*Discoveries* 274–75) displays his conviction that the logical, the common, and the general are not fit topics for the stage. Logic, and the attempt to make dramatic action and theme fit the limits of possibility and follow "general law" as found in realist theater, are both directed by and reinforce masculinist and imperialist ways of thinking. If stage representations of life reflect, even in a critical context, the social realities of actual masculinist, patriarchal, and colonial practices—real life's insistence on capitulation to norms of identity defined by science and reason—the "general law," Yeats's thinking went, would remain the standard. Typical of Yeats's reliance on opposition or conflict as the road to progress was his belief that theater, in the age of reason and science, needed at least to capitulate less completely and less frequently to the demands of logic or reason and should, moreover, provide alternatives to these ways of thinking. Thus, Yeats produced folk and mythic plays in which plots, themes, and characterizations went above and beyond the logical, possible, common, and general that keep us thinking along straight, and narrow, lines.

An important part of this process included the erasing, or at least the blurring, of gender and ethnic lines. Using the decidedly unrealistic and, for the time, relatively atypical formats of verse drama, folk stories, and Irish mythology, Yeats provided alternative models of literary social criticism in which, even while being tutored on an allegorical level about what Yeats saw as social injustices and problems, an audience member could, by partaking in the alternative philosophical or psychological reality of mythology, imagine an escape from the restrictions of that sociopolitical reality that reserved the right to govern one's most personal sense of identity. As Jack Zipes postulates in "The Changing Shape of the Fairy Tale," the reader (or spectator) of fantasy literature in the fairy or mythic mode, faced with a narrative and stylistic emphasis on "spells, enchantments, disenchantments, resurrections, [and] recreations," is encouraged to "wonder about the workings of the universe where anything can happen at any time" (11). *The Land of Heart's Desire, The King's Threshold, On Baile's Strand,* and *Deirdre* do not provide the happy ending standard in most fairy tales. However, the invocation of magical powers, figures, and enchantments do foster the possibility of wonder, if not about the specific fates of those in the play (the heroes meet tragic ends), then at least about the possibility of choosing forms of identity other than those suggested by convention. If the choice doesn't work out for these individuals, Yeats implies in the plays, the alternative identity is not to be blamed; rather—and here's where the social criticism comes into play—blood is shown to be on the hands of those who insist on conformity to the norm, and this usually for selfishly moralistic or materialistic reasons.

In its formal capacity, then, as a non-realistic work, the early Yeatsian folk or mythic play has the potential to perform a psychic healing function in that it "seek[s] to . . . evoke in a religious sense profound feelings of awe and respect for life as a miraculous process, which can be altered and changed to compensate for the lack of power, wealth, and pleasure that most people experience" (Zipes 11–12). In other words, Yeats reworked the tales of Mary Bruin, Seanchan, Cuchulain, Deirdre and Fergus in such a way as to display the possibility for alternative identities. That is, they represent the potential for men and women not to have to act as Victorian/Edwardian-defined men and women and for the Irish not to be relegated to the derogatory realms of femininity and bestiality. This not only rescues gender and Irishness from strictly defined categorization, but also suggests the potential for a positive transformation of the colonial present into a self-directed future.

Chapter Three
Progress as Material Gain
The Bourgeois Peasant as Invented Tradition in The Countess Cathleen, Cathleen ni Houlihan, *and* The Land of Heart's Desire

> *Class* is a more indefinite word than *rank,* and this was probably one of the reasons for its introduction.
> —Raymond Williams

> [Invented traditions] might foster the corporate sense of *superiority* of élites—particularly when these had to be recruited from those who did not already possess it by birth of ascription—rather than by inculcating a sense of obedience in inferiors.
> —Eric Hobsbawm

> [M]aterial progress does not merely fail to relieve poverty—it actually produces it.
> —Henry George[1]

INVENTED TRADITIONS, LITERARY AND CULTURAL

YEATS'S DISDAIN FOR AND LITERARY CRITIQUE OF THE MIDDLE CLASSES HAS been well documented by critics of his poetry and drama alike.[2] Many critics dealing with the issue of Yeats and class focus on his later years, in which Yeats's philosophical and social expeditions into fascism and eugenics rather cry out for analysis. However, the plays written in the 1890s and in the first decade of the 1900s not only offer insight into the early development of his anti-bourgeois sentiments; a study of the plays as class critique further advances their importance to Yeats's wider anti-colonial stance. Although, throughout the course of his career, Yeats wrote few plays of the self-representational, middle-class sort epitomized by Wilde's and Shaw's social satires and Ibsen's dramas, he did produce a handful of popular prose plays in which the middle classes play an overt role: *Where There Is Nothing* (1902) and *The Words upon the Window-Pane* (1934) being the most obvious examples.[3] Yet even where members of the bourgeoisie do not appear as characters, the representative bourgeois ideologies reveal themselves in many of Yeats's plays as major canonical themes. In this chapter, I will focus on a selection of plays from early in his career when he was still concerned with the wider audiences that were to be excluded in his later drawing-room performance days. Yeats's earliest produced plays, *The Countess Cathleen* (1892), *The Land of Heart's Desire* (1894), and *Cathleen ni Houlihan* (1902),[4] focus on peasant characters and concerns and, in the two Cathleen plays, exhibit overtly nationalist leanings. Despite their absorption in the working-class milieu, these plays reveal Yeats's initial inclinations toward what becomes a canon-wide theme of anti-bourgeois sentiment. I will not argue here that Yeats entirely despises the middle classes; to do so would be to miss the finessed nature of Yeats's arguments. Rather, I will focus on Yeats's attention to moralism, materialism, and philistinism as inherently bourgeois traits, and as inherently problematic trends at the turn of the century.

More specifically, in *The Countess Cathleen*, *The Land of Heart's Desire*, and *Cathleen ni Houlihan*, Yeats's representation of the "bourgeois peasant" catalogues the re-invention of the actual and literary Irish peasant in the bourgeois English mode as he saw the transformation unfold in the late nineteenth century. Closely tied to his beliefs about the social construction of gender, race, and class roles, Yeats's depiction of the hero in these plays echoes his evolving theories about the overweening power of bourgeois morality. Even more importantly, we see Yeats's early attempts to redefine for his generation the meaning of progress, a definition that had been strongly yoked to English, middle-class concerns.

The Irish Literary Revival's evocation of the peasant as hero and, in particular, of the peasant as representative of a proud and strong Ireland, constitutes what Eric Hobsbawm has called an invented tradition. Hobsbawm's notion of the invented tradition is useful here because of its application to the development of constructions of identity occurring at the time, specifically that of the English and Irish middle-classes in general and of the Irish Revivalist version of Irish identity in particular. That is, by examining them within the framework of Hobsbawm's theory of the invented tradition, we find palpable evidence of the following factors in the construction of middle-class and Irish Revivalist identity: a vivid self-consciousness in the forging of notions of class, gender, and ethnicity; the use of the past in order to create a self-controlled version of the present and the future; and the involvement of even those oppressed by the social constructions in their maintenance.

Aware of the damaging nature of literary and stage renderings of the Irish typical at the time, Yeats, Lady Gregory, John M. Synge, Douglas Hyde, Edward Martyn, George Moore, and AE provided the prototypes for the new stage Irishman, Irishwoman, and Irish play which in manner, dress, accent, syntax, setting, and plot were meant to represent the opposite of all that "stage Irish" had meant for centuries. The Stage Irishman, who began to appear with frequency in English theaters in the eighteenth century, was sometimes bloodthirsty but more often was either naive or well-intentioned but inept. As Christopher Fitz-Simon explains, the type generally was represented by two categories: "the lazy, crafty, and (in all probability) inebriated buffoon who nonetheless has the gift of good humour and a nimble way with words" and "the braggart (also partial to a 'dhrop of the besht') who is likely to be a soldier or ex-soldier, boasting of having seen a great deal of the world when he has probably been no further from his own country than some English barracks or camp" (94). Although the Stage Irishman becomes an increasingly comic figure throughout the eighteenth and nineteenth centuries, thus escaping, at least in part, the previously predominant stereotype of savagery, theater's degradation of the Irish as dim-witted and/or drunken nevertheless played upon earlier, negative views of the Irish as ignorant. While they used laughter as a disguise, English, American, and even Irish stages of the nineteenth century had continued to depict the Irish as uncivilized.[5]

Despite the fact that the Revival-era literary Irish peasant was no stranger to drunkenness and revelry—a fact protested most infamously during the *Playboy* riots of 1907—he also obtained a level of dignity, afforded by the popular representation of his natural (not exaggerated) speech patterns, dress, and rural ways of life with its concomitant concerns. This difference in perspective represents a literary and political transformation for the Irish, a self-conscious egress from the ideological control of colonial representation to that of self-representation (though admittedly, in many cases, of the Anglo-Irish representation of the Catholic, rural Irish). This change was made possible in part by the fact that, as Luke Gibbons observes, "[w]here the colonizer saw nature" (read: the more bestial Irish "race"), "the colonized saw culture" (*Transformations* 14). Just as importantly, the Irish could take pride in seeing themselves represented in theaters in the role of central figure, even hero, as well as content themselves with the decreasing presence of Irish servants, fools, and (foolish) traitors on the stage.

Having undergone a sociopolitical as much as aesthetic revision, the Irish Revival stage peasant, then, played an important role in the Irish re-invention of identity along Hobsbawmian lines. In the stage Irishman, a theatrical practice that widely affected the historical representation of the Irish, we have one of the many "traditional practices" that, as Hobsbawm explains, "were modified, ritualized, and institutionalized for new national purposes" (6). It might be argued that the Irish Revival's dramatic doings provide an example of the argument that "the conceptual coherence of Irish identity conceived in the nineteenth century derived paradoxically from imperialist discourse, thus propping-up through its organisational assumptions that which it claimed to oppose" (Smyth, "The Past" 244).[6] Although, from our position of historic hindsight, this claim holds much authority, it is also important to credit these Revivalists with the (intended) improvements—progress, as it were—that comprised their stage depictions of the Irish. That is, re-inventing an English-derived tradition of Irish stereotyping as a more politically and socially viable example of Irishness, the Revival playwrights strove to turn a negative into a positive. By replacing the buffoon and braggart with more heroic counterparts, and especially by borrowing heroes from ancient Irish mythology, these playwrights followed the pattern Hobsbawm recognizes in nationalist re-invention practices whereby "the use of ancient materials to construct invented traditions of a novel type for quite novel purposes" (6) partakes in the overall process of cultural and historical revision.

In the case of the Anglo-Irish proponents of the Literary Revival, the purpose was to reinvigorate the Irish people with a sense of the Irish self: a self that existed before the English colonized Ireland. The use of historically valued Irish heroes, names, places, and stories imbues not only Ireland's past but also its present and future with what John Hutchinson calls the traditionalist's "sense of unique identity" (33). When combined, as part of the Irish cultural nationalist movement, with the modernist "universal drive for progress" (34), this sense of identity would allow the Irish to construct "an integrated distinctive and autonomous community, capable of competing in the modern world" (34). Hutchinson concludes that cultural nationalists view history as proof that "social progress comes not from the imposition of alien norms on the community but from the inner reformation of the traditional status order. The recovery of national pride is a prerequisite for successful participation in the wider world" (34). Or, in Hobsbawm's terms, the Irish Literary Revivalists "use[d] history as a legitimator of action and cement of group cohesion" (12).

It is impossible, from the perspective afforded by the distance of one hundred years, to avoid the conclusion that the legitimation of the Irish peasant was classist in origin if not in sentiment: a product of the Anglo-Irish elitism that allowed the Irish Revivalist writers to feel they could use the image of the peasant for their own political purposes, their respect for the "traditional," rural way of life not withstanding. Contemporary critics of the movement did not miss this point either. As Lady Gregory tells us, the Irish Revivalists often fell under the indictment of those who perceived their "'attitude to the Irish peasant [to] arise out of class prejudice which ke[pt] [them] from seeing anything that is good in him'" (*Our Irish Theatre* 432). However, most also recognize in the Irish Revivalist agenda—that is, in its anti-colonial endeavor to show the world and especially England that Ireland has its own history, its own way of doing things and, therefore, its own powerful, independent future—an inclusivity, in the form of collusion against the common enemy of English imperialism, that outdistances the exclusivity inherent in classist thinking. Thus, more than a literary trope, and surpassing even the impetus to "preserve" the historical past (Hobsbawm 8), the Irish Revival's invention of the peasant can be seen as a tradition that aspired to "develop . . . a living past" (8) with which the Irish might proceed into a more secure future.

In most Revival renditions of the peasant, peasants are "peasants." That is, in Lady Gregory's *Spreading the News* (1904) and Hyde's Irish language play, *Casadh an tSúgáin* or *The Twisting of the Rope* (1901), for instance, the Irish peasant characters exist in a rural, domestic, Catholic-cum-pagan world in which agricultural and familial duties, games and sport, the Catholic church, and pagan spirituality circumscribe their daily lives.[7] The literary characters, like their real counterparts, are often shown to be not entirely pleased with this existence. Synge's *Playboy*, in which an isolated rural citizenry is as so event-starved as to find murder appealing, provides just one example. However, the appeal of Irish life *as* country life presents itself as a clear objective in the early Revivalist peasant plays.

Into this group of stage peasants who represented both the sentimentalism and nationalist fervor of their creators, Yeats introduced a new character: the bourgeois peasant, a further re-invention of the nineteenth-century stage Irishman. Emerging from the other more complacent versions of Irish Revival peasant, Yeats's depictions of the bourgeois peasant do cling, like those of Lady Gregory and Douglas Hyde, to sentimental notions of the peasant as the primary bearers of "an ancient idealism"— the representation of which the Irish Literary Theatre proclaimed as one of its goals (Gregory, *Our Irish Theatre* 378). This fact helps justify Joep Leerssen's contention that, with the exception of Synge and Shaw, Irish Literary Theatre playwrights used "stereotyped Stage Irish characters, almost as automatically and unthinkingly as they used a twenty-six-letter alphabet" (*Remembrance and Imagination* 172). However, I want to argue here that Yeats's version of the peasant reveals less of the idealism and sentimentalism than, for instance, the fairgoers in *Spreading the News* or Sheamus in *Casadh an tSúgáin*. While his Irish Literary Theatre partners busied themselves with their versions of the Irish peasant, Yeats took a slightly different tack in which praise of the peasant walked hand in hand with criticism of the same.[8] What some might call, positively or negatively, the modernization of the peasant—his or her entry into a global economy and its relative material comforts—Yeats saw, decidedly negatively, as a problematic movement of the rural populace away from spiritual (traditional) values and toward those of (bourgeois) moralism, materialism, and philistinism. Yeats's plays thus mythologize and demythologize peasants simultaneously.

The argument that his plays comprise, at least in part, a social critique of class as well as of nation can be supported by the fact that, in many ways, Yeats's bourgeois peasant represents the actual rural Irish inhabitants of the age who were struggling to maintain agrarian economic stability in an increasingly industrial and modern world.[9] As Deborah Fleming notes, "Far from being independent villages remote from what may be perceived to be urban corruption, peasant communities rely on the urban culture as the principal source of innovation, motivation, and prestige" (32). Although they have a long family and social heritage of farming, characters such as Shemus and Teigue Rua in *The Countess Cathleen* and Maurteen and Bridget Bruin in *The Land of Heart's Desire* reveal a growing dissatisfaction with their agricultural existence. They see themselves undeserving of such a fate, especially in the face of the material opportunities emerging around them that ostensibly could lead them up and out of a subsistence-level life. Fleming similarly contends that, whereas peasants are "fascinated by the opportunities the city offers," they also find the city a source of "helplessness and humiliation" (32). Because it is understandable, financially speaking, that the Rua and Bruin families would prefer to live a more secure and comfortable life, Yeats does not make this desire the center of his critique. Rather, Yeats's social critique in these plays focuses on the characters whose motives stem more from greed than necessity—those who prize material possessions, and its partner social status, above and beyond all else. Shemus and Teigue, who choose to irretrievably barter their souls in exchange for riches, and Maurteen Bruin, who works for a level of fiscal security that conspicuously includes a steady supply of ribbons for his daughter-in-law's hair, reflect the interests and desires of the turn-of-the-century, long-suffering Irish farmer who more and more frequently seemed to be setting his eyes on the prizes accrued by materialist aims. In this way, Irish farmers had much in common with what Alice Effie Murray, an economist writing in 1903, calls their "capitalist" English counterparts, with whom, moreover, Murray not so favorably compares the Irish (437). However, as Yeats's plays illustrate for us, the rural Irish were becoming every day more and more like their middle-class neighbors.

The instability of the Irish agricultural market since the Famine and tensions around issues of land ownership provided late nineteenth- and early twentieth-century farmers with a stark reminder of their mercurial economic position. L. M. Cullen tells us that although, throughout most of the 1870s, agriculture had been prosperous (148), after 1877, agricultural prosperity took a turn for the worse, especially in the relatively isolated west, southwest, and northwest of Ireland (150–51). With the 1890s came the development of higher prices, higher earnings for migratory workers in England and Scotland, and an increase in the quantity and price of eggs, an invaluable financial staple for the wives of small farmers (152). Land legislation further enhanced living conditions, with rent reductions of twenty percent occurring in 1881 and again fifteen years later. The Wyndham Act of 1903 "began the process of land purchase on a large scale; [and] by 1917 almost two-thirds of the tenants had acquired their holdings" (154). For Alice Effie Murray one of the most inspiriting of occurrences at the time was the growth of agricultural co-operatives, fostered by Horace Plunkett and others, which enabled the "peasant proprietary to exist in some sort of material comfort" (425). Furthermore, rural involvement in cottage industries such as weaving and lace-making, and the sense of hope for the future evinced at professional industrial meetings like the Cork Exhibition in 1902 (Murray 423), foretold a possibly brighter, if never entirely stable, fiscal future for

Irish workers. Finally, the increasing number of shops that appeared in rural areas in the second half of the nineteenth century, which served to replace monopolies with the competitive pricing of goods, represented the "increased purchasing power of the rural community and—scarcely less important—its enhanced mobility" (Cullen 156).

The position of small farmer, however, did not guarantee ease or complacency. Cullen points out that, by the end of the nineteenth century, although Ireland was "in many respects a highly developed country," nevertheless, "incomes compared with England and Scotland were relatively low" (167). Memories of the Famine and more recent worries like the Land League battles and the financially damaging Danish intrusion into what had previously been the primarily Irish butter market took their toll not only on material conditions but morale as well. Moreover, rural inhabitants of Ireland became desirous of the material benefits of urban and suburban society, about which, because of widespread improvements in communication and transportation, they became more and more aware—that is, more and more aware that they did not have access to such benefits.

Of the opportunities that rural Irish eyes had to observe other worlds, emigration, a trend begun during the Famine era, made one of the biggest impacts on those who stayed behind. I am not so much concerned here with the economic as with the social reverberations of emigration on the Irish psyche, and in particular with the extent to which it introduced the outside world to the hitherto relatively isolated rural communities. With family members and friends either permanently or temporarily leaving to work in England, Scotland, the United States, and elsewhere, the rural Irish had opportunity through letters, popular periodicals sent home, and (less often) travel to obtain access to the ways in which suburban and urban, English and American, and middle- and upper-class others existed.[10] The fact that these others did more than merely subsist could not help but become either an increasing irritant or perhaps an inspiration to those who continued to live the traditional farming life. Seeing what others had, many aspired to such material comfort themselves and worked to achieve the middle-class or town life of their so-called betters.

Cullen reinforces this point when he writes, "Heavier emigration and the earnings that emigrants, temporary or permanent, sent back were . . . important" contributions to improved living conditions; but "modernisation itself, by creating a greater awareness of outside areas and facilitating contact with higher living standards elsewhere, probably did more to reinforce the rise in emigration than to stem it" (153). Murray, writing in 1903, similarly concludes, "the continuous stream of emigration shows that in Ireland . . . the desire, or rather the necessity, for town life is a factor which must be taken into account" (424). Even when people chose not to or were unable to emigrate, most inevitably fell under the spell of the other places and ways of life in which living standards were higher. By the turn of the century, materialism had made a powerful headway into a group of people whose cultural, political, and geographical isolation had, for centuries, denied—or as Yeats would have it, protected—them from such vulgar interests. As a result of this perspective, Yeats's early peasant characters may have West coast ways, but they also, the less likable that is, have West End pretensions. It is in this way that Yeats's bourgeois peasant partakes in the re-invention of not only the Stage Irish stereotype but the Victorian English bourgeois tradition as well.

To take a step back in the bourgeois peasant's line of succession for a moment, we must consider the ways in which the Victorian English bourgeoisie is an invented tradition, constructed along the same Hobsbawmian structural lines as the Irish Revival peasant figure. Using the legitimating forces of scientism and rationalism, the bourgeoisie depended on the almost ubiquitous political and social domination by the imperialist English during the Victorian era in order to defend its ideological positions. This latter defense might be called the "sun never sets" paradigm, a political and military reality that transmutes into a rationale for nationalist and ethnocentric as well as classist behaviors. The supposed divine and/or natural sanction of English domination thus comes to express the certainty established in the conviction, also implied in the tautological notion of survival of the fittest, that because it is, it is right. Memmi further exposes the mythologization of both bourgeois and peasant, conqueror and conquered as correlative:

> Just as the bourgeoisie proposes an image of the proletariat, the existence of the colonizer requires that an image of the colonized be suggested. These images become excuses without which the presence and conduct of a colonizer, and that of a bourgeois, would seem shocking. But the favored image becomes a myth precisely because it suits them too well. (79)

The power favored by the bourgeoisie took the form of a moral, social, and political control that required the conscious participation of every individual and group within, or desirous of obtaining admittance into, its domain. In other words, the Victorian bourgeoisie aimed for—and achieved—a true hegemony in the Gramscian derivation of the term. Achieving power beyond that attained through the forced dominance of their ideologies, the Victorian bourgeoisie can be considered a hegemony precisely because "it presuppose[d] an active and practical involvement of the hegemonized groups, quite unlike the static, totalizing and passive subordination implied by the dominant ideology concept" (Gramsci 424). Terry Eagleton concurs with this assessment, writing in "Ideology and Literary Form" about the power of one of the most influential Victorian proponents of bourgeois ideology, Matthew Arnold: "[t]he thrust of [his] social criticism is to convert a visionless, sectarian bourgeoisie, pragmatically sunk in its own material interests, into a truly *hegemonic* class—a class with cultural resources adequate to the predominance it has come to hold in history" (172). Although Yeats would argue that the bourgeois class never transcended its material interests, he does display the ways in which it employs its cultural resources to augment the force with which its invented traditions of class, gender, and race eventually infiltrated all classes.

One could argue that all victims of a forced ideology partake in their own victimization. But what's important about this Victorian version about which I speak here is the way in which not only hegemonized groups, like the English middle classes, but also initially ostracized groups, such as the Irish and especially the Irish peasant class, partake in the championing of the dominant group's ideals. Terry Eagleton speaks to this point when he writes, "the liberal humanist notion of Culture was constituted, among other things, to marginalise such peoples as the Irish, so that it is particularly intriguing to find this sectarian gesture being rehearsed by a few of the Irish themselves" (365).[11] As we have seen, the Irish were considered the bestial, feminine other, or the opposite of the English norm of civilized masculinity, the hegemonic favoring of which made the hierarchy of colonial civilizations possible. However, many of the Irish insisted on partaking in the very same strategies that led to their being labeled, at best, complementary others—as in Arnold's reckoning of England and Ireland as Platonic opposites, respectively masculine and feminine and ideally suited to a match with one another—and, at worst, animals—as in Thomas Nast's popular depictions of the Irish as ape-like. In the latter rendering especially, the Irish appear hardly even human. As a result, in the nineteenth-century version of the great chain of being, at the apex of which resides English civilization, the Irish are of little account at all, superseding only those reputedly uncivilizable, dark-skinned inhabitants of the African continent.[12] The idea of being of account, of being countable in any social, economic, or political sense, manifests an influential metaphor of the era that represents the intertwined prejudices of the Victorian era's colonial and bourgeois ideals. Benedict Anderson explains the metaphor in his discussion of the nineteenth-century construction of census, map, and museum, constructions that are valuable in their

> illuminat[ion of] the colonial state's style of thinking about its domain. The "warp" of this thinking was a totalizing classificatory grid, which could be applied with endless flexibility to anything under the state's real or contemplated control: peoples, regions, religions, languages, products, monuments, and so forth. The effect of the grid was always to be able to say of anything that it was this, not that; it belonged here, not there. It was bounded, determinate, and therefore—in principle—countable. (184)

The accountability of each member of the large and varied group under British colonial rule to English bourgeois values, and the apparent interest on the part of British subjects to partake in this process, further reinforces the "inventedness" or consciousness of creation of bourgeois tradition. Hobsbawm points out that one of the main differences between "old" and "invented" practices lies in the following distinction: "The former were specific and strongly binding social practices, the latter tended to be quite unspecific and vague as to the nature of the values, rights and obligations of the group membership they inculcate: 'patriotism', 'loyalty', 'duty', 'playing the game', 'the school spirit', and the like" (10). Raymond Williams explains the derivation of one of the most important of nineteenth-century categories of membership in similar terms when he writes, "*Class* is a more indefinite word than *rank*, and this was probably one of the reasons for its introduction" (*Culture and Society 1780 - 1950* xv). A string of descriptors that could have risen directly out of the pages of Baden-Powell's Boy Scout handbook, *Tom Brown's School Days*, or Charles Kingsley's encomiums to muscular Christianity, the list provided by Hobsbawm uncovers as an overt socio-political ploy the hegemonic Victorian social constructions of class, gender, and race. With the signs of group membership able to be worn like so many Boy Scout merit badges, members of the English bourgeoisie could be confident of their membership in a group for which the function of patriotism and duty usually followed the form, or outward manifestation, of these values. For an example, we might turn to the historically if not nationally appropriate novel, *The Age of Innocence*, in which, Edith Wharton tells us, Old New York, a social group contemporaneous with and in social composition (if not in level of socioeconomic privilege) similar to the English bourgeoisie, emphasizes above all else "form" (8).

Tom Brown's Schooldays provides us with even more pertinent examples of the exercise and application of vague ideals and the fact that, in spite of the narrator's protestations to the contrary, in group solidarity lies the primary, though unspoken, power. Created as an exemplar of the mores of the day, *Tom Brown* offers the following lesson: "The object of all schools is not to ram Latin and Greek into boys, but to make them good English boys, good future citizens; and by far the most important part of that work must be done, or not done, out of school hours" (63). Does the novel go on to define "good English boys, good future citizens"? To a certain extent, yes, as when we hear of Squire Brown's paternal wish that his son Tom does not exert too much effort "'to make himself a good scholar,'" for "'he isn't sent to school for that—at any rate, not for that mainly.'" Rather, his father prays, "'If he'll only turn out a brave, helpful, truth-telling Englishman, and a gentleman, and a Christian, that's all I want'" (73). Though the qualities of bravery, helpfulness, honesty, and of being a gentleman and a Christian provide marginally more direction for a schoolboy in need of guidance than the suggestion to be a "good future citizen," they nonetheless leave much room for interpretation. For instance, a large portion of the "work" done "out of school hours" includes stalking and killing animals, stoning birds and skinning mice (66). In this case, the victimization of smaller creatures less able to defend themselves counts as a trial effort at feats of bravery and gentlemanly or Christian behavior. It also explains why one does not have to look too deeply for reasons that the colonization of peoples less able to defend themselves comes to be understood not only as a brave act but a morally righteous one as well. It is arguable that Thomas Hughes's, Rudyard Kiplings's and others' boys' stories *directly* inspire imperialist behaviors—though, as I have shown, the case is easily made. Still, one cannot help but recognize that the indeterminate definitions of correct behavior the novels encourage allow concepts like bravery and honor to suit whatever purpose to which a given individual chooses to put it, whether or not that purpose is defined as honorable by another (e.g., a father or a public school official).

Such vaguely defined and potentially imperialistic thinking also finds sustenance in the group solidarity taught to the public school boys. The significance of membership in factions ranging from one's school house to one's profession to one's county of origin cuts a clear path through the novel's other, weaker attempts at encouraging the equal treatment of all people regardless of class, gender, or race. For example, Squire Brown does not care "whether his son associated with lords' sons or ploughmen's sons, provided they were brave and honest" (52–53): but, here again are those vaguely defined morals. Similarly, the narrator of the novel chastises the characters', and by extension the readers', classism when he writes: "I never came across but two of you who could value a man wholly and solely for what was in him; who thought themselves verily and indeed of the same flesh and blood as John Jones the attorney's clerk, and Bill Smith the costermonger, and could act as if they thought so" (43).

However, such protestations ring false in the context of a novel in which, with the exception of gender, class and nation form the thickest of all group bonds. Depicted as a "hearty strong boy from the first, given to fighting with and escaping from his nurse, and fraternizing with all the village boys, with whom he made expeditions all round the neighbourhood" (Hughes 7), Tom maintains his virility—and establishes his place in the order of men—only by finally eschewing the care of his "dry nurse" for the company of Benjy, a respected, elderly man who was, importantly, distinguished in his day for his athletic prowess (27). Although gender solidarity, with the masculine gender at the social helm, remains the most obvious unspoken rule throughout the novel, other group identifications help the boys build not only their sense of identity but the social orderliness and concomitant security that such self-assuredness provides—for those in power, that is. A concern with both regional and national identification is shown in the following passage: "We were Berkshire, or Gloucestershire, or Yorkshire boys; and you're young cosmopolites, belonging to all counties and no countries" (7). Although this passage indicates that new and different group solidarities were emerging, the narrator's concern about this subject—and the disingenuousness manifested by a Victorian English narrator's lamenting insistence that nation is no longer an important category of identification—reveals in a he-doth-protest-too-much manner the actual prominence that national, and to a lesser extent regional, identity held for the English at the time. Class, too, appears to be important, when we discover that Tom was grilled about "birth, parentage, education, and other like matters" (96) after his first dinner at the school. All of this, as Andrew Sanders reminds us in his 1989 introduction to the novel, represents the "schoolboy fashion of solidarity with his order, his house, and his immediate circle of friends" (xvi)—a fashion that generates the more consequential power structures of adulthood.

In his theory of the invented tradition, Hobsbawm explains the impulse toward correct "form" and group solidarity in terms similar to the nineteenth-century authors discussed above. Utilizing a metaphor of fraternal/patriarchal collegiality with which Wharton's Newland Archer and a grown-up Tom Brown would have been equally familiar, he writes, "[t]he crucial element [in defining a tradition as invented] seems to have been the invention of emotionally and symbolically charged signs of club membership rather than the statutes and objects of the club. Their significance lay precisely in their undefined universality" (11). Thus, an important part of what makes the Victorian bourgeoisie an invented tradition is its refusal to define terms combined with its insistence on the fulfillment of those terms in order to maintain membership in the group. In this regard, the standard identification of the bourgeoisie with individualism requires some recasting. In one such rendering of this formula, Raymond Williams writes in *Culture and Society*, "'Bourgeois' is a significant term because it marks that version of social relationship which we usually call individualism: that is to say, an ideal of society as a neutral area within which each individual is free to pursue his own development and his own advantage as a natural right" (325). Further delineating the configuration of power in the bourgeois culture structure, Williams invokes the image of climbing a ladder as the "perfect symbol of the bourgeois idea of society, because, while undoubtedly it offers the opportunity to climb, it is a device which can only be used individually: you go up the ladder alone" (331). Whereas the accuracy of the assertion that individualism represents the bourgeoisie's ideal path to power and self-fulfillment cannot be denied, the reality, on at least one level, was much different. As the Tom Brown narrative shows us, while lip service is paid to the democratic ideal of social justice, which recommends that individuals are free to pursue their own development regardless of socioeconomic rank, gender, or race, the undefined "signs of club membership" offer the surest path to an individual's fulfillment as a social and economic being.

The outward signs of membership in the English Victorian colonial bourgeois class, what Gramsci calls the "formidable complex of trenches and fortifications of the dominant class" (380), thus might be seen as the invented traditions of a group determined to maintain its social cohesion and political hegemony through moralism in the guise of rationalism. As Foucault reminds us, aided by rationalism, any tradition will become necessarily hierarchical, for in the system of rationalism "every resemblance must be subjected to proof by comparison, that is, it will not be accepted until its identity and the series of its differences have been discovered by means of measurement with a common unit, or, more radically, by its position in an order"

(*The Order of Things* 56). By establishing a hierarchical system of values based on vaguely designated, self-defined notions of proper behavior, the bourgeoisie could ensure its dominance in a world only too eager, much to Yeats's chagrin, to follow in its footsteps.

And thus the bourgeois peasant was born. Initially a relatively marginal commentary in the primarily nationalist dramas *The Countess Cathleen* and *Cathleen ni Houlihan*, Yeats's bourgeois peasant takes the central role in *The Land of Heart's Desire*, where he serves, at one level, as a realistic—and negative—representation of Yeats's contemporaries. Blinded by his particular brand of progress, defined by the achievement of the material comforts of the middle classes, the bourgeois peasant becomes infected, as Yeats would have it, with the moralistic materialism (or materialistic moralism) that defines middle-class interests. The increasing range of bourgeois influence worried Yeats, not in small part because of the definitive judgments made about "correct" behavior under the guise of rationalism and/or morality, which safely barricaded the biased evaluations behind a supposedly universal and immovable front. With the bourgeois peasant, moreover, Yeats provides an allegorical representation of Habermas's depiction of the bourgeoisie as a fervent indoctrinator of others originally outside its bounds. "[C]onscious of being part of a larger public" and considering itself its "mouthpiece" and "educator," Habermas tells us, the bourgeoisie aimed to fulfill the role its self-proclaimed role as "publicist" (37). Although, in *Where There Is Nothing*, members of the middle class aim to "educate" or indoctrinate others in their group (a topic I will discuss in more detail in chapter five), in *The Countess Cathleen*, *Cathleen ni Houlihan*, and *The Land of Heart's Desire*, Yeats seems most concerned with the apparently, and in his view unfortunately, successful indoctrination of the peasant class.[13]

THE BOURGEOIS PEASANT: *THE COUNTESS CATHLEEN* AND *CATHLEEN NI HOULIHAN*

The most blatantly anti-bourgeois of Yeats's plays, *Where There Is Nothing*, *The Words upon the Window-Pane*, and *Purgatory* take their thematic cue, in part, from the plays that precede them, including the popular nationalist drama, *The Countess Cathleen*. Like many of his early poems and plays, the impetus for *The Countess Cathleen* can be traced back to Yeats's related interest and involvement in magical practices and the nationalist literary movement. He writes in an 1892 letter to John O'Leary that serves as a defense of the twinning of magical with literary/political pursuits, "If I had not made magic my constant study I could not have written my Blake book nor would 'The Countess Kathleen' have ever come to exist. The mystical life is the centre of all that I do & all that I think & all that I write" (*CL I* 303). And in "Apologia Addressed to Ireland in the Coming Days"—the poem that framed the collection in which *The Countess Cathleen* first appeared and that was later revised as "To Ireland in the Coming Times"—Yeats showed his intention to "fus[e] occultism and advanced nationalism in a manner calculated to appeal to Maud Gonne, and to irritate nearly everyone else" (Foster, *W. B. Yeats* 122). In the earlier version of the poem, Yeats writes of his desire to "be counted one / with Davis, Mangan, and Ferguson," of "dim wisdoms old and deep" that "round about my table go / The magical powers to and fro," and finally of "The love I lived, the dream I knew." These three lines represent the three major interests that most critics understand to have gone into the making of *The Countess Cathleen*: nationalism, religion or spirituality, and his desire for, and his desire to impress, Maud Gonne. The importance of the second of those interests to Yeats at the time is further elucidated when we consider the ways in which the line was revised. In "To Ireland in the Coming Times," the lines "round about my table go / The magical powers to and fro" become "the elemental creatures go / About my table to and fro." Although "elemental creatures" are, to be sure, blessed with magical powers (and therefore, indirectly, so is their homeland Ireland), the second version of the poem does little to suggest that the speaker may be similarly blessed. Whereas the first version describes the speaker as if he might be in the throes of casting a spell of his own, the second shows the speaker to be merely acted upon. Yeats's choice to include the more overt reference to ritualistic magic in the earlier version of the poem reinforces the centrality of magic as influencing *The Countess Cathleen* thematically, in particular the theme of spirituality and religion.

Yeats's use of religious elements and themes in *The Countess Cathleen* did not appeal equally to all spectators and readers. Roy Foster tells us that the play initially received many positive reviews, "including two ecstatic pieces by [Richard] Le Gallienne and [Lionel] Johnson" (*W. B. Yeats* 125), both members of the Rhymers Club and, more importantly, influential critics. However, dissenting and especially Catholic voices quickly made themselves heard, most loudly and infamously in the form of *Souls for Gold*, an angry pamphlet written and circulated by F. Hugh O'Donnell.[14] Adrian Frazier also points out that the earliest audiences condemned *The Countess Cathleen* for its depiction of certain "sins singled out in the play—lechery, robbery, and iconoclasm" (457). This response was as nationalist as it was religious, for both Catholicism and the mere fact of being Irish, for many, practically negated the potential for such crimes to take place on Irish soil—or at least made their appearance on Irish stages an uncomfortable event. As an alternative to the Catholic and nationalist audience's assessment, and in spite of Frazier's insistence that Yeats believed that "the Irish, unlike the English, were a spiritual people, caring little for material gain" (457), I want to argue here that, in *The Countess Cathleen*, Yeats in fact singles out for consideration by Irish theatergoers yet another sin: that of materialism.

Yeats appears to have denied the play a contemporary historical setting or social significance when he wrote in *Beltaine* that "the play is not historic, but symbolic" ("Plans and Methods" 8). David R. Clark also notes that, although the play has a specific historical setting in the first version (it is set in the sixteenth century), Yeats made "no attempt at historicity" and, moreover, set later versions in the vaguely worded "'in Ireland, and in old times'" (130). Yet Yeats's focus on materialistic motives, even its presence as a sub-theme, foreshadows the level of involvement in which Yeats's dramatic canon comes to be involved in social critique.[15] Further evidence of Yeats's interest in the materialism theme can be found in the increasing amount of time allotted, in subsequent revisions of the play, to the most materialistic characters in the play, Shemus and Teigue, who, significantly, do not even appear in the tale, recorded by Yeats in *Fairy and Folk Tales of Ireland*, that inspired the play. As Clark points out, not only do Shemus and Teigue become more central characters in the later 1913 version, "[i]n scene one Shemus and Teigue have become blacker characters and Mary whiter" (133), thus emphasizing the evils of materialism even more.

That the play is meant to shake up the status quo is supported by Yeats himself, who hoped the play's plot would be "'fantastic enough to wake [the audience] from their conventional standards'" (qtd. in Cribb 165).[16] Although the play's contemporary audiences and many literary critics, including Andrew Parkin, have interpreted the play as "scandalis[ing] Irish Catholics" (71), the most scandalous behavior in the play is not necessarily Catholic but bourgeois in origin. More specifically, *The Countess Cathleen* discredits those who follow in the footsteps of the middle class, abandoning themselves to materialism in the most absolute and irretrievable of fashions: by, literally in the play or figuratively, selling their souls to the devil. John Rees Moore believes the audiences' at times irate responses to Yeats's "object lesson in . . . morality" resulted from their realization that "Irishmen *were* selling their souls, and not only to the English. All compromises with the ideal were tacitly rebuked, just as all martyrs to the cause of Irish freedom were implicitly praised" (61). For instance, whereas the Countess Cathleen becomes both a Christian martyr and nationalist hero by sacrificing her soul for the purpose of saving the rest of the villagers, and Mary bravely chooses to starve to death rather than sell her soul for material gain, her husband Shemus and her son Teigue reveal themselves to be Yeatsian villains.[17]

Shemus and Teigue represent what for Yeats was one of the most unattractive of bourgeois qualities, materialism. Teigue betrays his propensity for capitalist interests early in the play. We first notice his obsession with capital through the sheer amount of time he spends talking about it. In the first scene, of Teigue's thirty lines, approximately one-third reflect a concern with his lack of money and desire to obtain it. "And the last penny gone" (13), "So that they brought us money" (27), "There is many a one, they say, had money from them" (31): Even when taken out of context, Teigue's words reveal his true obsession; and it's money he wants, not food, literally starving though he is. With the taste of silver always already in his mouth, it does not surprise us then when, at first word of the merchants' interest in buying souls, Teigue immediately offers his. Upon hearing mention of "a vaporous thing" also defined as "a second self / They call immortal for a story's sake" as the "merchandise" sought by the merchants (43), even Shemus, who later proves to be quite the complacent capitalist, hesitates for a moment. Not sure he understands the terms, he asks, "They come to buy our souls?" Teigue, however, does not fee the same compunction as does his father and quickly bargains his own soul. "I'll barter mine" (43), he announces suddenly, impatiently, almost as if he sees himself in competition with his father for the best price. In basing his decision to sell his soul entirely upon material needs and, even moreso, desires, Shemus reveals from whence his son's opportunism originates. Shemus has been starved almost to death by famine, a factor that could understandably lead to actions otherwise considered taboo. However, when he is offered a pile of gold by the mysterious merchants, Shemus's thoughts shift swiftly and calculatingly from the need to eat to the more exotic benefits of the gold. He is almost choked with (demonic?) glee as he boasts, "What sets me to laughing when I think of it, / Is that a rogue who's lain in lousy straw, / If he but sell [his soul], may set up his coach" (71).

The merchants, in fact, are emissaries of Satan or the "Master of all merchants" (37), a title that not so subtly reveals Yeats's level of disgust with the merchant classes, as does his depiction of the merchants as "vermin that our Master sent / To overrun the world" (49). The political symbolism of the merchants as English oppressors is also pertinent here. The merchants bear a striking resemblance to the Protestant missionaries who used the Famine to their advantage by coercing starving, Catholic peasants to capitulate to their demands in order to obtain food. As has been well documented, the demand consisted of forced conversion to Protestantism, an emotional and physical form of blackmail that consigned those desperate enough to give in to it to the disgrace of Souperism.[18] Andrew Parkin also sees reflections of English colonization of the Irish in the merchants' "bitter brutal streak which issues violence at the end of the first scene" and which reminds him of "melodramatic caricatures of ruthless landlords" (71). It is not likely that this point would be missed by many members of Yeats's contemporary audiences who were either involved in or at least aware of the land legislation battles that took place throughout the late nineteenth and early twentieth century.

Other critics give weight to the theory that the merchants represent imperialism in its wider context. For instance, David R. Clark points out that because their evil supernatural status makes them always other and their ability to buy and sell souls makes them always powerful, "wherever they go," the merchants "are foreign exploiters" (128) or the colonizer in control of the colonized. John Rees Moore departs from the imperialism metaphor, finding significance in the fact that, because they sit cross-legged on a carpet on the floor (*Countess Cathleen* 33), the merchants hail from the "Far East" (61) and have a "pre-Christian flavor" (60). Similarly, he reminds his reader that "Money . . . was the devil's lure for the desperate unwary long before Judas betrayed Christ for thirty pieces of silver" (60–61).

A glance into Yeats's interest in Noh theater and his affiliation with the Indian mystics and writers, Shri Purohit, Mohini Chatterji, and Rabindranath Tagore, shows us that, for Yeats, the Far East represented a civilization as ancient, spiritually-centered, and deserving of respect as ancient Irish civilization, before it had been corrupted by materialistic and progressivist values. Likewise, in "The Celtic Element in Literature," Yeats allies the Irish with other ancient cultures when he argues that Arnold's and Renan's theories about the alleged ethnic traits of the Celt apply to all "'primitive'" cultures (*EI* 182). Thus, although during this period Yeats included Irish nationalism in his belief system, his investment in a movement with a different sort of message stayed with him even longer. That is, at this point and throughout his career, Yeats believed not so much in the value of Ireland as "Irish" as in the function of Ireland as an ancient civilization which, like other ancient civilizations, was made up of individuals who lived "in a world where anything might flow and change, and become any other thing; and among great gods whose passions were in the flaming sunset, and in the thunder and the thunder-shower" (*EI* 178). Preferring this, a fluent world without the social handcuffs created by theories of science, rationalism, and progress, to modern civilization with its "thoughts of weight and measure" (*EI* 178), Yeats saw Ireland and the Orient in a fraternal (or, as befits Victorian gender construction of the other, sororal) relationship that decidedly did not include England.

When viewed from this perspective, the exoticization of the merchants exemplifies Yeats's growing recognition of the potential for betrayal amongst one's own kind. A reading of the merchants as representing both English imperialism and ancient idealism of the Far East/Ireland widens the significance of their role in the play. By twinning the imperialist with the native and making that particular conglomeration a soul-destroying merchant, Yeats further emphasizes not only the trouble with materialism but also the fact that Irish (peasants') capitulation to capitalism is, as postcolonial theorists after Yeats would argue, like most everything else, inseparable from the historical fact of England's imperialistic hold on Ireland. This reading of the merchants also supports my belief that, in *The Countess Cathleen*, Yeats means to show the Irish peasants as complicit in their own downfall, with materialism acting as means and end.

Whereas Yeats's condemnation of the political blackmail allegorized in the first scene of the play marks one level of socio-historical critique, another level manifests itself in the significance of the metamorphosis of Yeats's sympathy for Shemus. Any compassion Yeats elicits from the reader for Shemus's plight as starving victim of English oppression ends abruptly when Shemus's motive for selling his soul transmutes from the understandable one of need to that of greed. Delighting in the physical pleasures to which he has not for some time been privy, the hedonist Shemus shuns others' worries about his eternal damnation with a devil-may-care approach to the problem: "For souls—if there are souls— / But keep the flesh out of its merriment. / I shall be drunk and merry" (73). Continuing his ruminations over the existence of the soul, he concludes: "And if there is [a soul], / I'd rather trust myself into the hands / That have but shaken famine from the bag" (73). In other words, if it feels good, do it. Especially when compared to Cathleen's "impulsive [Christian] generosity" (Zwerdling 76) and Mary's Christian martyrdom, mercenary capitalists like Shemus, Teigue, and the merchants evoke little sympathy.

In *Cathleen ni Houlihan*, also written for a popular nationalist audience, Yeats likewise directs a critical eye toward the subjugation of the more noble pursuits of family, romantic love, and nationalist fervor to material gain. As in *The Countess Cathleen*, anti-materialism is not *Cathleen ni Houlihan*'s central theme.[19] According to Elizabeth Butler Cullingford, *Cathleen ni Houlihan*'s significance in literary history and in the history of Yeats's thought is the role it plays in making Yeats "one of the great modern propagandists of the notion of blood sacrifice" ("'Thinking of Her . . . .'" 4). Alex Zwerdling similarly identifies *Cathleen ni Houlihan* as the play that most closely resembles the propagandism Yeats elsewhere decries (118). Proof that Yeats himself recognized the play's nationalist propagandistic elements can be found in his late poem, "The Man and the Echo," in which he ponders, "Did that play of mine send out / Certain men the English shot?" (*CP* 345). Whether or not Yeats can or should be held responsible for inspiring men and women to join in the Easter Rising or to enlist with the Irish Republican Brotherhood, we can be certain that, with *Cathleen ni Houlihan*, Yeats advances his thesis about the relevance of a different type of sacrifice: Ireland's willingness to sacrifice itself to materialist aims.

In its depiction of yet another choice between self-directed desires and self-sacrifice—in this case between personal fulfillment and nationalist asceticism—the play dramatizes heroism not only through Michael's willingness to sacrifice first his money and then himself, but also, negatively, through his covetous parents, Bridget and Peter. Celebrating the good fortune of Michael's impending marriage to Delia Cahel, Bridget and Peter focus on the material boon the union will provide, including Peter's "grand clothes" (215) and the £100 dowry, with even a shilling of which Peter is loathe to part for the sake of the old, feeble, homeless woman who appears at his door. "Indeed, I'd not begrudge it to her if we had it to spare," Peter rationalizes, "but if we go running through what we have, we'll soon have to break the hundred pounds, and that would be a pity" (225). Unlike Michael, they do not have the sense to recognize that although "the woman [Delia] will be there always," the "fortune only lasts for a while" (219). Or perhaps their awareness is so acute as to make them all the more loathe to part with even a small portion of their recent windfall. In either case, Yeats relates with disapproval the parents' estimation of money over human compassion. It is true that Peter's and Bridget's choices "reflect peasants' values" (Fleming 163) to the extent that they are concerned with issues of land and family, both of which are of central importance to the tradition, lifestyle, and economic maintenance of the peasant. However, with heads always "full of plans" for their family's *financial* enhancement (220), in particular, Bridget and Peter more closely reflect the bourgeois conception of progress wherein individuals evolve (and devolve) according the balance of their bank accounts.

Although his elitist tendencies limit the comparison considerably, Yeats's antimaterialist theme warrants a comparison with Marxist theories about bourgeois or capitalist society. For instance, in the *Communist Manifesto*, Marx writes that the "essential condition for the existence, and for the sway of the bourgeois class, is the formation and augmentation of capital" (345). This is true also of family for, as Marx explains, the "bourgeoisie has torn away from the family its sentimental veil, and has reduced the family relation to a mere money relation" (338). Because of the primacy of capital, the "bourgeoisie cannot exist without constantly revolutionising the instruments of production, and thereby the relations of production, and with them the whole relations of society" (338). Here Marx speaks to both the centrality of material wealth to the bourgeoisie—even (or especially?) the bourgeois peasantry—and the concomitant need to increase its prominence, or evidence of its prominence, in one's own personal life and in society in general. According to the scientific notion of survival of the fittest as translated into the economic theory of capitalism, the more money (or better, easier ways to make it) the better.

The realistic formal elements of *Cathleen ni Houlihan* support a reading of the play as social criticism, though critics disagree on this point. Even though its historical setting, the 1798 Rising, gives the play historical credence, John Rees Moore reads *Cathleen ni Houlihan* as primarily a "myth play" (69) that appeals on a nationalist level "more to mob instinct than to a traditional understanding of community" (14). The play's appeal to the mob has also been recognized by Marjorie Howes, who understands the play to "embod[y] Yeats's historically specific anxieties about Irish nationalism as mass politics," a reading suggested in part by "the ever present but never visible cheering crowd" (75). As Howes explains, Victorian crowd theorists like Gustave Le Bon associated the mob with feminism and socialism (81) because social Darwinism and other like-minded theories pronounced these women and the working classes "more likely to succumb to the group mind than others" (81). As "political subject[s]" theoretically less capable of reason, these individuals were seen to be "motivated by unconscious, irrational and emotional forces" (81). As Howes insightfully details for us, Yeats bought into the insights of Victorian crowd theory, at least in part, and felt threatened by mobs composed of the underclass and female would-be hysterics.

However, theories about Yeats's fear of groups who have "succumb[ed] to the group mind" as displayed in *Cathleen ni Houlihan* must also include his apprehensions about the middle classes. It is true that, on one level, the play depicts Yeats's very real fear of mob politics. But the play also reveals his fears about the indoctrination of the lower and middle classes into the elementally group-minded structure of the materialist bourgeoisie. In this way, *Cathleen ni Houlihan*'s realistic elements—its historical significance, the family drama plot line, the dialogue[20]—help foreground the social critique embedded in an otherwise mythical play in which nationalist sentiment marries an indictment of materialism as part of the Victorian obsession with progress. This is not to deny the mythic levels of the play, which, if we consider the early audiences' responses in the form of nationalist fervor, clearly prevail. Yet to ignore the realistic critique of the materialist ethos would be to deny the relevance of an important message in the play and in Yeats's early involvement with theater.

Susan C. Harris also recognizes the importance of the realist elements in the play when she characterizes the play's inclusion of both melodramatic and realistic elements as an important moment in theater history. Harris explains that one of the ways in which Yeats departs from melodramatic conventions is through his "displacement of the male villain" by Bridget (479). Although the identification of the "strangers" who have occupied Ireland's "beautiful fields" (*Cathleen ni Houlihan* 226) with the English-as-enemy is obvious, the strangers do not partake in the play's primary dramatic action or conflict. Rather, Harris argues, "the opposition to [Cathleen's] union with Michael comes from his materialistic mother, Bridget, who claims her son for the world of domestic responsibility" (479). Although the play represents English imperialism as a formidable enemy, Yeats's choice to overturn melodramatic convention in ways that foreground Bridget and Peter's materialism makes this the major on-stage conflict. Yeats's decision in this regard both highlights the prominence of the anti-materialism theme and further emphasizes Yeats's construction of materialism, in the guise of progress, as an imposing, and related, threat to the present and future of Ireland.

PROGRESS AS MATERIAL GAIN: *THE LAND OF HEART'S DESIRE*

The Land of Heart's Desire is readily interpreted as representing the clash between pagan and Christian values. The major conflict in the play might also be described as that between a spiritual (pagan) world and that of material existence, the latter of which Yeats colors specifically as Christian, bourgeois, and given the Catholic context of the play, somewhat ironically as reflective of the Protestant work ethic.[21] Alex Zwerdling has already noted that "church and priest in this play seem to represent all organized religion rather than any specific sect" (85). I would take his argument one step further (or back) to insist that, in spite of their decidedly Catholic heritage, the play's characters reflect the more generally Christian, even particularly Protestant, belief that one must work diligently for one's salvation. Most of the characters in the play—namely Bridget, Maurteen, and Father Hart—consider idle, lazy, and frivolous the pagan existence of fairies and those who choose to join them, especially when compared with the hard-working life of the Christian. In the words of

John Rees Moore, they practice a "joyless puritanism" (9). Yeats exhibits contempt for these individuals who entirely exclude the mystery of life, such as that found in books and the use of the imagination, for the industry that not only meets current needs but concerns itself primarily with the (over)filling of pockets with capital—capital to be used for the fulfillment of a material desire always in some future moment and in order to ensure the continual progression of the family in the class continuum.

As part of his anti-materialist agenda, Yeats depicts those either enmeshed in (Bridget, Maurteen, and Father Hart) or entrapped by (Mary) the bourgeois, Christian notions of proper living as unhappy, as sick as the Blakean rose in the play's epigraph. That Yeats opens the play with an epigraph from *Songs of Experience*, the first line of Blake's poem "The Sick Rose," is of particular significance. In its entirety, the poem runs as follows:

> O Rose, thou art sick!
> The invisible worm,
> That flies in the night,
> In the howling storm,
>
> Has found out thy bed
> Of crimson joy,
> And his dark secret love
> Does thy life destroy. (216–17)

It would be easy to read into the poem support for the claim that the pagan world is a dangerous place with poisonous values: Mary (the "Rose") not only sickens but also dies from the "dark secret love" of an "invisible" creature that "flies in the night" which, in Blake's case is a worm, and in Yeats's a fairy. This reading assumes the reader's complicity with the values of (the holy trinity of) Bridget, Maurteen, and Father Hart.

If we look more closely at the play, however, we see that the poem more likely represents another perspective. That is, Mary has not been sickened or had her life destroyed by her day-dreamy interest in the otherworld but by the "old and godly and grave," the "old and crafty and wise," and the "old and bitter of tongue" (184) who insist that she capitulate to the real world's bourgeois values. In this case, the "dark secret love" is love of money, and the sickness that of materialism. Yeats himself allies materialism with illness in his notes in *The Works of William Blake*, which he edited with Edwin Ellis between 1889 and 1893. In his notes on "Lafayette," he defines "doubt of imagination and belief in nature" as a "disease of the soul" (287). Support for this interpretation lies in Maurteen's espousal of filling one's pockets over and instead of (not even in addition to) the necessity of fulfilling one's imagination. He advises Mary in this regard:

> ... Had I
> Or had my father read or written books
> There were no stocking stuffed with yellow guineas
> To come when I am dead to Shawn and you. (183–84).

The depiction here of the pursuit and fruit of artists as a waste of time and as utilizing effort better put to use elsewhere—that is, in more practical pursuits such as those which lead to the making of money—reveals the bourgeois origin of the Bruins' definition of productivity as closely tied to wealth.[22] Here, as with Shemus and Teigue in *The Countess Cathleen* and the parents in *Cathleen ni Houlihan*, money is valued not for its ability to fulfill basic needs but for the sake of accumulation and its subsequent ability to provide the pleasures and security of a middle-class lifestyle.

One might put a practical spin on Maurteen's faith in money. As patriarchal head of the household, responsible for ensuring the present and future care of his family, Maurteen reflects a trait common to most parents: the desire for one's children to do better, economically speaking, than oneself. Yet Maurteen's attempts to evoke Mary's compliance with her new family's expectations of her reveal an understated desire not only to achieve an economic level of comfort, but to do so in a fashion that would allow the family not only to keep up with but to surpass the Joneses. That this is his goal manifests itself, in one instance, in his wife's unqualified resentment toward her husband and the focus of his attentions: Mary, whose youth and attractiveness, Maurteen believes, will help the family to display the outward manifestation of his wealth both during his lifetime and in the future. Complaining that she must "spare and pinch that my son's wife / May have all kinds of ribbons for her head" (190), Bridget exposes Maurteen's promotion of the more frivolous and showy of material goods over mundane necessities, thereby naming her husband as embracing the middle-class consciousness Yeats would like his audience to renounce. Maurteen himself reinforces this character sketch by designing, in the same scene, to convince Mary to "put away [her] dreams of discontent" because, he promises, after his death she will be "the wealthiest hereabout" (189). Maurteen's emphasis here and elsewhere on superlative prosperity flies in the face of Fleming's reading of his "vision of the best life" as "naïve, homey, comfortable" (99). Rather, consoling Mary with what he thinks she desires, the lure of future material pleasures, Maurteen goes so far as to disregard the more prosaic familial pleasures of the glowing turf fire, available to all but the poorest of the classes, for the day when Mary can rest assured and happy, if not with the support of a loving father-in-law, then with the possession of more money than that of anyone of her acquaintance.

Moreover, in revealing his espousal of Victorian gender prejudices, which are related through the value of productivity to both the Protestant work ethic and more general bourgeois notions of progress, Maurteen equates the reading of books with weakness, femininity, and witlessness. "Persuade the colleen to put down the book," he pleads when Mary speaks longingly of the world of mythic heroes. "My grandfa-

Progress as Material Gain

ther would mutter just such things, / And he was no judge of a dog or a horse, / And any idle boy could blarney him" (184). A bourgeois peasant, Maurteen depicts imaginative literature as a potential threat to the social fabric that must maintain its productive and future-gazing integrity, and thereby unmasks himself as philistine as well as ardent materialist. Maurteen's advice likewise upholds traditional Victorian notions of masculinity that belittle literary knowledge in favor of more overtly (read: fiscally) rational capabilities such as the ability to "judge" the market value of an animal and, more importantly, not to be "blarney[ed]" by an even less masculine specimen than himself, an "idle boy," with all the connotations of childishness, wastefulness, and socially-draining indigence this image implies.

In its connotation as non-functioning, idleness ironically performs an important function in *Land*. The absence of activity, idleness represents the lack of participation in productive social enterprise, which is frowned upon in a world in which active functioning holds social, economic, and spiritual value, as the works of Victorian writers ranging from Karl Marx to Thomas Carlyle attest.[23] From the perspective of the Bruins and Father Hart, Mary's idleness marks her as an immature woman, an addition to their home who is more burden than help and who, more importantly, threatens the social contract of marriage by not fulfilling her end of the bargain. For instance, Bridget chastises Mary as "old enough to know that it is wrong / To mope and idle" (185). She feels particularly put out because Mary does not, as she had expected her son's bride to do, "[g]et up at dawn like me and mend and scour" (182). Maurteen similarly, though more sympathetically, represents Mary as "driven . . . to hide among her dreams / Like children from the dark under the bedclothes" (185). In either case, Mary's choice to fill her hours with the "idle" activity of book reading allies her, negatively, with artists whose "childish" imaginative capacity makes them, in terms of the Victorian hegemonic course of progress, useless.[24]

The relegation of Mary to the role of child also reveals Yeats's perception and antipathy toward the social coding of Victorian gender, whereby women were classified as being innately closer to the natural state of man-as-animal and, subsequently, as potential sites of anarchy-inducing hysteria. Clearly no Angel in the House, Mary is described by Yeats, through the other characters' perceptions, as not only vague and dreamy but, more threateningly, as quarrelsome (182), "[r]estless and ill at ease" (185). Interestingly, in both of the preceding instances, the Bruins calm their fears about Mary's unsettled and unsettling presence in the house with the time-tested belief that Mary will grow calm after her first pregnancy. For instance, Maurteen predicts that

> . . . she will grow
> As quiet as a puff-ball in a tree
> When but the moons of marriage dawn and die
> For half a score of times. (182)

The biological facts of conception and gestation, reflected in the references to monthly cycles and Mary's rounded appearance, introduce that which Maurteen thinks will help, or rather force, Mary to settle down. According to the standard Victorian line of thinking about women's relationship to creative processes, Mary wastes her time (or her seed, to borrow a phrase from the masculine version of this argument) nurturing intellectual or imaginative pursuits at a time when her energies should be directed toward the *pro*creative process of childbirth.

The puff-ball passage also iterates the bestial state of womanhood and her supposedly inescapable tie to her own body. The implication is that Mary *will* become quiet; it is her biological destiny. As Father Hart explains, women's "hearts are wild, / As be the hearts of birds, till children come" (182). Maurteen further acknowledges the power of social indoctrination when he likens Mary to all the women who, over the years, "grew like their neighbours and were glad / In minding children, working at the churn, / And gossiping of weddings and of wakes" (185).[25] Maurteen's ruminations reveal his sympathy for Mary's plight in their implicit acknowledgement that a newly married, childless woman has reason to feel ill at ease in her own skin. The pagan belief that women in Mary's state of life are especially vulnerable to fairy abduction, moreover, strengthens his biological and social defenses of Mary, for Maurteen warns, "Remember they may steal new-married brides / After the fall of twilight on May Eve" (186). However, in spite of their acknowledgements, the Bruin family and Father Hart have little patience for Mary, whose uneasiness is paired with a willful rejection of the Angel in the House role, the very tradition to which her new family strains to make her submit.

The Bruins understandably consider insurgent Mary's intractability when it comes to subsuming herself into the traditional female role: she will not, after all, help with the most necessary of chores, refusing to "mind the kettle, milk the cow, / Or even lay the knives and spread the cloth" (182). Yeats, however, does not attribute Mary's rebellion entirely to her idleness or dreaminess, or what Bridget would have us see as her desire to be taken away on the wings of flighty fairy irresponsibility. In fact, Mary in some ways appears to be the most reliable witness, the person most aware of what occurs around her. She is not only more perceptive than her housemates but also more in control of her fate than she first appears to be. For example, Mary is the only character not fooled by the fairy child that the Bruins unwittingly invite into their home. Even Maurteen, bastion of common sense, does not recognize the truth. When the fairy child appears, he proclaims, "Being happy, I would have all others happy," and asks her in from the cold (195). Even giving credit where credit is due, the slightly patronizing tone with which the kind deed is offered reveals a relationship between the offer and Victorian bourgeois values regarding charity. That is, feeling comfortable in his role as patriarch, Maurteen, like any (aspiring) self-respecting member of the middle class, wants to do his part for the less fortunate.[26]

A look into the philanthropic and charitable habits of the Victorian age illuminate my reading of Maurteen's motives. As Alan Kidd notes, the motives of the charitable in the nineteenth century ranged from "sympathy and fellow feeling to the desire to be well thought of, from religious piety to a sense of guilt, from the desire for a well-regulated society to the fear of the mob, from the feeling of having done your duty to a sense of personal gratification at helping others" (69). Of the preceding list of motivations, we would be justified by the play in ascribing most if not all of them to Maurteen, whom Yeats characterizes as sympathetic, pious, and fearful of the mob (in the form of the fairies who, as inhabitants of a pagan world, form, as he sees it, the only class of being lower than himself). And, as with all who perform charitable acts, Maurteen gains a sense of personal gratification and feels as if he's done his duty by letting the seemingly homeless "child" into his home. Maurteen obtains pleasure from making the girl happy—a fact evinced by his capitulation to her every wish including her request to remove the crucifix from the wall. (Father Hart actually removes it, but Maurteen's sympathy for the girl's horrified reaction manifests itself clearly.)

But Maurteen also feels so pleased that his invitation has provided him with the opportunity to rectify her complete ignorance of Christianity ("Her parents are to blame" [199]), he gives her the ribbons he had been saving for Mary. This act is meant to make the fairy child feel at home, as does his telling her that he loves her (201), both of which serve to console not only the fairy child but Maurteen as well. For here, with the exercise of patriarchal power that comes from providing for one's family, Maurteen has widened the family circle and made himself, at least for the moment, an even more substantial patriarch. Maurteen's ribbon offering, like his efforts to tame Mary, metaphorically represents his "desire for a well-regulated society"—the ribbons are "[t]o tie up that wild hair the winds have tumbled" (201)— as well as his belief that materialistic endeavors are the best path to that regulation. Likewise, Maurteen's intended use of the ribbons correlates with what, in *Capital*, Marx calls the bourgeois fetishism of commodities present in bourgeois societies. Or, as the *Encyclopedia of Marxism* entry on bourgeois society so clearly explains, "just as tribal peoples believed that their lives were being determined by trees and animals and natural forces possessing human powers, in bourgeois society, people's lives are driven by money and other commodities, whose value is determined by extramundane forces; instead of ethics and morality being governed by traditional systems of belief and imagined spiritual forces, there is just the ethic of cash-payment."

Another theorist of Victorian philanthropy, Olive Checkland, sees an important distinction between philanthropy and charity, one that Yeats also seemed to recognize. She defines philanthropy as a "broader" concept than charity, "concerned to better human conditions." Victorian charity, on the other hand, was "heavily impregnated with moral judgments of those who became its objects" (2). She singles out Christian charity for special attention in this regard, remarking that "Christian charity was often a social observance, designed rather for the re-assurance of the giver than for the good of the receiver. It was regarded as a thank offering made by those with a surplus to those less fortunate than themselves" (2). In light of these definitions, Maurteen's continual pairing of gift-giving with talk about his role in the transformation that such gifts provide—again, "[b]eing happy, [he] would have all others happy"—identify Maurteen less with the role of philanthropist than that of charitable Christian, a complex and not entirely positive designation, as I will display in more detail in my discussion of Father Hart below.[27]

Mary, who has made the philanthropic moment possible by offering milk and light to the fairy outside the front door (thereby, according to folk tradition, giving the fairy power over the house), and who in the end proves susceptible to the otherworldly summons of the fairy child, nevertheless recognizes who/what it is the family has invited into their midst. Whereas ever-cynical Bridget, surprisingly charmed by the fairy's apparitional appearance as a little girl with "white hands and [a] pretty dress," sees in the fairy a "child of the gentle [upper-class] people" (197)—perhaps she is blinded by her desire for a daughter-in-law of this sort—Mary sees, or rather hears, the truth. Open to knowledge beyond the sensory or the scientifically validated, Mary warns,

> Just now when she came near I thought I heard
> Other small steps beating upon the floor,
> And a faint music blowing in the wind,
> Invisible pipes giving her feet the tune. (201)

"I hear them now," she insists in response to the others' doubtful rebuffs of her insight. "The unholy powers are dancing in the house" (201). In this scene, the commencement of the play's climax at which Mary joins the fairies, Yeats reverses the roles set up earlier by the characters' judgments of one another: Mary is wise well beyond the years and comprehension of the Bruins and Father Hart.[28] Her intuition and imaginative capabilities, not insignificantly fed by her reading of mythology and her openness to alternative spheres of existence, obtain more value than a sensory, rational, and material comprehension of the world.

Mary's comparative wisdom at this moment is ironic in that she has, to this point, been portrayed as puerile and foolish. However, Yeats makes Mary stronger still by foregrounding her complicity in her entrance into the fairy world, a transformation made in part through bewitchment, but not entirely without Mary's conscious cooperation. In other words, Mary chooses to join the fairies; nor does Yeats invalidate her choice by having her make it without the careful deliberation that signals rationality. Mary's sense of agency emerges in part from self-awareness. She reveals an especially relevant insight into the composition of her identity when she admits that she has "always loved [the fairy's] world" (208). Yeats reinforces this apparently intrinsic attachment at the opening of the play by situating her physically between the two worlds: Whereas the Bruins and Father Hart sit under the crucifix, enjoying the warmly domestic "glow of light from the fire," Mary is separated from them by her choice to sit by the doorway, through which she can see into the dark wood as she reads a book of ancient Irish mythology (180). Her physical placement and choice of activity emblematize Mary's sensitivity to the allure of the "vague, mysterious world," which has beckoned her for some time.

The strongest evidence of Mary's self-agency occurs at the end of the play. Just before her death, Mary's husband Shawn has pleaded with her to choose her love for life and for him over her desire to "ride the winds." "Beloved, I will keep you," he avows. "I've more than words, I have these arms to hold you, / Nor all the faery host, do what they please / Shall ever make me loose you from these arms" (208). The security and solidity of Shawn's arms, though tempting, are not enough to sway Mary, who subsequently makes the following openly rebellious declaration to the fairy: "I will go with you" (207). The fact that Shawn's appeals to her draw her in, if only briefly, evinces that, even at this late point, Mary possesses the faculty of reason. Torn between her reason, which urges her not to relinquish her human life, and her emotional and spiritual connection to the imaginative world of the fairies, however, Mary chooses to go to the land of her heart's, not her mind's, desire. She pays with her human life, the renouncement of which is necessary for her rebirth into the fairy world. Although some critics argue that Mary has been "possessed" by the fairy's magic (Parkin 57) or "acted upon" (Moore 9), a common fate of new brides in Irish folklore, I suggest this more positive interpretation of Mary's self-agency.

At this point, we must consider the implicit comparison Yeats makes between Mary, who martyrs herself for a pagan existence, and Jesus Christ, whose image and teachings the Bruins and Father Hart evoke throughout the play. There can be no doubt that Yeats intended his protagonist's name to resonate the story of Jesus Christ on many levels. As martyr, *Land*'s Mary represents both Jesus Christ and his mother Mary who, in effect if not by choice, became a martyr for her son's life. [29] The irony, of course, is that Yeats's Mary martyrs herself in order to opt out of the Christian life that the earlier Mary, in part, made possible. But Christianity plays a larger role in *Land*. In addition to the obvious presence of Father Hart, Christianity influences the life philosophies of the Bruin family, who preach the doctrine of love, both love of God and of other humans. Maureen, for example, heartily believes that all people eventually settle down to "find the excellent old way through love, / And through the care of children, to the hour / For bidding Fate and Time and Change good-bye" (190). The centrality of the family in Christian life is represented by the frequent references to, and attempts to enforce, family gatherings by the hearth fire beneath the loving and watchful eye of Jesus, ever-present in the form of the crucifix. "Stir up the fire, / And put new turf upon it till it blaze," Maureen enjoins in an effort to soothe the family wrinkles caused by Mary's refusal to succumb to their ways. "To watch the turf-smoke coiling from the fire, / And feel content and wisdom in your heart, / This is the best of life"—this and, significantly, "a hundred acres of good land" (190).

As innocuously agreeable as contentment, wisdom, and a warm turf fire sound, Yeats does not allow Maurteen's description of idyllic family life to go unchallenged. For the "best of life," according to the Bruin family, also necessarily means living according to the standards of the nuclear family, the Christian family, the hardworking, philistine, bourgeois-aspiring (if not in socio-economic fact) family. In other words, in defining the best of life, the bourgeoisie also controls to whom and in what ways the relaxed state implied by the warm turf fire scenario applies. More specifically, the middle class aims to achieve the ease and relaxation that prosperity affords without having to contend with the social complexity and disquietude that the relaxed conditioning of social roles, such as those of gender, race, and class, would create.

Yeats does not let the Bruins have the last word. He not only shows the value in alternative ways of life—represented in the play by those who live, or at least do not disdain, the pagan, imaginative, and intellectual life—but also exposes the disingenuousness practiced by Christianity and its followers. For instance, in acknowledging the fairies' powers, Father Hart reveals the significant force pagan beliefs hold over even the most devout of Christian followers, when he admits:

> We do not know the limit of those powers
> God has permitted to the evil spirits
> For some mysterious end. You have done right . . .;
> It's well to keep old innocent customs up. (186)

Referring to Bridget's rush to hang the fairy prophylactic, quicken wood, on the door, in this passage Father Hart displays the extent to which Christianity in Ireland has subsumed into its belief system the pagan folklore it elsewhere mocks. Although he understands ultimate power to lie in the hands of God, Father Hart nonetheless betrays his fear of the fairies' capacity to influence humans. Pagan powers, therefore, still hold sway even in this world in which Christians rule. Though the prominent presence of both Father Hart and a crucifix appear to point to Catholicism as Yeats's specific target, the hypocrisies I show here indicate that he directs criticism not only at the Catholic Church but at Christianity, Protestant and Catholic alike. This depiction marks a departure from the more specifically anti-Catholic theme in *The Countess Cathleen*, in which Yeats equates Protestantism, represented by the Countess Cathleen, with generosity, while many if not all Catholics (Mary Rua is the exception) represent the corrupting influences of selfishness, greed, and materialism.

Yeats further exposes the weaknesses of Christianity by portraying some of its subtler hypocrisies. When Father Hart perceives that the fairies have achieved dominance in the situation, he savagely lashes out at them, calling them "children of the Fiend" whom "God shall fight . . . in a great pitched battle / And hack . . . into pieces" (187). Such harsh, violent language reflects the Old Testament's and Revelation's wrathful tone rather than Christ's doctrine of peace, the latter of which include the directives, here made ironic by Father Hart himself, to turn the other cheek and to do unto others as you would have them do unto you. Father Hart's "Christian" malice appears even more ironic when contrasted with Mary's behavior, which better fulfills the traditional Christian ideal. Responding to Father Hart's and the Bruins' spurning of the creature they had welcomed into the house when they thought it was one of their own kind, Mary admits, "I am glad that I was courteous to them," reasoning, albeit naively, "[f]or are not they, likewise, children of God?" (187). In light of Father Hart's admission that the "evil spirits" exist with God's permission, Mary's question does not seem as un-Christian as it does legitimate.

Mary's desire to see everyone loved and happy continues with the wish that God "will smile, / Father, perhaps, and open His great door" (187) to everyone including the fairy child. Father Hart, more fully master of Christian doctrine than the already half-pagan Mary, frightens away Mary's questions with his insistence that if she opens the door to the "lawless angels" (187), she will be forced to "drive through the same storm" with the fallen (188). Although, in this instance, Father Hart out-reasons Mary within the context of Christian doctrine, the scene nevertheless forces the reader or spectator to consider the hypocrisy behind a doctrine of forgiveness that does not apply in all circumstances. What in any other case would reflect Mary's Christian upbringing—providing for the needy—becomes, when she shares with an individual from an unauthorized group, an instance of collusion with the enemy. It is also interesting to note that the Christian church, through its representative Father Hart, takes the same stance on poverty as do *The Countess Cathleen*'s Satanic merchants who, with an understood satirical wink, lecture about "the evils of mere charity" (41). This ironic, meta-textual twist merely serves to reinforce Yeats's message, in *The Land of Heart's Desire*, about the duplicity of a religion that, at times during its long history, has shown partiality in choosing the recipients of its beneficence.

A continued analysis of the 29 January 1876 version of *Leisure Hour*'s "Varieties" column is instructive here.[30] In his column, Thomas Walker reflects the religious and class bias Yeats highlights in *Land* when, from his self-elected superior position, he hierarchizes, according to vague moral distinctions, those who exist on a lower socio-economic level. Whereas "poverty," he argues, is a "natural appetite," is "sincere," and has a "naturally proud spirit," "pauperism" is a "ravenous atrophy," with a "base, . . . servile . . . [and] insolent spirit." Never stopping to consider the circumstances that might have befallen individuals in each type of indigence, he punctuates his moralistic, classist distinctions with the following hubristic declaration: "Poverty has the blessing of Heaven as well as those who relieve it—pauperism, on the contrary, has nothing in common with the Christian virtues" (80). Walker's

"Christian" philosophy, like Father Hart's, again sounds much like that of the merchants in *The Countess Cathleen* who pay out varying amounts of coin for each soul they buy. Like the conferrers of Victorian charity Alan Kidd discusses, they make "charity . . . conditional upon status rather than need" (69). More specifically, in their supposition that certain souls or people are more valuable or worthy than others, the philosophies of all three entities thus embody virtue, even humanity, as a market commodity. With this satiric example of Christian virtue, we too, like the fairy child, might begin to pity the image of Christ on the crucifix as a "tortured thing!" (199), at least in terms of what he represents for the Victorian bourgeois peasant.

The depiction of Christ as a tortured creature corresponds to Mary's state in the play, but it also might be said to represent, for Yeats, Christianity's martyrdom to contemporary bourgeois values.[31] The crucifix, for example, loses its reputed power to shield the house from the fairy child's influence when the fairy convinces Father Hart to physically remove it from the wall. Understanding the child's fear as bred from ignorance of the significance of what she calls the "ugly thing on the black cross" (198), Father Hart takes pity on her and removes the cross at her behest. He chooses to "[h]ide it away," as she asks, because of the following conviction: "We must be tender to all budding things. / Our Maker let no thought of Calvary / Trouble the morning stars in their first song" (199, 200). Judging that the child merely lacks the experience that eventually opens all innocent eyes to the wonder of God (and to an orderly bourgeois life), the priest offers to "instruct [her] in our blessed Faith" (200). Once indoctrinated into the ways of the region, he implies, the child—like Mary—will become an acceptable member of society. Until such time, however, these individuals pose a threat to a system that has no place for anyone but born believers and converts.

The limited nature of her life in the Bruin household draws Mary further and further into what becomes a dangerous world. According to folk legend, because she is unhappy with her new role as Bruin bride and is childless as well, Mary is especially vulnerable to the threat of fairy abduction.[32] Mary's previously innocent employment of imaginative and intellectual capabilities—that is, her thoughts of other worlds and her reading of Irish mythology—become her socially-defined downfall when she takes on the role of Shawn's wife. Expected to entirely forego her imaginative life for that of mundane reality, Mary feels trapped by the rules of a world not suited to her needs. Forced to choose one world over the other, she opts for the otherworld and thereby leaves the Bruins behind.

Many critics of the play also see Mary's choice as twofold. John Rees Moore depicts both Mary's and the Countess Cathleen's choices in the following terms: "Man would like to seize the moment of most perfect beauty, pleasure, peace and forget his heartaches, but he is bound to the wheel of life and cannot stop its turning" (211). Susan C. Harris similarly recognizes a "paradigm" in Yeats's early plays in which "there is no third option: the hero chooses glorious death or ignominious life" (480). Although the aforementioned comments were extracted from Harris's arguments about *Cathleen ni Houlihan*, their relevance here lies in the fact that they also adequately represent most critics' interpretations of *The Land of Heart's Desire*. In terms that reflect Moore's, Harris contends that the hero in Yeats's early plays must choose between "the world of the glorious ideal and the world of limiting domesticity" (480).

I argue, however, that Yeats offers a subtle third alternative to life according to Bruin/bourgeois/Christian rules or fairy freedom, one that does not enforce an either/or choice between, on the one hand, Christianity, materialism, and philistinism and, on the other, paganism, imagination, and passion. This third possibility, envisioned by Mary as well as by her husband, makes room for both the imaginative and the material life. Yeats does not allow Mary's plea to "Let me have all the freedom I have lost; / Work when I will and idle when I will" (192) to stand on its own merit. Reinforcing the plausibility of Mary's preferred way of life, the more stable and therefore more trustworthy source, Shawn, admits to the possibility of a world in which "quiet hearths" exist alongside of the "bewilderment of light and freedom" (193). Yet, for Mary, a life of the twinned pursuits of reason and imagination, of work and idleness, of hearth and bewilderment is not to be. In a world of inflexible rules and gender roles developed to satisfy the bourgeois ideal, Mary's attempt to be true to her own needs and desires must necessarily fail.

In Lacanian terms, we might say that Mary exemplifies the difficulties women face in having to exist under the strict social codes enforced by the patriarchal promotion of the Name-of-the-Father. Although obviously not a Lacanian theorist, Yeats nonetheless posits two rather Lacanian possibilities for Mary at the end of the play: She can either relinquish herself to Father Hart "[b]y the dear Name of the One crucified"—in Christian terms, the ultimate Name-of-the-Father—or choose to go with the fairy child "in the name of [her] own heart" (206). According to the Lacanian theory of self-constitution, whereby we recognize ourselves as subjects and enter into communal reality, Mary's refusal to live in a society organized according to the "dear name of the One crucified" or the Name-of-the-Father would represent her choice to stay within the confines of the pre-symbolic or Imaginary realm of existence—a state entered by adults primarily through mental illness and, thus, not the preferred state for most individuals.[33] Mary does not end up mentally ill but, depending on your perspective, damned or freed in the otherworld, a world in which, like Lacan's Imaginary realm, the intuitive and imaginative senses reign.

Lacanian theory provides further insight into *Land* when we consider the significance of Father Hart's appeal to Mary, which is made *in the name of the Father*. For it is this very appeal, and the fairy child's offer to let Mary abide by the calling of her own heart, that ultimately pushes Mary in the direction of the fairy child. What it comes down to, for Mary, is the "name" under which she chooses to exist:

her own or that taken from another, intrinsically patriarchal cause. This Lacanian reading, moreover, fits Yeats's notion of progress as a necessarily individual, not other-prescribed, path. Only by choosing to follow her heart, whether or not its wishes coincide with the role afforded her by hegemonic definition (or by the Symbolic Order), will Mary grow. Only by facing her opposite—that is, by choosing to partake of the fairy form of life that so fascinates her—can Mary continue on the independent path of her personal progress. In her willingness to entertain more than one lifestyle choice—to accept those ruled by the hearth, by bewilderment, or preferably by both—Mary is a Yeatsian hero.

When read, like *Cathleen ni Houlihan*, at the level of realist play, *Land* depicts what Yeats perceived as a real social problem for his era, the inability or refusal of the predominant class to allow any deviation from the materialist, rationalist, philistine norm. Several critics have touched on the fact that *Land* has realistic elements. James W. Flannery, for instance, describes the play as "relatively representational," but notes, "the dramatic line is broken periodically by lyrics that cause us to reflect or meditate upon the action" (84). The break in realistic action no doubt provides one answer to why, as Flannery tells us, Yeats's contemporary audiences rejected the play for its "remoteness from life" (89).[34] Andrew Parkin also allies the play with formal dramatic realism, when he writes, "[t]he play begins with a realistic domestic situation very much in tune with the commercial theatre of the day" (58). Similarly, David R. Clark counts *Land* as one of Yeats's plays that "show 'real' folk characters, in whom we can believe" (121). And John Rees Moore calls the play "a fantasy . . . firmly in touch with reality" (64), marking the mixed generic elements of its formal structure.

None of these critics, however, view the realistic elements of the play as especially significant or recognize the realism as evidence of Yeats's intention to formulate a social critique. For example, Moore explains that Yeats's choice to end the play at a point that impedes us from witnessing the family's grief over the loss of Mary indicates that he is on the side of the fairies (67). While I believe that, in this instance, Yeats is on the side of the fairies, I offer a different but no less relevant interpretation of Yeats's choice to end the play at the point that he does: Yeats halts an otherwise realistic plot line (fairies excluded) mid-point—that is, without providing closure for Maurteen, Bridget, Shawn, and Father Hart—in order to show that these characters, having been the cause of Mary's suffering and ultimately her choice of death over life in the Bruin household, deserve to wallow in their grief. In other words, Yeats manipulates the medium of realistic theater in order to make a thematic point about the evils of bourgeois materialism and conformity.

More specifically, the realistic elements of *The Land of Heart's Desire* present Mary as representative of all individuals who feel trapped by their socially codified roles of gender, class, and race. This is not to say that Yeats fosters suicide (the choice Mary made, one might argue) or even that he suggests that societal norms might altogether be avoided. Instead, he chooses, on the one hand, to depict the Bruins and Father Hart—who are, significantly, representative of hegemony or, in Lacanian terms, the Symbolic Order—as mouthpieces for self-interested bourgeois materialism, and, on the other hand, to depict the supposedly selfish Mary as insightful, caring, and accepting of others. By doing so, Yeats turns the tables on the invented traditions of bourgeois moralism and materialism, unmasking them as villains and their digressors as victims.

Although the bourgeois peasant provided the initiatory moment in Yeatsian class criticism, Yeats's critique of middle-class values went on to include, in *The King's Threshold* and *On Baile's Strand*, the satirization, with tragic consequences, of the aristocracy's capitulation to bourgeois values of materialism and philistinism. In these two plays, as in *Deirdre*, Yeats continues and expands his attention to gender as a bourgeois-enforced social construction—a theme, as I have shown here, Yeats also addresses, though less centrally, in *The Land of Heart's Desire*. Following Yeats's thematic cue as presented in the plays, I continue my discussion of Yeats's critique of bourgeois values and notions of progress in chapter four. More specifically, I analyze the ways in which, in *The King's Threshold*, *On Baile's Strand*, and *Deirdre*, Yeats details for his readers and audiences alike the reasons that the identificatory category of gender, like class and race, must be recognized as being socially (specifically bourgeois) constructed and therefore politically and economically motivated (specifically constrictive) in form.

Chapter Four
Recovering the Feminized Other
Psychological Androgyny in The King's Threshold, On Baile's Strand, *and* Deirdre

> The becoming of androgynous human persons implies a radical change in the fabric of human consciousness.
> —Mary Daly
>
> The unity of the subject is thus already potentially contested by the distinction that permits of gender as a multiple interpretation of sex.
> —Judith Butler
>
> Blasphemy protects one from the moral majority within, while still insisting on the need for community.... Irony is about contradictions that do not resolve into larger wholes, even dialectically, about the tension of holding incompatible things together because both or all are necessary and true.
> —Donna Haraway[1]

EARLY IN HIS WRITING CAREER, YEATS PROMOTED THE IDENTIFICATION OF Irishness with the rural, the imaginative, and the feminine, thereby linking himself with Matthew Arnold and Ernest Renan, who argued that Ireland was best suited to the secondary and inferior position of "wife" to the masterful "husband" figure of England. This fact evinces itself, in part, in the anti-materialist peasant plays, *The Countess Cathleen, The Land of Heart's Desire,* and *Cathleen ni Houlihan,* in which Yeats can be said to have judged not too dear the "opportunity cost of an identity based on the domestic, local, and rural, which valorised the ... generally selfless feminine virtues" and which devalued "the competitive, masculine 'virtue' of selfishness, the supposed *sine qua non* of economic progress" (T. P. Foley 22).[2] Marjorie Howes elaborates an interesting argument in terms of Yeats's espousal of the Arnoldian depiction of the Irish, an argument that emancipates Yeats from the contention that he strictly favors one gender identity over another, though not from his belief in the dualistic nature of gender identity. More specifically, Howes tells us that Yeats's evolving theories about the Irish vacillated between two poles: the

"Arnoldian, feminine and particular" and the "anti-Arnoldian, masculine and universalist" (25). Yeats's espousal of an essentialist and hierarchical conception of gender, however, was never unequivocal. His personal correspondence, public prose, and several of the plays written in the first decade of the twentieth century reveal the extent to which Yeats struggled, in matters personal, political and aesthetic, to come to terms with and, I argue, counter conceptions of femininity, Irishness, and imagination as innately subordinate to masculinity, Englishness, and reason.

Although his vision of history and personality as preordained in character support the contention that Yeats's views on gender originate in traditionally essentialist conceptions of femininity and masculinity, this is not to say that he believed actual individuals to be fixed in their biological status as men or women. For that which in Yeats's system is innate is not necessarily inescapable. As Janis Tedesco Haswell puts it, for Yeats, "gender is marked by fluid and perpetual action, with masculine and feminine finally defined not by fixed attributes but by their ever-changing and dynamic relationship to each other" (8). When we consider that the doctrine of the mask not only allows but enjoins individuals to encounter a series of opposites that create an ever-widening or multiply configured personality, we can begin to see the ways in which such a system provides the potential for escape from essentialist definitions of gender. That is, attempts to achieve Unity of Being are evolutionary in that they convert the essentialist origin of Yeats's understanding of gender into a theory of gender as transformable and socially constructed—and, therefore, one element of identity over which we have at least a limited amount of control. In this way, Yeats defines gender in terms set out by Bonnie Kime Scott one hundred years later in *The Gender of Modernism*, in which she writes, "Gender is a category constructed through cultural and social systems" and "is more fluid, flexible, and multiple in its options than the (so far) unchanging biological binary of male and female" (2). I would add that Yeats saw—and meant to expose—bourgeois progressivism as the specific "cultural and social system" with the most powerfully negative influence on the construction of gender during the late nineteenth and early twentieth century.

Yeats's dramatizations of the social construction of gender identity in *The King's Threshold* (1904), *On Baile's Strand* (1904), and *Deirdre* (1907) put these theories into action, displaying the tragedy that results from the blind acceptance and blanket enforcement of biological and social givens of gender identity as well as the potential benefits to be attained by the refusal of them. The fixed gender identities to which I refer, and which I discuss in more detail in chapter one, include the designation of femininity or femaleness as, somewhat contradictorily, the state of being 1) highly emotional (more likely to be a victim of, because less able to control, the emotions that we all, men and women, have), 2) intuitive (able and willing to discover truth through procedures other than those governed by reason), 3) closer to the animalistic side of our human nature (and, therefore, potentially wild or hysterical), 4) domestic (interested in love, family, care-taking), and 5) fragile (in need of physical protection and intellectual guidance). Traditional Victorian definitions of masculinity or maleness required one to be 1) in control of his emotions, 2) a believer in the infallibility of reason and science, 3) interested in maintaining a settled, ordered, and orderly existence (an impetus again dictated by the example of reason and science), 4) a powerful player in the public sphere, and 5) physically as well as emotionally brave and strong (a fearless protector of women and social justice). Yeats, on the other hand, chose to portray alternative, even anarchistic—or as Haswell puts it, "radical" (5)—forms of gender identity. That is, Yeats represents gender as socially constructed, multiple, fluid, and capable of expansion, not biologically determined, normative, immutable, and restrictive. In doing so, I argue, Yeats attempted to recover the feminine from its culturally derived ancillary position and, more specifically, to replace conventional and essentialist definitions of gender with an idealized, but nevertheless attainable form of androgyny.

My delineation of Yeats's philosophical and theatrical approach to androgyny does not concern androgyny in its physical or sexualized aspects (e.g., not as represented by hermaphroditism, transsexuality, or drag culture) but with psychological androgyny as it relates to the social construction of identity. The closest contemporary theoretical construct would be Joyce Trebilcot's conception of a psychological form of androgyny she calls "polyandrogynism." Distinct from "monoandrogynism" in which the "single ideal for everyone" is when "both feminine and masculine characteristics . . . exist 'side by side' in every individual" (162), polyandrogynism differs "in that it advocates not a single ideal but rather a variety of options. . . . According to this view, all alternatives with respect to gender should be equally available to and equally approved for everyone, regardless of sex" (163). Although he would not have used these terms, Yeats did display a willingness for society to move toward a more open acceptance of a wider range of gender traits in the fashion described by Treblicot. In this regard, I contest Janis Tedesco Haswell's argument that androgyny

> provides little guidance in reading Yeats, who believed himself to be androgynous insofar as he was inhabited by a female daimon, not because he sought to transcend social stereotypes of male behavior. Yeats's expression of 'the woman in me' . . . impelled him to create gendered masks . . ., not personae of an androgynous nature. (9)

While Haswell's book provides a fascinating and important interpretation of Yeats's personal gender identification and gender theory as related to his feminine masks, my argument about Yeats's plays here displays that Yeats, in fact, was working out his gender theory, at least in part, through his development of dramatic "personae." *The King's Threshold*, *On Baile's Strand*, and *Deirdre* provide particularly convincing examples of Yeats's desire to validate attempts to transcend social stereotypes of gendered behavior.

An April 1904 letter to George Russell evinces the disquietude that gendered renderings of imagination elicited in Yeats around the time he wrote and produced *The King's Threshold, On Baile's Strand,* and *Deirdre.* In the oft-quoted letter, Yeats condemns his previous work as "unmanly"—a notion he allies with "weakness," "sentiment," "decadence," "subjectiveness," and "womanish introspection," and which finds its opposite in "energy"—energy of "the spirit" and of "the will." At this point in his career, Yeats's attempts to distance himself from the Romantic Celticism found throughout his first three volumes of poetry included the desire to avoid poetry "that speaks to me with that sweet insinuating feminine voice" (*L* 434). Marjorie Howes points to this derogation of femininity as an important moment in Yeats's changing conceptions of gender identity (17–18).[3]

A look at the original manuscript version of the letter reveals a related, important finding. In one small but insightful moment of self-editing, Yeats records himself as conflicted about the cultural meaning of femininity. More specifically, Yeats's use of the term "voice" in the phrase "sweet insinuating feminine voice" is an emendation to his first thought, which called for the elimination of poetry that speaks with "sweet insinuating feminine *wiles*" (POS 15,600, emphasis added). Although both versions of the passage depict femininity in negative terms, the original, in its implication of femininity's conscious and almost devious attempt to influence men and art, reflects, on Yeats's part, more animosity towards—or is it fear of?—his "feminine" side.[4] The fact that Yeats first chose the term "wiles" tells us much about the commonly derogative connotation of femininity in its conventional connotation: "wiles" was Yeats's first choice and, therefore, I argue, the one most deeply embedded in him through the process of enculturation. That Yeats chose to cross out "wiles" and replace it with "voice" displays just how much he struggled, even in that moment of composition, to come to terms with what he saw as a powerful (and, in cultural terms, negative) side to his subjective, ethnic, and artistic identity. Although Yeats ultimately chose the less insulting diction of "voice" over "wiles," he nonetheless counsels in the letter's postscript, "Let us have no emotions, however absurd, in which there is not athletic joy." Here Yeats swings back to the other side of the gender pendulum, manifesting the conventionally masculine urge to obtain a measure of control over himself. The inextricably gendered, if erratic character of these judgments reflect Yeats's sometimes complicity with Victorian bourgeois notions of the masculine and feminine and, as Marjorie Howes puts it, with "the imperial gendering of the Irish as feminine" (18).

Around the turn of the century, and even before the letter to Russell, Yeats had begun to revise his definitions of the Celt and of gender codes in ways that problematized the hierarchical dualistic structures that subjugated both forms of identity. In this way, Yeats helped widen the realm of possibilities open to the individual subject. For instance, in "The Celtic Element in Literature" (1897), his public response to and restatement of Renan and Arnold, Yeats repudiates comparisons of the Celt with the feminine, essentially by writing the negative connotation of femininity out of the equation. He achieves this by allying the traits Arnold and Renan define as Celtic/feminine with the tradition of all great, ancient societies, thereby making substantial and honorable what in the Victorian era had been devalued by the hegemony of science and reason. Marking similarities between "all the fountains of the passions and beliefs of ancient times in Europe, the Slavonic, the Finnish, the Scandinavian, and the Celtic" (*EI* 185), Yeats reclaims as heroes "[m]en who lived in a world where anything might flow and change, and become any other thing; and . . . great gods whose passions were in the flaming sunset, and in the thunder and the thunder-shower, [and who] had not our thoughts of weight and measure" (*EI* 178).

Howes explains Yeats's changing views as follows: "Rather than reject femininity as pathological or lock it into a hierarchical, complementary relationship with British masculinity, Yeats allied femininity with racial specificity, both Irish and English, and claimed that beneath Irish particularity lay a masculine universalism" (27–28). That is, by "disrupting the imperialist equation of femininity with subordinate political status, and by failing to establish a stable relationship between gender and the Irish national character" (28), Yeats redefined hierarchies of gender and race. By doing so, Howes argues, he also, to a certain extent, rejected imperialism. Yeats's refusal to equate femininity with inferiority and masculinity with superiority, then, enacts a social critique with the potential for changing the ways in which both gender and the Irish are viewed in the early twentieth century.

The three plays that comprise the focus of this chapter typify Yeats's attempts to revise gender and ethnic roles during the first decade of the twentieth century in ways that illustrate, through their themes, character structure, and form, that gender identity ideally evolves out of a process whereby one can: 1) make individual choices about one's affiliation with traditionally female or male traits, regardless of one's sex, and 2) make even unconventional choices without fear of invoking the ridicule, hostility, or rejection of those who favor more orthodox customs. Yeats's Cuchulain and Deirdre, just two of Yeats's characters who negate stereotyped gender coding by being emotional and intuitive as well as logical and capable of great physical endurance, display that, for Yeats, one's "sex," in terms of biological determination, appears to be much less of a factor in the creation of personality than one's "gender" is.[5] Because biologically male and female dramatic characters frequently, and profitably, share traditionally male and female traits, I would define Yeats's ideal gender as androgynous. In other words, Yeats partakes in the imaginative and aesthetic but nevertheless sociopolitical "troubling" of gender that Judith Butler describes as necessary to "counter the violence performed by gender norms" (xxiv). By showcasing the essentially anarchistic state of psychological androgyny in a positive light, thereby problematizing conventional constructions of gender, Yeats creates a model of androgyny that suggests the possibility, even the beneficiality, of "cross[ing] over if not cross[ing] out the binary" (Gelpi, "Sex as Performance" 186). In this way, Yeats moves closer to erasing the normative structure of gender identity and, by extension, of other forms of identity as well. As with what Donna Haraway calls the underused "rhetorical strategy and . . . political method" of irony, the ideal construction of identity, as portrayed in Yeats's plays, "is about contradictions that do not resolve into larger wholes, even dialectically, about the tension of holding incompatible things together because both or all are necessary and true" (149).

Androgynous characteristics have long been part of the constitution of Irish mythological figures. Fionn mac Cumhaill, for instance, has been associated with the refined, domestic and therefore feminine—he is an epicure—as well as with the masculine world of conquest—he is a renowned lover and fighter. And Maeve, Aoife, and Deirdre serve as merely representative examples of a long list of Irish warrior queens and strong women characters. Yeats, however, makes androgyny a central feature in his plays by narrowing and focusing the lens of Irish mythic history on the social constructedness of gender. *The King's Threshold*, *On Baile's Strand*, and *Deirdre* do concede, in part, to Victorian conventions of masculinity and femininity. For example, Yeats follows Lady Gregory's and Standish O'Grady's lead in leaving out some of the brutally violent aspects of the stories that would show the heroes to be more savage and uncontrolled than Victorian and Edwardian audiences would generally like. He writes out Cuchulain's use of the cruel *ga bolga*, which the hero uses to bloody purpose against his son in *The Yellow Book of Lecan*. Likewise, he revises Deirdre's choice to commit suicide by throwing herself off a carriage in order to smash her beautiful face into pieces against a rock. We might also point to Yeats's characterization, in the Preface to *Cuchulain of Muirthemne*, of Lady Gregory's Deirdre as a woman "who might be some mild modern housewife" (16) as evidence that he agrees with what Jacqueline McCurry more negatively calls Gregory's "de-feminization" of the independent-minded Deirdre of more traditional versions (34). However, I would caution against taking Yeats's assessment of Gregory's Deirdre as one that fits his own. In that regard, I would disagree with McCurry's depiction of Yeats's *Deirdre* as a "patriarchal love stor[y]" (34), in part because her reading is based too heavily on Yeats's comments in the preface and not enough on the text of his play. Rather, as I argue later in this chapter, Yeats's conscious representation of the patriarchy in negative terms is one of the play's major themes.[6] Another example that points to Yeats's conscious fashioning of these myths as allegorical tales of contemporary struggles with gender identity is the reason Cuchulain suspects the Young Man is his son. In many traditional Irish language versions of the tale, it is Emer who cautions the hero that the threatening invader might be his son, a plot element that plays on the notion of feminine intuition. In *On Baile's Strand*, we find Cuchulain listening intently to his own intuition. Instead of de-feminizing the tale, this change serves the revolutionary purpose of feminizing—or making androgynous—the male hero.

Yeats's re-creation of standard Irish mythic characters in an androgynous form partakes in the overturning of what Judith Butler calls the portrayal of identity as a "normative ideal rather than a descriptive feature of experience" (23). Individuals with "'discontinuous'" or "'incoherent'" gender identities or those who "fail to conform to the norms of cultural intelligibility by which persons are defined," she continues, "call into question the very notion of 'the person'" as a unified subject (23). Yeats did not himself contest the unity of the subject, as his theory of Unity of Being tells us quite clearly. However, he did create many nonconformist characters, such as those in *The King's Threshold*, *On Baile's Strand*, and *Deirdre*, who choose gender identities other than the standard. Cuchulain's reliance on instinct as a survival tactic, Seanchan's devotion to imagination as an invaluable element of social progress, and Deirdre's refusal to "read" the world or to be "read" from a conventional point of view provide just three examples of individuals struggling to maintain what come to be seen as socially heretical identities in a world obsessed with "normative ideal[s]" (Butler 23). Significantly, Yeats's choice to refocus the lenses of mythology, literature, and history on society's obsessive compulsion toward what Butler calls "stablilizing concepts" (23) situates the illness not in the individual but in the society.

As emotional (typically hot-headed), intuitive, and/or imaginative—that is, feminine—beings, characters like Yeats's Cuchulain and Seanchan are "'incoherent'" by virtue of their lack of stable gender identity. That is, they refuse to identify completely with the gender with which they are biologically affiliated and, in turn, allow their "feminine" sides to make regular appearances in the arenas of decision-making and action. Thus, these characters are involved not only in the literary and cultural destabilization of gender identity but in the unfixing of identity itself as a stable cultural construct. By manifesting the social and political constructedness of perhaps the most fundamental form of identity, gender, at a time when norms were being erected as evidence of the existence of, or even as monuments to, the secular gods of science, reason, and proto-psychiatry, Yeats partook in the outing of identification as "an enacted fantasy or incorporation" (Butler 173). In Yeats's plays, if identity is incorporated—as, in the negative sense, co-opted by hegemonic forces—it is also, in the positive sense, fantastic—as in made-up, constructed, and performed. That is, identity is shown to be not entirely biologically determined and therefore capable of revision.

Before I continue to elaborate Yeats's gender theories, I must return for a moment to the, for many, troublesome concept of androgyny. In the last decade or so, androgyny has not maintained the status it attained during the 1970s and 1980s, when numerous feminist theorists, following Carolyn Heilbrun, sang its praises. Some more recent writers, like Donald A. Harris, Nancy Topping Bazin, and Alma Freeman, perceive androgyny as a sexist, particularly masculinist attempt, in Bazin and Freeman's terms, to achieve "Feminine oneness" (186) in addition to maintaining patriarchal control. These critics point out, and rightly so, that most androgynes in mythic and literary history are feminized men rather than masculinized women, a fact that continues to privilege the male or patriarchal point-of-view.[7] Others, like Cynthia Secor, understand androgyny to be "rooted in a static image of perfection, in eternity" (164). Evelyn Hinz sums up these arguments in the following description. Unlike those who see androgyny as "a mode of resistance to established sexual norms and as a positive and liberating concept," androgyny antagonists see it as "a nefarious anodyne and a 'myth' that must be resisted" (vii).

I believe Yeats's version of androgyny rebuts these critics on several points. First, it is true that, as with his literary predecessors, most of Yeats's androgynous characters are biologically male: the Seanchans, Cuchulains, and Ferguses outnumber the Deirdres. While I do not have the space here to discuss the entire history of androgyny, I can make an important point where Yeats is concerned. I believe the preponderance of male-sexed over female-sexed androgynous characters in Yeats's works has more to do with his historical and cultural positioning (as Irish, Victorian, Edwardian) than with any masculinist agenda on his part. As his doctrine of the mask evinces, Yeats maintained that progress could occur, on an individual or communal level, only through the advent of conflict or opposition. In an age overwhelmed by logic and reason, or by "masculinity," the conventionally feminine traits of passion and intuition came to be seen by Yeats as elemental for social and individual progress. Yeats's biologically male androgynous characters thus represent an idealized version of Western society in which the logical, "antithetical" modern era has been put into balance with its opposite. Thus, Yeats might argue, the cultural proclivity toward creating "male" androgynous characters is itself a condition of history that, nevertheless, can either be accepted or rejected.

The allegedly static nature of androgyny likewise stumbles before Yeats's examples. "[L]imiting," "reactionary," and capable only of "conjur[ing] up the image of a person devoid of social context," the androgyne, according to Secor, has little to do with "real change, change that is cultural as well as individual" (162, 163). Secor prefers more palpably gendered characters. Witches and amazons, for instance, appeal to her "because they suggest energy, power, and movement; they are active, self-actualizing images rather than images of static completion" (165). While I am unsure through what conduit witches and amazons are ostensibly able to achieve a more direct route to "real change" than androgynes, I do see Yeats's androgynous characters as entirely and evocatively suggestive of energy, power and movement. Deirdre is as active and alert as any of Yeats's male heroes, and no character's diligence matches Cuchulain's attempts to achieve self-actualization—until, that is, they are forced to give up the traits that make them androgynous. Only then does their life force begin to ebb, only then are they edged into the most complete stasis of all: death. On the other hand, the characters who elicit the most complete sense of stasis-in-life are the powerful and strictly gendered King Guaire and King Conchubar.

Indignantly refusing to allow or even recognize any deviation from the norm, including or especially the androgynous behavior of the heroes, Guaire and Conchubar represent the most reactionary, limiting (as well as limited), and consequently static point-of-view. By comparison—an act into which Yeats's characterizations and plot structure practically pushes us—Yeats's androgynous heroes represent the strongest potential for progress or movement of any sort.

To borrow phrasing from Marjorie Howes's discussion of his theories on racial hybridity, Yeats's model of androgyny reflects, in part, the "dialectic between hybridity as the elimination of difference and hybridity as the intermingling of distinct entities [that] was central to the period's racial theory" (21). In the case of gender, Yeats does not want to eliminate differences so much as to celebrate their intermingling.[8] As hybrid or multiple beings, Yeats's androgynous characters thus move beyond the essentialist, neo-Platonic, or Arnoldian idea of feminine-Irish/masculine-English marriage, also a model of nationalist conciliation. Instead, they represent the intermingling or union of distinctive qualities that lead to—or, rather, must be preceded by?—a celebration of differences. Yeats's androgynous characters are therefore a prototype for the androgyne celebrated by twentieth-century literary critic Linda Lamont-Stewart as "a trope which figures refusal to conform to hierarchical binary oppositions of all sorts" (129).

One telling example of Yeats's dedication to the revision of gender stereotyping on the Irish stage can be found in his public response to the famous *Playboy* riots.[9] As Irish nationalists and/or Catholics, the rioting members of the 1907 audience for Synge's *The Playboy of the Western World* objected to the depiction of Irish men as cowards, fools, and liars and to the mere mention of Irish women in their "shifts." According to this contingent, Irish men were to appear on stage at all times as powerful, brave, and virile while Irish women were to be pure, sexless creatures, always willing to do their fathers' or husbands' bidding. Not to be condoned, then, even in Synge's satiric form, were Christy's and Pegeen's weaknesses: his indolence, cowardice, and fear of women; her sexual awareness, rebelliousness, and disregard for her father's authority. The crowd's riotous reaction to Synge's play disappointed Yeats, in large part, because it reflected their firm and insistent endorsement of conformity to what he perceived to be unattainable as well as undesirable ideals of masculinity and femininity. Calling the crowd's summons to close the play an "annihilation of civil rights" (*UPII* 351), Yeats displayed his strong and lifelong indictment of artistic (and gender) censorship.

More subtly, however, Yeats's defense of "civil rights" reflects his concomitant concern with the social legislation of individual identity. Yeats blamed the Victorian and Edwardian dedication to group identity such as that found in ideals of nation, race, county, or school—or what he called "the tyranny of clubs and leagues"—for abandoning "individual sincerity" in favor of a world in which all would "crouch upon the one roost and quack or cry in the one flock" (*Explorations* 228). In order to counteract the "one flock" mentality, Yeats advises in *Per Amica Silentia Lunae* that we assume a "second self" (*Mythologies* 334). The recognition of a second self—an other, or in Yeats's doctrine of the mask, an opposite—exposes us to points of view not previously experienced which, in turn, will widen our knowledge of others as well as of ourselves. This act, which shares both the limitations and the advantages of what Patrick Colm Hogan calls "empathic universalism," represents an important step in Yeats's evolving theories about the identity of self and other. For although, as Hogan warns us, empathic universalism holds the danger of "confus[ing] projection of one's own viewpoint with empathic adoption of another viewpoint" (323), Yeats shows empathic universalism to be preferable, nonetheless, to the resolute unwillingness to, as it were, walk a mile in someone else's shoes.

THE KING'S THRESHOLD

As a sympathetic portrayal of a royal poet's unjust removal from his time-honored place at court, *The King's Threshold* is traditionally and correctly read by critics as a defense of the poet and his or her imagination.[10] Yeats's intention in this regard makes itself apparent, first, in his sympathy for Seanchan's motives, an element of the play invented by the playwright. Yeats's notes on the play tell us that he "took the plot from a Middle Irish story about the demands of the poets at the court of King Guaire, but twisted it about and revised its moral that the poet might have the best of it" (*VP* 315). The play succeeds in representing Seanchan in a sympathetic light not only because of the valiant and noble efforts he exerts in the defense of poetry but also through Yeats's quite obvious intention to make the enemies of imagination appear just as, if not more, shallow and selfish than the materialist characters in *The Countess Cathleen*, *Cathleen ni Houlihan*, and *The Land of Heart's Desire*. But in case any readers or spectators, by the end of the play, have missed that point, Yeats makes sure they are aware that, as Seanchan says, "[t]he man that dies has the chief part in the story" (309) by making these meta-conscious words part of the hero's last speech.

Second, Yeats includes many passages in which the sympathetic characters—primarily Seanchan, his Pupils, and his old servant Brian—not only extol the power and virtues of imagination but also disparage strictly materialist interpretations of life. For instance, the relative power of imagination over materiality can be seen in the following passage, spoken by Seanchan:

> . . . when the heavy body has grown weak,
> There's nothing that can tether the wild mind
> That, being moonstruck and fantastical,
> Goes where it fancies. (263)

Another passage, spoken by Seanchan's Oldest Pupil, honors poetry's majesty, grace, and venerable authority:

> . . . the poets hung
> Images of the life that was in Eden
> About the child-bed of the world, that it,
> Looking upon those images, might bear
> Triumphant children. (264)

Other characters in the play go so far as to ally poetry with witchcraft or magical powers, like the First Cripple who reverently, tremulously suggests, "Those that make rhymes have a power from beyond the world" (270). The theme of poet-as-prophet, which reflects Yeats's elitist (and Romantic) belief that the lower and middle classes require the administration of those more talented and educated than themselves, also evinces itself in Seanchan's contention that "the Courtly life / Is the world's model" (266)—words which recall Yeats's faith in the leadership powers of the Countess Cathleen. Seanchan's teachings, however, also reveal the poet's astute awareness that his beliefs do not correspond with those of the rest of the world and that, in order to make his arguments understood, he must articulate them in terms the typical person can comprehend. His Oldest Pupil's declaration that poetry must be vouchsafed "as the Men of Dea / Guard their four treasures" and "as the Grail King guards / His holy cup" (265) manifests his and Seanchan's perception, moreover, that the terms must indeed be those of the language of materialism.

The poets' materialist rendering of the value of poetry provides just one example of the ways in which the play's gendered subtext reflects the generally problematic confluence of rationalism, materialism, gender coding, and morality in Victorian and Edwardian society. The significance of gender to *The King's Threshold* announces itself early, within the first few lines, in fact, when the King discusses art in gendered terms, describing music and poetry as "the one kind / Being like a woman, the other like a man." Of further significance is the fact that the King addresses this speech to artists, whom he praises as having "mastery / Of the two kinds of Music." At first glance, it would seem from this opening address that the King and the society he represents have a great deal of respect for artists, those masculine specimens who have earned the status of "master" through their ability to "understand stringed instruments / And how to mingle words and notes together" (257). However, if we look as closely at the speech as Andrew Parkin does, we too will recognize in it the development of Guaire's "devious" and "wily" as well as "genial" characteristics (86) and see that Yeats has set us up for a fall. The actual level of respect afforded to artists under King Guaire's rule soon becomes evident.

As the play opens, we learn that Seanchan has been ejected from his traditional spot as court poet because the

> Bishops, Soldiers, and Makers of the Law—
> . . . long had thought it against their dignity
> For a mere man of words to sit amongst them

At the great council of the State and share
In their authority. (259)

The use of the word "mere" only hints at the feminization of the poet that, elsewhere in the play, occurs more obviously. The courtiers' lack of respect for Seanchan's talent and social significance becomes compounded when, in response to the King's capitulation to the demands of his court, Seanchan decides to follow an ancient custom by which

... if a man
Be wronged, or think that he is wronged, and starve
Upon another's threshold till he die,
The common people, for all time to come,
Will raise a cry against that threshold,
Even though it be the King's. (258)[11]

Although this action sets in motion a downward spiral of social chaos—in itself, evidence of the poet's power—both the residents of the King's court and of Seanchan's home town of Kinvara nonetheless persist in allying imagination and poets with the politically disempowered construct of femininity. King Guaire, for example, criticizes Seanchan for giving in to "wild thought that overruns the measure" (261). The Mayor of Kinvara calls Seanchan's heroic quest "a matter of no importance, a matter of mere sentiment" (273). Furthermore, although doing so inadvertently uncovers his own ignorance, the Mayor attempts to insult Seanchan with the impudent statement, an embarrassing admission really, that he "never understood a poet's talk more than the baa of a sheep" (276). And the Soldier expresses his disgust with Seanchan's refusal to eat—or, rather, his mortification, as an otherwise victorious and cocksure warrior, over his failure to convince Seanchan to eat—by remarking contemptuously, "If he's to be flattered, / Petted, cajoled, and dandled into humour, / We might as well have left him at the table" (288). Seen from this angle, Seanchan is, by bourgeois Victorian standards, hardly a man at all.

The derogatory nature of the preceding statements proceed from the socially constructed alliance of the imagination with the feminine and, by extension, the feminine with the hysterical ("wild thought that overruns the measure"), emotional ("sentiment"), animalistic ("baa of a sheep"), and fickle (the need to be flattered and petted). Moreover, because the King and his court see Seanchan as excessive, out of control, childish, unreasonable, physically weak, and reflective—in other words, as feminine—they also see him as out of place in the public sphere in which warriors and lawyers rule. Logic dictates, then, that Seanchan would have to be ousted into the private sphere where he supposedly belongs. This Medieval society tinged with Victorian bourgeois values—what John Rees Moore calls an "uneasy no-man's-land between the archaic times it evokes and the present" (Moore 102)—then, represents the philistine impulse of Yeats's era. Like the kingdom of Gort, Victorian and, to a lesser extent, Edwardian England was run by men who exerted conformist pressure in the name of the self-aggrandizing assessment that "it was the men who ruled the world, / And not the men who sang to it, who should sit / Where there was most honour" (48–50). The courtiers' choice to further tighten their already small circle by homogenizing its constituency and expelling the other (in the form of Seanchan) forms an us-versus-them situation, a dichotomy between "[m]aking . . . deeds," on the one hand, and "words" on the other (81).

The play's plot consists of Seanchan's gradual decline into death, cataloging along the way the various individuals who visit him and their reasons for attempting to convince him to end his fast. Their reasons, more often than not, are entirely selfish and, more importantly, smack of the "one roost" mentality Yeats despised. Invoking the heroic qualities of Seanchan's hunger strike, Yeats invokes further sympathy by emphasizing the negative—that is, selfish, materialistic, and philistine— qualities of those who have made Seanchan's suffering possible. For instance, if we return for a moment to the concept of empathic universalism, we find one significant example of the ways in which the "one roost" mentality fosters more social exclusion than, as the phrase implies, inclusion. King Guaire had assumed that Seanchan would happily consent to his royal decision to retire the poet from his long-held and esteemed position; but, as we know, Seanchan chooses to die rather than to relinquish the poet's right to be seated officially in the king's court. Guaire, who cannot comprehend Seanchan's motives, designates as "light" (259) the issue over which Seanchan has chosen to fast until death, and even attempts to persuade him to eat with the "Promise [of] a house with grass and tillage land, / An annual payment, jewels and silken wear, / Or anything but that old right of the poets" (262). Understanding Seanchan's stance, like his own, to have material as opposed to ethical and spiritual origins, Guaire displays a complete inability to empathize with Seanchan's motives—though he thinks he does understand them. In Hogan's terms, Guaire has confused "projection of [his] own viewpoint with empathic adoption of" Seanchan's. If Guaire had been able to keep his point of view separate from that of Seanchan and had been successful in what Hogan calls the imaginative adoption of Seanchan's incommensurate perspective (323), the theory goes, he might have understood Seanchan's motives—which is a step in the right direction (toward inclusion or acceptance of the other) even if it would not necessarily have led the King to rule in Seanchan's favor. However, Guaire's inability to empathize with Seanchan leads him, in Yeats's terms, to choose "the passive acceptance of a code" over "[a]ctive virtue" which, like the taking on of a second self, is "theatrical, consciously dramatic, the wearing of a mask" (*Mythologies* 334). Guaire's decision to remain passive in the face of the bourgeois-inspired demands of his court, then, leaves him with no choice but to agree to the eradication of that "second self." In this case, the "second self" that threatens the King's and courtiers' passive acceptance of a code—specifically the bourgeois code that renders traditional gender identification the only acceptable option—is Seanchan.

That Seanchan's status as a "second self" or an other can be equated with his role as court poet does not bespeak historical accuracy. Traditionally speaking, bards wielded enormous power in their clans, a fact allluded to in the play by Brian's implication that Seanchan and his pupils "can give a great name or a bad one" (283). Visitors to Ireland in the sixteenth century wrote frequently and with awe on the subject of bardic authority, in letters and poems that evince the integrality of bards to ancient Irish culture. Thomas Smythe, for example, said of the bards in 1561 that they cause people "'to be rebellious theves, extorcioners, mutherers, ravners, yea and worse if it were possible'" (qtd. in Leerssen, *Mere Irish* 53). John Derricke's 1581 poem, *The Image of Irelande*, offers a similar appraisal of bardic power:

> This Barde he doeth report, the noble conquestes done,
> And eke in Rhymes shewes forthe at large, their glorie thereby wonne.
> Thus he at randome ronneth, he pricks the Rebells on:
> And shewes by suche externall deeds, their honour lyes upon.
> And more to stirre them up, to prosecute their ille:
> What great renowne their fathers gotte, thei shewe by Rimying skill.
> (qtd. in Leerssen, *Mere Irish* 44–45)

Clearly, these impressions of the bards, recorded when bardic power remained extant, reflect the subjective point of view of the unsympathetic English oppressors who penned them. Read with this fact of historic subjectivity in mind, the passages indicate the immense influence levied by bards not only in aesthetic but in political, economic, and military circles as well. Using their art to honor the great and heroic deeds of past and present chieftains and warriors, as well as to inspire communal pride, fear, and anger that could be used to preserve and enlarge their kindgoms, the bards had a substantial role in the construction of Irish society, culture, and history.

Such is not the case in Yeats's version of Gort, in which Seanchan, purveyor of imaginative powers and talents, has been summarily shoved aside to make (even more) room for the mercenary pursuits of war, law—and even, as Bishops and the Monk display, organized religion. This fact in itself provides us with an important clue to the setting of the play in allegorical if not actual historical terms. The relative power of the bishops, soldiers, and lawyers and their attempt to exile the sole artist from their midst easily evinces the play's socio-critical sensibility and, more specifically, aids in the play's constructive criticism of the Victorian and Edwardian era's philistinism as well as its strict adherence to the traditional construction of gender roles. From this perspective, Seanchan emblematizes the imaginative and therefore feminized other, exiled from the court of men with masculine achievements so that they alone may rule. However, because he is not only the protagonist but the prototypical hero of the play—he undergoes physical and emotional trials and ultimately faces death for the sake of his own beliefs and honor as well as for the sake of his people—Seanchan also represents masculinity. His fearlessly public defense of what convention does not value—that is, his conscious embracing of otherness in a traditionally heroic and therefore "masculine" manner—ironically allows him to obtain a level of "sameness." What is important about Yeats's depiction of this hero is that Seanchan's manly valor, in the form of a fast and death in defense of his "othrness," does not invalidate the feminine, in the form of the imagination. Instead, Seanchan's actions rescue the feminine from its subordinate position, thereby imbuing femininity, otherness, and imagination with cultural value. Moreover, because he evinces both masculine and feminine traits, Seanchan represents a step toward Yeats's creation and advocacy of androgynous dramatic characters.

My argument that *The King's Threshold* is, on one level, a vehicle for social criticism is supported by the language of the play which, in the mouths of all who attempt to coax Seanchan from his fast, mimics that of Victorian proponents of rationalism, like Thomas Huxley, who yearned to invest humanity with the rather robotic character of "a clear, cold, logic[al] engine, with all its parts of equal strength, and in smooth working order" (193). Yeats represents Huxley's masculinist ideal in the play by having almost every character advocate the exclusive use of reason. The mere profusion of words like "reason" and "argument" in the vocabulary of all who attempt to convince Seanchan to give up his fast clearly are not the result of poor proofreading on Yeats's part because, like the bulk of Yeats's plays, *The King's Threshold* was revised many times; rather, they represent the target of Yeats's criticism. In just one short statement, for example, the Mayor invokes reason three times, including twice insisting that he and the others who beg Seanchan to eat simply ask "nothing but what's reasonable" (272). Seanchan, however, is not convinced by reason or, rather, what he knows to be faulty reason, and throws the words right back into the Mayor's face: "Reason, O reason in plenty," he practically spits. "How comes it that you have been so long in the world and not found reason out?" (273). Knowing the Mayor's advocacy of reason—and reasons for desiring him to eat—to be materially/materialistically based, Seanchan refuses to even listen to his arguments. Brian, Seanchan's former servant who has also come from Kinvara to see his master of old, is second only after Seanchan in fathoming the futility of the Mayor's approach: "What's the good in saying all that, haven't they been reasoning with him all day long?" (273), he censures. Finally (ten pages later) coming around to Brian's perspective, the Mayor admits defeat and concocts a new plan involving Seanchan's fiancée. "[W]hen the intellect is out," he maintains, "Nobody but a woman's any good" (283). This statement evinces the Mayor's dependence on the standard affiliation of intellect and reason with the masculine and of emotion with the feminine.

These desperate attempts to convince the poet of the folly of his ways demonstrate the fact that, from the perspective of the self-absorbed members of court, the harm the poet does to himself during his hunger strike pales in comparison to that done to them. By choosing to stand firm in his role as androgynous other in a decidedly patriarchal kingdom, Seanchan disempowers himself on every level. More importantly, however, Seanchan's refusal to sit on the "one roost" represents not only a personal gender transgression but a general social transgression as well. By refusing to comply with the ruling force of reason—and by extension masculinity—he blurs the distinction between the masculine and feminine spheres. This turns all the other characters' worlds upside down in numerous ways. To begin with, the presence of Seanchan's starving figure on the King's threshold threatens the King's peace, his reputation, and the stability of his kingdom. As the Chamberlain perceives, not only has Seanchan's "work," in the form of his hunger strike as well as his poetry, "roused the common sort against the King, / And stolen his authority" (284). "The State" also

> Is like some orderly and reverend house
> Wherein, the master being dead of a sudden,
> The servants quarrel where they have a mind to,
> And pilfer here and there. (284)

Evidence of Seanchan's disturbance of the body politic likewise evinces itself in the state of chaos into which the regular business day has deteriorated. In place of the normal run of things, there is, much to the chagrin of the Monk, "Dancing, hurling, the country full of noise, / And King and Church neglected" (291–92). The Oldest Pupil manifests the psychological origin of the social unrest when he exclaims, "My head whirls round; I do not know what I am to think or say" (258–59). And, providing a prelude to King Conchubar's fears about Cuchulain's wild and passionate nature in *On Baile's Strand*, the Monk bemoans the lack of "orderliness of life" (291) that Seanchan's refusal to conform has brought to pass in the kingdom.

Individual characters' motives for urging Seanchan to give up his fast also reveal a desire for a more orderly life, but the selfishness and materialism that accompany the understandable desire for the return of normal life undermine any compassion we might initially feel for the characters. Yeats paints the Mayor of Kinvara in the least sympathetic light, showing him to be the most self-centered, self-important, and arrogant of the characters. The Mayor arrives at court to plead with Seanchan on the grounds that his hunger strike has endangered the likelihood that the King will grant his hometown the grazing lands once promised. The mayor's fears appear to be justified: if the King is willing to sacrifice lives in this situation, we can assume that he surely would not balk at rescinding a gift. However, in spite of this possibility and his self-professed selfless motivation of meeting with Seanchan "for the sake of the town" (272), the Mayor ultimately reveals himself to be much more concerned with the threat to his own authority than with the fate of Seanchan or of the townspeople of Kinvara. His entrance, in which he repeats the following words in an attempt to memorize his diplomatic address, provides the first clue to Yeats's mocking portrayal of the Mayor as self-important, upstart, middle-class buffoon: "'Chief poet, Ireland, townsman, grazing land', those are the words I have to keep in mind, 'Chief poet, Ireland, townsman, grazing land'. I have got them all right now, they are all here cut upon the Ogham stick, 'Chief poet, Ireland, townsman, grazing land', and that's the right order [*He keeps muttering over his speech during what follows.*]" (269). So obsessed with his appearance that he never even pretends to care about Seanchan's personal fate, the Mayor bumbles through the remainder of the scene, his actions alternating between hushing others, muttering "stock phrases" (Flannery 303), and mostly forgetting his own carefully planned speech. The Ogham stick adds a subtle irony to the scene.[12] That the Mayor represents the materialistic modern order is made manifest by his occupation with economic matters and his use of political plea bargaining to get what he wants, as when he begs of Seanchan, "We ask you for the sake of the town to do what the King wants and then maybe he'll do what we want" (272).[13] That the power and organization of his presentation depends on speech notes transcribed in Ogham, the oldest known written language in Ireland, makes his complicity with middle-class ideals that much more laughable: the speech of modern sentiment has been composed in a language created well before such sentiments became predominant. Reinforcing my assertion about the centrality of the Mayor to Yeats's social critique, S. B. Bushrui tells us, in his study of the manuscript versions of *The King's Threshold*, that the Mayor's role took prominence only in later versions of the play, a fact that leads him to similarly conclude that the Mayor is the "chief target of Yeats's attack" (80).

The Mayor's anxiety about Seanchan's refusal to live up to what he calls the "honour" of "liv[ing] and prosper[ing]" (273) and the effect this refusal will have on his town likewise reveals itself to be somewhat selfish in origin. Only slightly more concerned with the "honour" of his town than the potential death of his townsman, the Mayor sees Seanchan's hunger strike/death primarily as his own political homicide. When his irritable inability to comprehend Seanchan's metaphoric responses to his materialistic arguments prompts Brian to ask him to leave, the Mayor responds with the puffed-up anger and resentment that eventually compels him to admit his true modus operandi, swaggering pride: "Is it get away?" he booms indignantly. "Is that the way I'm to be spoken to? Am I not the Mayor? Am I not in authority? Am I not in the King's place?" (278–79). But for all his protestations, and even after he provides the unsolicited and self-protective statement that he is "not to blame" (283) for what Seanchan has done, the Mayor continues to play fool to Seanchan's hero.

With the exception of his mother and Fedelm, the remainder of characters who pass before Seanchan with offers of food and reasons for eating display similarly selfish and materialistic motives.[14] In one of Yeats's bitterly satiric twists, the local girls are upset because, due to the recent state of emergency invoked by Seanchan's hunger strike, they've been deprived of their favorite activity, dancing: no one will play for them, and, the girls whine, "they will never do it if he die" (291). Suffering from stiff bones and other debilitating effects of age, Seanchan's father, on the other hand, at first elicits sympathy from the reader. But it is not long before we realize that, like the Mayor, his motivation for persuading Seanchan to give up his fast reflects less of a concern for his son's life than for his own reputation and for his rights as an authority figure. Brian tells Seanchan that his father "bade me tell you that . . . the people will be pointing at him, that he will not be able to lift up his head if you turn the King's favour away, that he cared you well and you in your young age, and that it's right you should care him now" (275). Here we have more talk about reputation and rights, but none about the poet's rights, or even about Seanchan's right to live in a world that welcomes his difference. King Guaire likewise pipes in about his rights, proclaiming that because he is "a king" and Seanchan "a subject" (307), he even has the right to sacrifice the lives of Seanchan's pupils and supporters in order to force Seanchan to do his bidding. "Speak to your master; beg your lives of him," he orders (307). Although, after Seanchan dies, Guaire eventually relents and releases the men from the halters that hold them prisoner, this passage nevertheless shows us the extent to which Yeats thinks individuals will go in order to preserve their "right" to enforce conformity on others.

Brian, however, silences these loaded protestations about rights when he complains that the behavior of kings and their representatives issue from their modernizing impetus, from their bourgeois definition of progress. "Then show the people what a king is like," he sarcastically challenges the Mayor. "[R]oot up old customs, old habits, old rights" (279). Here Brian (and Yeats) blame the social disruption that occurs in the play not on Seanchan's hunger strike but on the act that originated the strike. The implication is that it is the king's revisionist history—that is, his choice to delete the ancient tradition of court poet from Irish culture—which must be held responsible for the disorder that has plagued the body politic of the kingdom of Gort. Rather than maintain the balance made possible only with the inclusion of the bard (or feminized other) on the royal court, King Guaire and his courtiers have capitulated to the modern trend Yeats so despises, the definition of progress along masculinist and logical lines, as obsequiously as the Mayor literally and figuratively kowtows to the king (283). In postcolonial theoretical terms, the King's and courtiers' actions reflect Western imperialists' advocacy of the "homology between sexual and political dominance," which gained support from the "denial of psychological bisexuality in men in large areas of Western culture, [and] beautifully legitimized Europe's post-medieval models of dominance, exploitation and cruelty as natural and valid" (Nandy 4).

One last character who deserves mention here is the Monk who, unlike the others, does not even attempt to urge an end to Seanchan's hunger strike. From his pompous position on high, the Monk sees in Seanchan only the sins of "wanton imagination" and "pride and disobedience" which, if allowed to go "unpunished," would incite others' disobedience (285). Let him hang, the Monk says, metaphorically and almost literally. However, Seanchan's satiric manipulations show that the Monk, like the others at court, is a hypocritical and, therefore, unreliable narrator of Seanchan's, or anyone's, faults. Playing on the Monk's stated desire for "orderliness of life" (291), Seanchan accuses him of not only capitulating personally to the materialistic advances of the court but of having sold out the Church itself. "Has that wild God of yours, that was so wild / When you'd but lately taken the King's pay / Grown any tamer? He gave you all much trouble," Seanchan whispers sarcastically to the Monk (292). Seanchan also develops an extended metaphor of God as a bird that obediently "perches on the King's strong hand" (293). He continues to bait the Monk, causing him to flee after saying that this bird

> ... maybe has learned to sing quite softly
> Because loud singing would disturb the King,
> Who is sitting drowsily among his friends
> After the table has been cleared. (292–93)

As he leaves, Seanchan clings to his robes and continues his attack on the Monk's materialism. Moreover, with the falsely sympathetic statement," You must not weary in your work" (293), Seanchan mocks the Monk's and the rest of the courtiers' continual efforts to tame wildness, both by banishing wanton imagination in the form of Seanchan and by forcing God to submit to the will of the King. Seanchan's alliance of himself with God is not, however, an act of hubris but a powerful and rightful indictment of the King's, Monk's, and court's conformist and materialist actions.

In *The King's Threshold* Yeats makes it clear that the King Guaires of the world, those who enforce compliance to a social norm that they legislate, only serve to weaken the society in which they hope to foster prosperity. This is not to say, though, that the leaders are entirely to blame. As I have shown, the general populace seems eager and ready to comply. But perhaps most interestingly, Yeats does not make this an entirely us/them situation in that he provides evidence that Seanchan is himself partially complicit in his own downfall. The key scene in this regard can be read as a defense of bardic power and, somewhat ironically, an indictment of the same. More specifically, Seanchan reminds the Chamberlain, who uses his status as amateur poet to try to bond with the bard:

> ... Well, if you are a poet,
> Cry out that the King's money would not buy,
> Nor the high circle consecrate his head,
> If poets had never christened gold, and even
> The moon's poor daughter, that most whey-faced metal,
> Precious. (289–90)

From one perspective, the passage from which these lines are taken provides a laudatory estimation of bards as essential to the social and economic promotion of kings and their treasures. Viewed from another angle, it implies that any poet who "christen[s] gold" helps breed the monsters whose materialistic goals created the selfish, masculinist, and unremittingly conventional society that, somewhat ironically, no longer has a place for Seanchan, its greatest poet. However, I do not believe Yeats's goal in displaying the hero's complicity in his own downfall was to make us see the error of his ways so much, perhaps, as the error of our own. When read in a cultural and historical context, *The King's Threshold* displays the dangers of "morally pretentious rationality"—or in Yeats's terms, of choosing to accept an imposed discipline rather than to engage difference and choose our own set of rules by which to live. Moreover, the play exhibits the ease with which even the most autonomous of others (or we) can be implicated in the tyrannical process by which social norms are rigidly and narrowly defined, performed, and legislated.

By the end of the play, Seanchan's choice to die for his non-conformist beliefs, though it temporarily unsettles his society, does not appear to promise the desired effect. Other than the poets, none of the common people who, according to the legend of hunger strikes held on thresholds, were expected to lay blame at the foot of the king, seem to blame the king. The Gort residents' obvious lack of concern for Seanchan's fate implies that they will not only allow, but that they hunger for, the return to normalcy, even if it means acclimating to the new-found tradition of a court without its poet. We can only assume, for instance, that the local girls breathed a sigh of relief at Seanchan's death, which would ultimately facilitate the return of dancing parties to the area. Poetry, on the other hand, clearly holds little or no interest for these hedonistic materialists. Finally, Yeats's choice to end the play with even Seanchan's pupils disagreeing about the potential survival strength of poetry as an implement of social power leaves little hope for poetry to have any assured future.

I believe Yeats ends *The King's Threshold* on what, for him, is a pessimistic note because, as a play that serves in part as social criticism, the ending must be realistic. John Rees Moore contends similarly that in the play's ending "one can feel Yeats's satisfaction in prophesying the worsening of the world and the alienation of the poet" even as he contemplates "the ultimate justification of the bard's superior wisdom" (90). More importantly, by taking Seanchan's and not King Guaire's side, Yeats manages to refashion the myth into a sympathetic treatment of the other. That is, with Seanchan's twinned status as psychological androgyne and hero, Yeats restores the feminine to its rightful place: not above but alongside of the masculine.

ON BAILE'S STRAND

Several critics have read *On Baile's Strand*, the first in Yeats's cycle of Cuchulain plays, in ways that would appear to contradict my contention that this play, like the others written in the years between 1900 and 1910, represents Yeats's attempt to rescue femininity from its secondary and disparaged position. In *The Cuchulain Plays of W. B. Yeats: A Study*, Reg Skene maintains that, on one level, *On Baile's Strand* is "about" Aoife and the "evil shadow" she casts "over those who dare to love her" (43). Representing Cuchulain as a victim of the "burning wheel of love" (44) that can as easily set one's heart afire with joy as burn one to death, Skene makes a woman who does not even appear on stage one of the play's central villains. John Rees Moore appears to agree with Skene when he asserts that *On Baile's Strand* is "Yeats's most militant and masculine tragedy" and that, in the context of the play, "it is the feminine principle which destroys" (108, 105). My reading of the play will demonstrate the limited nature of these assessments. While no one could deny Aoife's influence on the events that take place on stage, her role as agitator clearly takes a second seat to the central conflict in the play, that between Cuchulain and Conchubar.

In *On Baile's Strand*, Yeats provides another example of the immense pressures exerted by those who subscribe to the "one flock" philosophy of life in the tale of yet another King whose attempts to enlist a nonconformist and atypically gendered hero in his narrowly prescribed vision of the future ends in tragedy.[15] King Conchubar has called the great hero Cuchulain to his "assembly-house" at Dundealgan in order to force him to take an oath of obedience (459). Yeats establishes Conchubar's status as patriarchal authority in the opening scene in which, more generally, the Fool and the Blind Man educate the audience about the goings-on in Conchubar's kingdom. The Blind Man tells us, for instance, that Conchubar, who rules "over all the rest of the kings of Ireland" will, after Cuchulain swears his allegiance to him, "be Cuchulain's master in earnest from this day out" (463). Not content with others' assessments of his power, Conchubar himself later remarks to Cuchulain in a somewhat defensively posturing tone, "I am High King" and

> you . . .
> Are but a little king and weigh but light
> In anything that touches government,
> If put into the balance with my children. (481)

Here Conchubar falls back on the dual security afforded him in the role of supreme commander and father—his progeny and ancient Irish culture's version of the divine right of kings promise continued power in the future—in order to inflate the strength of his position and thereby fortify himself against Cuchulain. Conchubar's defensive self-importance shows that he is clearly apprehensive about Cuchulain, whose actions display an independent-minded, even insurrectionary element. For instance, Cuchulain boldly declares to the King, "I'll dance or hunt, or quarrel, or make love, / Wherever and whenever I've a mind to" (477, 479). He has also, we are told, felt self-assured enough in the past to kill men "without [the king's] bidding" and to reward others "at [his] own pleasure" (477).

The Blind Man also predicts that the oath Cuchulain has come to take will make him "as biddable as a house-dog and keep him always at [Conchubar's] hand" (463), an image that recalls *The King's Threshold* and Seanchan's bitingly satiric dismissal of the Soldier as the "King's dog," after which he sneers:

> ... Go to the King, your master.
> Crouch down and wag your tail, for it may be
> He has nothing now against you, and I think
> The stripes of your last beating are all healed (287).

Hinting at the cruelty of leaders, like Guaire and Conchubar, who demand complete loyalty, Seanchan's words also indict the Soldier as obsequious. Although no one could accuse Cuchulain of slavishness, the dog reference that allies him with this character from Seanchan's tragic tale nonetheless foretells the similarly tragic outcome of Cuchulain's choice to take the oath.

Whereas the Blind Man depicts the oath Cuchulain is to take in negative terms, Conchubar sees it as a form of progress. The King, "linking national security with the preservation of the family unit" (S. C. Harris 481), seeks the stability of an orderly and obedient society: As the King himself puts it, he wants to "leave / A strong and settled country to [his] children" (479). However, Cuchulain's disruptive presence in the country leaves little hope for the possibility of this legacy. His predilection for opening up boundaries—portrayed metaphorically in his desire to "scatter [men of the province] like water from a dish" (586), his attempt to befriend an enemy (the Young Man), and his transitory way of life—stands in direct opposition to the aims of Conchubar and his family, who wish to tighten and preserve their circle. Furthermore, "the wildness of [Cuchulain's] blood" (481) and his penchant, as Conchubar sees it, to "mock at every *reasonable* hope" (485, emphasis added) leads Conchubar's children to complain, "How can we be at safety with this man / That nobody can buy or bid or bind?" (479). Cuchulain, it seems, cannot be bribed into compliance with others' notions of social orderliness or their insistence on conformity to traditional gender roles.

Here, as in *The King's Threshold*, the conventional and convention-making characters paint the hero in negatively defined feminine terms, their measure making an other of the passionate Cuchulain. And, as is the case with Seanchan, the hero's "feminine" characteristics and his refusal to comply with the masculine model of level-headedness (his refusal to be reasonable), threatens the social stability of his community. In fact, Cuchulain's passion or potential hysteria (in the mercurial wildness of his blood) seems to threaten the literal as well as metaphorical ground upon which the others stand. As Conchubar's offspring explain nervously to their father, "We shall be at his mercy when you are gone; / He burns the earth as if he were a fire, / And time can never touch him" (481). The fears expressed here are twofold: The Young Kings cower from Cuchulain's passion, alarmed by its unpredictability, and, though less consciously, by his status as androgynous other. Exhibiting both "might of hand and burning heart" (491), Cuchulain is syncretistic, androgynous, a hybrid: a wild colonial boy who appreciates the metropolitan advantages of Conchubar's court, a virile warrior/lover who does not feel compelled to shirk his (feminine-coded) intuitive leanings, though convention would have him do so. Yeats's portrayal of Cuchulain as passionate and strong, intuitive and brave is, like that of Seanchan, a positive one. However, what Yeats and Cuchulain find perfectly "natural," Conchubar and his court perceive as anti-social.[16]

The differences between Cuchulain's and Conchubar's philosophies of life reveal themselves in many, often subtle ways, as in their discussion on the merits of women. When Conchubar contemptuously calls Cuchulain's former lover Aoife "a fierce woman of the camp," he spurs a tirade from Cuchulain that exposes Conchubar's narrow-mindedness. Conchubar's derisive evaluation of Aoife's lack of stereotypically lady-like characteristics causes Cuchulain to jump to her defense with celerity—and to return the favor of Conchubar's contempt to its owner:

> You call her "a fierce woman of the camp",
> For, having lived among the spinning-wheels,
> You'd have no woman near that would not say,
> "Ah! how wise!" "What will you have for supper?"
> "What shall I wear that I may please you, sir?"
> And keep that humming through the day and night
> For ever. (487)

Using Cuchulain to mock the bourgeois, patriarchal mentality that drives Conchubar to seek out the "subservient, domestic wife who flatters and serves her husband" (Cullingford 78), Yeats also provides yet another example of Conchubar's impetus, as insecure leader, to "debas[e]" so-called inferiors in order to "exalt [himself]" (Sartre xxvi)—a personality flaw that nevertheless has serious political implications. For those like Cuchulain, whose otherness Conchubar cannot comprehend and therefore does not respect, one's distinctive otherness—being a woman or a psychologically androgynous male, for instance—becomes the tool with which one is battered into submission by those demanding the debsement of otherness.

However, allowing Cuchulain to unfold a more inclusive, less selfish, and clearly less traditional appreciation of women, Yeats organizes an insightful comparison between the two men's perspectives that cannot help but make Cuchulain the victor in this battle. He describes Aoife lovingly, remembering:

> . . . that high, laughing, turbulent head of hers
> Thrown backward, and the bowstring at her ear,
> Or sitting at the fire with those grave eyes
> Full of good counsel as it were with wine,

Or when love ran through all the lineaments
Of her wild body . . . (487)

Whereas Conchubar perceives women as objects subject to his patriarchal authority, Cuchulain acknowledges women as subjects in their own right—a difference of opinion that reflects their more general views about the treatment of others. Aoife is an other not only by virtue of her status as a foreigner but also because she is a warrior queen, an androgynous or "hybrid" figure "whose existence," Susan C. Harris acknowledges, "threatens the structures that safeguard Conchubar's kingdom" (481). Being psychologically androgynous, Cuchulain has access to sympathy that allows him not to fear but, in fact, admire individuals, men and women, who have the capacity to be both turbulent (hysterical-leaning) and serious (reasonable and logical) and who would prefer to be individuals rather than stereotypical "men" or "women." Conchubar prefers the psychological safety and social equilibrium—or what Yeats might call the sterility—afforded by others' guaranteed obedience to his will.

Cuchulain does not limit his mocking commentary to Conchubar, however. Like Seanchan, his eyes perceive what S. B. Bushrui identifies as the "opportunis[m]" (51) at all levels of society, and he does not hesitate to expose the Young Kings' kindred capitulation to their father's narrow, conventional point-of-view. Their perspectives narrowed by bourgeois values, they have become "of one mind" (Yeats 493). The change in the men with whom Cuchulain used to frolic surprises him. At one time they readily would have agreed to accompany him, the "horses," and the "harp-players" in their quest to give up the serious business of oath-taking and instead "find a level place among the woods, / And dance awhile" (491). However, at the point of time at which the play takes place, the Young Kings make manifest Conchubar's contention that "There is not one but dreads this turbulence / Now that they're settled men" (493). And they have settled: settled down and, according to Cuchulain, settled for less. Cuchulain comes to this realization in the following lines:

Are you so changed,
Or have I grown more dangerous of late?
But that's not it. I understand it all.
It's you that have changed. You've wives and children now,
And for that reason cannot follow one
That lives like a bird's flight from tree to tree. (493)

This passage offers two possible interpretations. From a common sense perspective—that is, for those content to follow the traditional path set out before them by bourgeois protocol—the "reason" for choosing not to live as a bird does, flitting from branch to branch, is self-evident: settling down is simply part of the process of maturation. From this perspective, Cuchulain appears to be fixed in adolescence. On the other hand, from the perspective of those who value life qualities other than the stability gained through the procurement of material possessions and the continuation of the family line, the passage manifests the sad and lonely state of those who do not make the "changes" required by the conventional life plan—and especially of those who never fit in at all. Although I do not propose that there is an exact parity between settling down and settling for less, I believe Yeats suggests here that settling down, in the conventional usage of the phrase, would perforce mean settling for less in the case of Cuchulain and those like him—individuals who, *coerced* into relinquishing their passionate and wide-ranging appreciation for, and embodiment of, unconventional gender roles, lose their very selves.

What then do we make of Conchubar's avowal that he has heard Cuchulain

> . . . cry, aye, in [his] very sleep
> "I have no son", and with such bitterness
> That [he] ha[s] gone upon [his] knees and prayed
> That it might be amended. (483)

This, compounded with Cuchulain's palpable desire to affiliate himself with the Young Man does, in fact, render suspect the following declaration by Cuchulain:

> I think myself most lucky that I leave
> No pallid ghost or mockery of a man
> To drift and mutter in the corridors
> Where I have laughed and sung. (483)

However, his assessment of Conchubar's children, as well as his reasons for liking the man who in actuality is his son, display that even if he were to take on the role of parent, he would never "settle down" in the ways being asked of him. He reveals his disgust with the sort of offspring the middle-class lifestyle breeds when he declares to Conchubar, "I do not like your children — they have not pith, / No marrow in their bones, and will lie soft / Where you and I lie hard" (481). Cuchulain and the Young Man, on the other hand, speak the same language: "That's spoken as I'd have spoken it at your age," Cuchulain tells him at one point (510). More importantly, the language he shares with the Young man admits to more of an interest in living "like a bird's flight from tree to tree" than in drifting and muttering in corridors. This scene indicates that, even as a parent, Cuchulain would not capitulate to bourgeois childrearing practices and would instead insist on being, and encouraging his son to be, his androgynous self.

But the loss of self, in the form of his progeny as well as his sanity, is precisely the price Cuchulain pays for conceding to Conchubar's insistence on conformity. Forced to concede his position as "rebel" (McCarthy 61) to the majority power of the "settled men," Cuchulain demonstrates the pull peer pressure has on even the most individualistic of people when he surrenders: "It's time the years put water in my blood / And drowned the wildness of it, for all's changed, / But that unchanged. —I'll take what oath you will" (493). Although he here relinquishes his own power, it is clear from Yeats's imagery in this scene that Cuchulain perceives taking the oath as a form of suicide: the water will drown his wildness and weaken his blood. Next, having accepted his place as a member of the larger collective, Cuchulain has no choice but to do as he is told, in this case, to defend his new-found master's domain from the threat of a Young Man from enemy lands far, far away. Setting off to battle the unnamed invader, Cuchulain is stopped in his yet unbloodied tracks by his recognition of an intuitive connection with the Young Man. "I'd have you for my friend" though "I cannot tell the reason" (505), marvels Cuchulain.

That the connection is intuitive, and that the intuition is Cuchulain's is an important factor in Yeats's play. As I noted above, in many versions of the myth, as in *The Yellow Book of Lecan*, Cuchulain initially becomes cognizant of a potential paternal affiliation with the Young Man (who, in other versions, is generally called by his name, Conlaoch) through his wife Emer's warning. In the version given the most credit for influencing Yeats,[17] Lady Gregory's "The Only Son of Aoife" from *Cuchulain of Muirthemne*, the hero does not connect with his son until after he has dealt the youth a fatal blow. He laments to his dying son, "'If I and my fair Conlaoch were doing feats of war on the one side, the men of Ireland from sea to sea would not be equal to us together'" (240). This example of (albeit potential) strength, when paired with Yeats's choice to invest Cuchulain with the "feminine" virtue of intuition reinforces my contention that Cuchulain is meant to be a model of androgyny. Or, as Yeats's theory of the mask would have it, Cuchulain the virile warrior has faced his opposite, made it a part of himself, and thereby widened his understanding or personality.

Acknowledging kinship with his ought-to-be foe, Cuchulain at first attempts to deflect the Young Man's challenge to fight to the death and even offers to become his friend and mentor. Conchubar, however, insists that Cuchulain accept the challenge because he wants to "leave" the legacy of a "throne too high for insult" (507). Like Conchubar, whose motive is, in part, one of vanity, the Young Man similarly argues that he must fight or else appear to have "turned coward" (508). Unconcerned with these outward signs of masculinity, Cuchulain perseveres in his endeavor to engender peace between the two nations. In order to divest the Young Man of his fears of being considered a coward and Conchubar of his concern that Aoife will continue to wage war on him, Cuchulain offers to "give [the Young Man] gifts / That Aoife'll know, and all her people know, / To have come from me" (508). Then he offers, "O! tell her / I was afraid, or tell her what you will" (508). Here Cuchulain displays indifference toward the others' perception of his masculinity. This willingness to relinquish his warrior or ultra-masculine reputation signifies his nonconformity, in that he does not care what others think about him. It also evinces his androgyny, in that it signals an embrace of his feminine side as emblematized, in this instance, by his choice to forge and protect fragile human and social bonds (that is, with the Young Man), like an Angel in the House, rather than continue in the course of political and military conflict, like a warrior. Yet Cuchulain's next actions show just how convincing the arguments of the majority can be, even for one so independent-minded as him. Formerly ruled by gut instinct, or by the feminine-typed characteristics of passion and intuition, the "settled" Cuchulain displays just how "watered-down" and insecure his recent capitulation to convention has made him. Whereas he once would have stood his guns, defending his intuition and therefore the Young Man, Cuchulain, having agreed to the exclusive and strict rule of reason, becomes stripped of the previously balanced perspective imparted by his androgynous inclinations. Weakened by his oath to conformity, Cuchulain suffers from a diminished ability to recognize the real truth behind the fiction created by those around him. That is, he is at the mercy of the hypocritical and biased machinations of those who claim reason as god, and of witchcraft, both of which are employed for the purpose of inducing Cuchulain to give up "tree to tree" flight for the benefit of the "one flock." Early in the play, Cuchulain has no fear of defying Conchubar. Before he takes the oath of obedience, when he still lives by instinct, Cuchulain proudly stands up for what he believes in, as when he staunchly defends the character of Conchubar's enemy Aoife, and when he urges the Young Kings to abandon what he sees as ridiculous talk of oath-taking for a celebration in the woods. But as the play progresses, Cuchulain's ability to stand on his own diminishes. He does make efforts to evade Conchubar's war-making directive to kill the Young Man: as we have seen, his intuition initially wins the battle against all arguments in favor of fighting. Eventually, however, Cuchulain loses the battle to maintain peace with the Young Man as well as the struggle to follow his intuition and to preserve his psychologically androgynous nature.

Yeats represents Cuchulain's loss to majority rule in an interesting way. Traditional depictions of this portion of the Cuchulain myth blame Cuchulain's change of heart on a sort of pagan *deus ex machina*. In these versions, Cuchulain capitulates to Conchubar's entreaties to fight the Young Man because he falls under the spell of a géasa or, as Yeats calls it here, "witchcraft" (508). In Yeats's version, Cuchulain also comes to believe that witchcraft is involved, but not right away. In fact, he balks at the first mention of witchcraft, which occurs immediately after he admits he is not afraid to say he "was afraid" (508) in order to save the peace. "Some witch of the air has troubled Cuchulain's mind" (508), Conchubar conjectures, because he cannot fathom any other possible reason why Cuchulain would voluntarily, as he sees it, emasculate himself. But Cuchulain replies matter-of-factly about the Young Man's obvious influence over him, "No witchcraft. His head is like a woman's head / I had a fancy for" (508). Here Cuchulain refuses to see his intuition as anything other than completely natural. Yet when talk of witchcraft returns fifty lines later, Cuchulain suddenly becomes convinced by their arguments that he has been put under a spell by someone or something related to the Young Man. It is only then that Cuchulain rejects his intuition, a conciliation that results in the death of his son by Cuchulain's own hands.

What occurs between these two scenes that might have caused Cuchulain to change his mind? During this time, Cuchulain and the Young Man have continued to bond, even going so far as to pledge with a ring to "stand by one another from this out" (510). When commanded by Conchubar's "*loud voice*" (511) to put a stop to the friendship, Cuchulain not only "lay[s] commands" on Conchubar but also his hands: he seizes Conchubar, demanding "You shall not stir, High King. I'll hold you there" (511–512). Only then does Cuchulain perceive his treatment of the Young Man with the eyes of those for whom intuition has no value. This time, Conchubar's allegation that "Witchcraft has maddened you" persuades Cuchulain, who cries out, "Yes, witchcraft! witchcraft! Witches of the air!" (512) before he bounds off to take revenge on the Young Man.

Yeats's handling of this scene, in the context of my arguments about Cuchulain's status as androgynous figure, provokes the following question: Are Cuchulain's actions at the end of the play the work of witchcraft, or are they the result of having been brainwashed by the materialism, moralism, and rationalism of those to whom he pledged allegiance?[18] His actions up to the point that he chooses to kill the Young Man, after all, are very much in character with Cuchulain's faith in intuition. Yet he becomes convinced with a word that his heretofore intuitive character—and the peace-keeping actions influenced by it—are, ironically, as anti-social as the others would have it, which causes him to go into an hysterical rage and kill his own son.

My reading of *On Baile's Strand* as a social critique of the restrictive nature of Victorian gender construction suggests that, although we cannot deny the role of witchcraft in the play—all characters including Cuchulain outwardly recognize its presence—it would be a mistake to ignore the significance of the other powers at work on Cuchulain. More specifically, we must recognize that it is only when Cuchulain has been forced to concede to Conchubar's political manipulations, when he has gone over fully to the other side of the intuition/reason barrier, that the most anti-social and unreasonable of acts occur. The evidence in the play thus suggests that the weakness that allows Cuchulain to fall under the spell of witchcraft originates in the moment Conchubar insists he take an oath of obedience. Having agreed, in essence, to eradicate those so-called feminine qualities of wildness, passion, and intuition for which Conchubar has no use, Cuchulain destroys an entire half of his self-identity, thereby opening himself up to the influence of the materialism, greed, and pride that have convinced the others that there is no other way to maintain their peace and prosperity but to kill the Young Man. From this perspective, *On Baile's Strand* depicts the physical threatening of a king and the murder of a son, which typically are categorized as crimes of passion, as crimes of *reason*. Likewise, Cuchulain's conversion to reason and convention is portrayed not as progress but as degeneration. That is, by following the path set out by Conchubar— a conventional, bourgeois path the King would have all his subjects take regardless of any inclination otherwise—Cuchulain loses his son and his sanity.

It will be helpful, at this point, to take a step off the page to consider what might have happened had Cuchulain been allowed to follow his intuition. All evidence in the play points to a less violent conclusion to the play—and, therefore, potentially (and ironically) to the "settled country" Conchubar claims he would like to leave to his children.[19] It is true that the Young Man has come, under order of his mother, to kill Cuchulain. However, if allowed to blossom further, the shared intuitive recognition between father and son might have, Yeats implies, led to peace for Conchubar's kingdom. Already loathe to do battle with one another after only moments of acquaintance, Cuchulain and the Young Man are quickly well along the path toward conciliation. In the end, Cuchulain even goes so far as to take the Young Man's side by promising to defend him from all other challengers (510). Along each step of the way, Cuchulain's every effort to avoid battle has its desired affect: he convinces the Young Man to work with him (and, by extension, Conchubar), not against him. This, it would seem, holds hope for doing more by way of establishing a truce than Conchubar's methods for establishing peace—that is, via war.

But to forge an agreement between Cuchulain, Conchubar, and the Young Man would be to change the myth. It would also, following my reading of the play as an allegorical representation of the Victorian and Edwardian social structure, be to provide a revisionist version of reality. Like *The King's Threshold*, *On Baile's Strand* must end tragically in order to fulfill its role as social criticism. The reconciliation of gender characteristics within the individual, as seen in Cuchulain and Seanchan, garnered little sympathy from the conventional set. After all, if men and women were not allowed to occupy the same "sphere," the presence of a range of gender characteristics in one person would certainly not be considered acceptable. As with many of Yeats's dramatic heroes from this era, Cuchulain's (pre-oath) personality in *On Baile's Strand* represents what Yeats hoped eventually would be the winning side in the battle against the influential, convention-ridden rulers who upheld the dualistic, hierarchical, and socially divisive traditional structures of gender, class, and race. As an androgynously gendered hero, then, Cuchulain stands as an example of the more widely varied, more inclusive forms of identity Yeats would have replace the narrow, essentialist norm.

DEIRDRE

The pressure to conform to traditional gender roles is also central to the action and thematic content of *Deirdre*. In this play, Yeats challenges the validity of conventional gender characteristics by offering exceptions to the rule in the characters of Deirdre, the (female) musicians, Fergus, Naoise, and Conchubar. In Yeats's version of the Deirdre myth, the characters' various failures and successes depend in large part on whether or not their awareness of social convention is merely an espousal of the same, as is the case with Conchubar, Naoise and especially Fergus. On the other hand, because they recognize the conventions on a conscious level, *as conventions*, Deirdre and the musicians are able to manipulate them rather than be (entirely) manipulated by them. On another level, the play is about reading signs, intuitive and logical: the benefits afforded to those who can and will, and the tragic consequences of those who cannot or will not.[20] As with *The King's Threshold* and *On Baile's Strand*, embedded in this mythic retelling of Deirdre's tragic end, then, lies a rejection of the equation of femininity with inferiority, as well as a critique of the legitimacy of the social scripting of gender, in general, and of the Irish, in particular. My argument, based on the standard version of the play, also includes a reading of two early manuscript versions that display, like the aforementioned letter to George Russell, at what level of psychological and aesthetic reckoning Yeats struggled to come to terms with these issues in the first decade of the twentieth century.

As we know, the late Victorian period brought with it a loosening, to a certain extent, of restrictions on gender, class, and race identities—as exemplified, for instance, by the advent of Decadence and the negative response, on the part of the orthodox majority, to its homosexual elements as seen in the Wilde trial. These changes, accompanied in Ireland by arguments over and redefinitions of cultural, religious, and political borders (although not yet of the physical sort), brought with them a certain level of uncertainty which, as Elaine Showalter notes, reinforced the desire for the security of old and comfortable boundaries. She explains in *Sexual Anarchy: Gender and Culture at the Fin de Siècle* that "in periods of cultural insecurity when there are fears of regression and degeneration, the longing for strict border controls around the definition of gender, as well as race, class, and nationality, becomes especially intense" (4).

Yeats's *Deirdre* presents us with three such reactionaries: Fergus, Naoise, and Conchubar who, as men and leaders of other men, are shown to have a burgeoning awareness of the limits of their power. Conchubar's insecurity, which arises out of Deirdre's refusal to marry him, provokes his use of royal privilege to resolve his scheme to get her back. Having lost Deirdre to the young and handsome Naoise—and therefore having lost some of his stature as a man and as a king—seven years before the time of the play, Conchubar insists on his right to, in Showalter's terms, "control" the "borders." Even at the end of the play, when he has been forced to relinquish Deirdre to the death that will (physically) take her from him forever, he rigidly contends, "I, being King, did right / In choosing her most fitting to be Queen, / And letting no boy lover take the sway" (388). Fergus's and Naoise's actions reflect a similar belief in convention and, more specifically, in the traditional encoding of gender characteristics. In the case of each character, the habit of reverting to the safety of custom and convention in times of danger or confusion becomes a tragic flaw that has repercussions for every character in the play. Deirdre and the musicians, on the other hand, escape this particular tragic flaw (although not, in Deirdre's case, tragedy) by rejecting the legitimacy of one of the "border controls"—the social encoding of gender in which the feminine is allied with the weak, sentimental, illogical, and possibly hysterical, and in which to be masculine is to be strong (or to use Yeats's word "athletic") and logical.

These are the very notions of gender identity to which we see Naoise and Fergus subscribe. Both characterize women as nervous and jumpy, their potential for logic overpowered by their supposed frailty. For example, when the musicians question the presence, outside the house, of "dark men, / With murderous and outlandish-looking arms" (349) as those sent to greet Deirdre and Naoise in their supposed welcome to Conchubar's land, Fergus rejects this perfectly logical suspicion as a "trifle [that] sets [the women] quaking" (350). He continues to equate the feminine with the high-strung in his retelling of the legend of Lugaidh Redstripe who, with his wife, sat quietly playing chess, not coincidentally at the very board that sits in Conchubar's house, as they awaited their end. He explains that, had Redstripe's wife been "merely" a woman and not part sea-mew with cold blood of the sea in her veins" (375), the calmness she exuded would not have been possible.

Deirdre's husband Naoise shows himself to be as limited as Fergus. For instance, when Deirdre (insightfully) perceives that same fated chess table as an ominous sign of their own deaths, he dismisses her as being "startled by a cloud or a shadow" (357). Like the characters in *On Baile's Strand* who disparage the faculty of intuition, however, he will be proven fatally wrong, for Deirdre's belief that "gods turn clouds and casual accidents / Into omens" (356–57) is an unerring one. The two men agree that the women, *as women*, read too much into what the men think that they themselves are logical enough to recognize as common or coincidental occurrences. In addition, because her upbringing necessitated a life in which her "house has been / The hole of the badger and the den of the fox" (355) Deirdre is, by Naoise's and Fergus's reckoning, doubly crippled. Not only is she a woman; she also has been raised without the illustrative guidance of social convention. Ironically, Deirdre's unconventional upbringing is the very circumstance that ultimately comes to her aid in her dealings with Conchubar, for it is that which allows her to see through Conchubar's attempts to manipulate her and the others. As men invested in being "men," however, Naoise and Fergus choose to ignore the obvious signs that they are being tricked and instead put their trust in Conchubar's word, which they assume, as the word of a man and of a king, to be honest.

The number of times Fergus and Naoise feel it necessary to testify to their faith in Conchubar (their enthusiasm parallels that of the most ardent convert witnessing his or her faith in God) speaks to the deep, perhaps subconscious doubt activated by the strange and unconventional actions of their leader who, for instance, has not bothered to send anyone except brutal-looking soldiers to greet Deirdre and Naoise after their long journey. However, in spite of all evidence to the contrary, the men insist on defending Conchubar as a scrupulous and ethical man with a character unsullied in all its aspects: as a friend, a host, a maker of promises, an aged man, and a king. That he is "Conchubar's near friend," Fergus tells us, ought to "weigh . . . somewhat" (349) in terms of his ability to trust the King. That Conchubar has invited them to be his guests recommends social propriety as another reason to trust the High King: "Being his guest, / Words that would wrong him can but wrong ourselves" (357), Naoise argues. That their conventional upbringing has secured their faith in the inviolate nature of promises, not to mention the venerability of old age, leads Naoise to contend that the others' doubts "[w]rong this old man who's pledged his word to us" (358). But the strongest reason Naoise and Fergus find to trust Conchubar—which also, ironically, is the one that makes it so easy for him to deceive them—emanates from their filial respect for his patriarchal authority. In this regard, Naoise silences all proffered suspicion with the following:

> And being himself,
> Being High King, he cannot break his faith.
> I have his word and I must take that word,
> Or prove myself unworthy of my nurture
> Under a great man's roof. (355)

Having satisfied themselves and one another that the code of proper manhood, which says a man will never cheat, swindle, or manipulate one of his fellow men, is still intact, the men proceed to congratulate one another for having the sense allotted only to men. Naoise counsels:

> We must not speak or think as women do
> That when the house is all abed sit up
> Marking among the ashes with a stick
> Till they are terrified.—Being what we are
> We must meet all things with an equal mind. (358)

Confident that he has been able to set Deirdre straight (or so he thinks!), Naoise then retreats with Fergus to speak with the "dark men" guarding the door. They want to ensure that these men, whom they assume to be as gullible as themselves, do not do what they think the women have done, which is conflate gossip or "[s]ome crazy fantasy of their own brain" with Conchubar's wishes—wishes that, in their naïve estimation, could only be honorable. In Naoise's and Fergus's faith in the steadfastness of the male/male social bond, we find a strong indictment of the Victorian bourgeois phenomenon Showalter terms "Clubland," a literal and metaphorical network of male social clubs that helped separate men from domestic life (11) and the "illogical" women who ruled that sphere.

Fergus proves himself to be more gullible than Naoise, however, in that his faith in Conchubar goes deeper and lasts longer. Fergus's subordination of all else to his belief in the bonds between men is fueled in part by pride. Over and over again, Fergus reminds us of his role in obtaining Conchubar's ostensible forgiveness of Deirdre and Naoise. Conchubar, he tells us, was

> . . . so hard to cure that the whole court,
> But I alone, thought it impossible;
> Yet after I had urged it at all seasons,
> I had my way, and all's forgiven now. (348)

Elsewhere he explains, "If I had thought so little of mankind / I never could have moved him to this pardon" (359). It is clear from these testimonials that Fergus's trust in Conchubar's honorable nature, in what he sees as their "like" minds (371), and in their friendship is almost unshakeable. Even when the king's messenger announces that Naoise is an absolutely unwelcome guest, Fergus rationalizes that "[s]ome rogue, some enemy, / Has bribed [the messenger] to embroil us with the King" and vows to "find out the truth" (371). Refusing to hear the truth even as it is spoken boldly into his own ear, Fergus remains deaf to Conchubar's treachery until almost the very end of the play. The prominence of male/male bonds in Fergus's philosophy of life, thus, precludes all other possibilities for truth, even those that are more logical or obvious.

The irony of Fergus's and Naoise's stance is evident to the audience or reader: Fergus and Naoise, who pompously think themselves to be of "equal" or rational mind, are the characters furthest from this laudable quality. Yeats emphasizes their self-delusion by having Naoise speak the following metaphorical lines before they go to set the "dark men" straight: "Come, let us look if there's a messenger / From Conchubar. We cannot see from this / Because we are blinded by the leaves and twigs." Here Yeats shares a little joke with the reader, playing on the clichéd notion of not being able to see the forest for the trees. Unaware of the reader's and Yeats's complicity against him, however, Naoise continues to expound condescendingly, "It is but kind that when the lips we love / Speak words that are unfitting for kings' ears / Our ears be deaf" (358–59). Having closed their ears to "feminine" intuition, they also blind themselves to the rational evidence of Conchubar's duplicity that presents itself at every turn.

To the musicians and Deirdre, however, nothing could be more obvious than the fact of Conchubar's treachery. Even as Naoise and Fergus condescend to them, the women characters show themselves to be quite aware of the social script their male counterparts use to disparage them. When Deirdre acknowledges one of the musicians' metaphoric narratives with, "I catch your meaning" (361), she suggests one of the play's strongest themes, which is that there are multiple layers of meaning in every statement and occurrence. Only those able to "put . . . meaning upon words / Spoken at random" (361)—that process of reading between the lines that makes use of both "feminine" intuition and "masculine" logic—have access to the truth. Of course, in the play, no one speaks at random, and nothing occurs by chance. The chessboard, the "dark men" guarding the house, the empty house that greets Deirdre and Naoise after their long voyage, and the preparations for a visitor to the king's castle and bed all clearly betoken Conchubar's betrayal of Deirdre, Naoise, and Fergus. Yet only Deirdre and the musicians can identify the signs; only they recognize the traitorous order beneath seeming chance.

But Deirdre and the musicians go beyond merely recognizing the existence of the socially constructed gender codes with which they are labeled. They co-opt these codes, using their knowledge against those less enlightened in an attempt to save Deirdre and Naoise from the death that Fergus, Naoise, and Conchubar bring closer. Whereas Naoise and Fergus accept at face value woman's nature as depicted in stereotypes, because Deirdre and the musicians are more astute "readers," they recognize the possibility of revising the codes for use in their favor. In Showalter's terms, rather than fall back on the safety of old "borders," Deirdre and the other women reestablish them.

Attempting to inflame Naoise's jealousy in the hopes that the strong emotion will snap him out of his so-called rational faith in Cuchulain's word and convince him to escape, Deirdre plays the role that is expected of her: that of vain, fickle female. She taunts Naoise:

> Look at my face where the leaf raddled it
> And at these rubies on my hair and breast.
> It was for him, to stir him to desire,
> I put on beauty; yes, for Conchubar. (365)

Her seeming treachery initially engenders its desired effect: Naoise takes the bait. Incredulous and infuriated, he demands to know "What frenzy put these words into your mouth?" (365). Her response reinforces what may have been only a suspicion on the reader's or spectator's part that she is using social convention, and, more importantly, her husband's confidence in it, against him: "No frenzy," she teases, "for what need is there for frenzy / To change what shifts with every change of wind, / Or else there is no truth in men's old sayings?" (365). Fergus, for once able to read between the lines, foils her plans by warning the temporarily emotionally distracted Naoise, "Fool, she but seeks to rouse your jealousy / With crafty words" (366). Here, Deirdre's manipulations do not work with Naoise, but this one failure does not deter future attempts.

She plays the same trick on Conchubar later in the play when she attempts to convince him to allow her to "lay out" the dead Naoise (384), which is really just a ploy to be near him so that she may, Romeo-like, commit suicide at his side. She first flatters Conchubar by telling him, "You'll stir me to more passion than he could" (385). In order to convince the King further, Deirdre once again manipulates the stereotype of women's inconstancy, this time with the help of the women musicians, whom she here urges to defend her ostensible decision to marry Conchubar:

> . . . I will have you tell him
> How changeable all women are; how soon
> Even the best of lovers is forgot
> When his day's finished. (385)

His personal vanity and trust in social convention fortified, Conchubar grants Deirdre's appeal and loses her to the knife she has had hidden in her clothes during the entire time she has been speaking to him. The reason Conchubar allows her to go to her lover, of course, is because he is not a good reader of signs, people, or metaphors. This fact is made more obvious when he misconstrues as another instance of flattery what essentially is Deirdre's farewell to the musicians:

> Now strike the wire, and sing to it a while,
> Knowing that all is happy, and that you know
> Within what bride-bed I shall lie this night,
> And by what man, and lie close up to him,
> For the bed's narrow, and then outsleep the cockcrow. (387)

Able to "put meaning" on these words, we all know to "what bed" and "what man" she refers—all of us, that is, except Conchubar.

Changes Yeats made in early and later manuscript versions of *Deirdre* reinforce my argument that, on one level, this play dramatizes the problematic nature of blind complicity with the patriarchal social contract. One of the early drafts portrays a Fergus who is even more willing than his later incarnation to bolster the preeminence of the male/male social contract over all other bonds through his complete dismissal of passionate love. In the beginning of this version Fergus downplays the significance of passionate love by announcing, "I await Queen Deirdre / And Naoise once the foremost of all men / But now her lover only" (POS 7491, "early draft" 3). This passage tells us that, in Fergus's eyes, the post-Deirdre Naoise has lost stature in the world of men: a "lover only," he is good for nothing else. He further demonizes not only passionate love but Naoise as well in a scene in which Naoise doubts the benignity of Conchubar's motives. Fergus casts Naoise's doubt as an illness, a degeneration of logical capacity, almost hysteria: "If passion had not put an enmity / Between mankind and you . . .," you would still be a man, he implies. But ". . . now there[']s so much fever in you[r] eyes / You find out malice in mere accident / And plan in casual things" (POS 7491, "early draft" 13). These being precisely the complaints made about the women in the play, here Fergus allies Naoise with the feminine. A bit later in the same manuscript, Fergus continues to describe their infamous relationship along bitingly critical lines:

> For there will be thousands to point at her
> And tell how with a kiss that even now
> Is shrilling like a trumpet in your blood
> She drew you . . . from the manful natural life
> Into a useless wilderness. (POS 7491, "early draft" 26)

Naoise's response, "You called me coward but a moment since / And now . . . you have laid the blame on Deirdre" (POS 7491, "early draft" 26), reinforces Fergus's conclusion that the feminized Naoise is merely Deirdre's pawn and not his own man; in fact, he is not at man at all.

This section and, indeed, others like it, which indicate an almost overwhelming disgust for Naoise on the part of Fergus, were written out of the play. I believe Yeats chose to do so because the dismissal of passionate love and of Naoise makes Naoise a traitor to *man*kind, a move that would weaken the bond between him and Fergus. These sections would upset the complicity of their faith in the essential identity of men and women, thus undercutting the play's message about why such faith is problematic. In the standard, later version, the conflict between the destructive/creative force of passionate love with more settled conventions, which Virginia Rohan has labeled as a central theme (41), still stands. For instance, we see that Naoise's choice of passionate love, in fact, does dispossess him of the opportunity to take part in the "manly" activities of drinking, sport, and battle games he enjoyed before being forced into exile. What remains in the standard version of the play—Naoise's admission that he "gave up all for love" (373) and Deirdre's comment that she returned to Emain for Naoise's sake, only at the command of "her husband's will" (354)—clearly shows that he misses partaking in these communal bonding moments. While this example serves to uphold the earlier manuscript's theme of the oppositional nature of passionate love and conventional male bonds, the later version allows the conflict mentioned by Rohan to exist without intruding on the complicity between the two men, and thus on the play's social critique.

Yet another manuscript version of the play allies Fergus with the feminine in a different scene. In the standard version, in the scene in which Fergus and the musicians await the arrival of Deirdre and Naoise, the heated nature of Fergus's defense of Conchubar's honor leads him to need to "*Suddenly restrai*[*n*] *himself and spea*[*k*] *gently*" (351). The use of "restrain" and "gently" indicate a certain level of potency on Fergus's part, as if he fears he might physically or verbally hurt the women but has instead chosen to protect them. Furthermore, he does restrain himself or call himself back to order, and therefore follows the conventionally masculine path laid out for proper Victorian men. The earlier version, however, manifests an almost hysterical Fergus, rambling and confused. He confesses to the musicians, "Forgive me, women if I have been harsh, for all my thoughts are broken loose, grown wild, / With thinking on this good deed done at last / And I have lost the reins" (POS 7491, 14ff 9–10). Here, with his thoughts run amok, Fergus reflects conventional Victorian notions of the feminine, not to mention the hysteric. That Yeats chose to revise Fergus's hysteria into self-control, one of the signatures of masculine rationality, shows that Yeats perceived with growing importance the need to critique strict social constructions of gender. Writing the feminine out of Fergus's characterization, thereby making him more conventionally male, might appear to indicate Yeats's own conformity to traditional gender roles. However, in the context of the argument I outline in this chapter, we see that the alliance of a male character with the feminine is written out of the final, printed version so that the men may mock the women for acting *as women* without the added complication of having acted "as women" themselves. As completely masculine beings, from the perspective of social standards, Naoise and Fergus more readily represent the strict coding of gender that Yeats perceived to be one of the major problems at the base of his era's identity crisis.

A comparison of the revised version of Yeats's *Deirdre* with other versions of the myth written in the Victorian and Edwardian era also informs the interpretations I have elaborated here. As Herbert V. Fackler shows, the tale of Deirdre and the sons of Usnach was a popular subject in the late nineteenth and early twentieth centuries. Deirdre, her husband, and his brothers were featured, for instance, in Sir Samuel Ferguson's "The Death of the Children of Usnach" (1834) and *Deirdre* (1880), R. D. Joyce's *Deirdre* (1876), P. W. Joyce's "The Fate of the Sons of Usna" (1878), Aubrey de Vere's *The Sons of Usnach* (1882), William Sharp's *House of Usna* (1900), Herbert Trench's *Deirdre Wedded* (1901), Lady Gregory's "The Fate of the Sons of Usnach" in *Cuchulain of Muirthemne* (1902), A. E.'s *Deirdre* (1902), and T. W. Rolleston's "Deirdre and the Sons of Usna" (1911). However, in these versions, Deirdre was not often featured as the knowing hero in comparison to her male counterparts. Of particular note as regards my argument are the works of R. D. Joyce and William Sharp, who chose to depict Deirdre as a minor character in the legend. Naoise takes the role of protagonist in Joyce's epic poem, *Deirdre*, while in Sharp's version of the story, Deirdre plays no role whatsoever. Interestingly, in the 1880 version of *Deirdre*, Ferguson depicts Naoise as what Fackler calls an "optimistic Victorian" who has been "deceived, but only through an appeal to his rational nobility" (19). Ferguson's portrayal of Naoise's faith in reason in this work, thus, makes it a sort of predecessor for Yeats's version of the myth. Overall, however, this brief review reveals how radical Yeats was at that time to fashion his version of the Deirdre myth as, at least in part, a social critique of his time.

The major targets of Yeats's criticism in this play are also the character's tragic flaws. Because of Conchubar's treachery and Naoise's and (even moreso) Fergus's blind faith in reason and in conventional renderings of gender, Deirdre and Naoise die, and Fergus is forced to swear revenge on his former, beloved, yet trust-betray-ing "near friend," King Conchubar. On a more positive note, by the end, all of the characters have at least learned to "put meaning upon words spoken at random"—all, that is, except Conchubar, who unwaveringly demands his rights as a royal authority. At the end of the play, Conchubar continues to rail against circumstances, refusing to see how the misreading that led him to believe Deirdre did or could love him ironically caused him to lose what he had spent his life trying to obtain. Yeats defines one of the key problems in the play, and indeed in society, as blind faith in conventional definitions of gender and social contracts that foster the notion that men, and especially political and other leaders, do not betray other men. The play thus highlights the necessity to maintain a high degree of awareness of, and consequently not to swallow whole, socially constructed classifications. If you do you not follow this advice, Yeats suggests by literary example, you become complicit in the strict and often negative classification of gender and, by extension, of other socially encoded categories such as race, class, and nation. Suggesting an alternative to this mode of thought and action, with *Deirdre*, Yeats not only takes the "weakness" out of "femininity"; even more importantly, he exposes stereotypes, not women or femininity, to be blind, deaf, and dumb.

Chapter Five
"[N]ice little playwrights, making pretty little plays"
Yeats, Irish Identity, and the Critical Response

YEATS AND IRISH IDENTITY

IN HIS OBJECTION TO THEORIES OF PROGRESS THAT ATTEMPTED TO ENFORCE THE same moral discipline on all, Yeats found ethnicity an especially troublesome issue. Victorian and Edwardian definitions of race that made one's success as an "English" or "Irish" person dependent on the maintenance of prescribed character traits restricted the development of what Yeats saw as the welcome diversity of individual personalities. The Irish at the turn of the nineteenth century, moreover, were caught among three contradictory significations: 1) imperialist categorizations that allied Irishness with inferiority, femininity, and savagery, 2) political and cultural nationalisms that attempted to counter these imperialist categorizations with comparatively positive but oftentimes equally essentialist constructions of the Irish as descendents of an ancient and honorable race, and 3) socioeconomic demands that defined progress in increasingly materialistic ways that were considered English or modern or both. Clearly, anyone who tried to obtain to more than one of these identities at the same time would find himself or herself conflicted, fragmented, and culturally disjointed.

Yeats regretted, as Oscar Wilde articulates it in "The Soul of Man Under Socialism" (1891), "that society should be constructed on such a basis that man has been forced into a groove in which he cannot freely develop what is wonderful and fascinating, and delightful in him" (21).[1] According to Wilde, the existence of "[s]elfishness," which "always aims at creating around it an absolute uniformity of type" and which refused to recognize "an infinite variety of type as a delightful thing" (43) was a consequence of capitalism: of the "recognition of private property" which led to "confusing a man with what he possesses" (20). Although, as my explication of *The Countess Cathleen, Cathleen ni Houlihan,* and *The Land of Hearts'*

Desire displays, Yeats agreed wholeheartedly with this sentiment, he also perceived colonial and anti-colonial constructions of identity to contribute to the problem. That is, by using difference or otherness as a social and political tool, both colonizer and colonized reinforce the value of sameness. Richard Rorty's depiction of the ways individuals use otherness to bolster their self-esteem and perceived status suits the colonial situation in particular:

> Most people . . . simply do not think of themselves as, first and foremost, a human being. Instead, they think of themselves as being a certain *good* sort of human being—a sort defined by explicit opposition to a particularly bad sort. What is crucial for their sense of who they are is that they are *not* an infidel, *not* a queer, *not* a woman, *not* an untouchable. (178)

According to Yeats, however, any ideology that enforced sameness or "uniformity of type," regardless of its political origin, required revision. Yeats's attempts to find ways out of the intransigent strictness of identity formation that evolved out of the colonial situation led him to suggest, in his early plays and prose, a philosophy that presupposed the existence of a *range* of acceptable lifestyles and moral choices. By calling into question the attainability and desirability of a uniform conception of identity, including and especially that of Irishness, moreover, Yeats anticipated current theoretical discussions about the possibilities and limitations of variously defined notions of hybridity and authenticity within Irish Studies.[2] In this way, and to paraphrase Edward Said, Yeats can be credited with having provided an early historical alternative to the "authenticist" impasse.[3]

This is not to say that Yeats discredited the possibility of certain, particularly class-based notions of Irish authenticity, as evinced by his faith in the peasant and the aristocrat to help lead Ireland to new spiritual and artistic heights. However, alongside of and beyond that faith emerged another belief, Yeats's fight to free Ireland, specifically, and the Western world, more generally, from what he saw as their enslavement to socially-enforced stereotypes. As products of the bourgeois public sphere which, as Jürgen Habermas explains, has been engaged since the eighteenth century in the "political task of . . . the regulation of civil society" (52), these narrow (and gendered) constructions of race emerged as powerful implements of control. Using the tools of science, psychology, and reason to force individuals into standardized groups, with themselves as model for the mean and median, the dominant middle classes reinvented the traditions of patriarchy and English cultural superiority, thereby devising a regulatory process reflective of their own social wants and needs. With counter-cultural fervor typical of the author in his early years, Yeats advanced a reparative strategy meant to de-regulate: to loosen the social compulsion toward cultural conformity.

Yeats's attempts to motivate a heterogeneous culture in which individuals would not be judged predominantly by their compliance with social standards might locate him in the "Cultural Traditions Group" of literary and cultural theorists defined by Richard Kirkland in "Questioning the Frame: Hybridity, Ireland and the Institution." In this critical reassessment of trends in postcolonial theory, Kirkland's investigation of the uses and abuses of the notion of hybridity in contemporary Irish critical discourse calls attention, as did Yeats a century earlier, to the problematic because limiting nature of the concept. The problem occurs when initially boundary-breaking notions such as that of cultural diversity coalesce with the institution they were meant to oppose, thus becoming, as Kirkland puts it, "symbol[s] of monolithic cultural formation denying the possibility of historical method" (211). More specifically, Kirkland points to Luke Gibbons's and Declan Kiberd's identification of the "recognition of hybridity" with "the final stage of a teleological narrative yet to be fulfilled" as one such instance of insurgence become "a monument to its own permanence" (211). He continues, "it is of no surprise that celebration is seen as the natural response: the fallen present, gripped by essentialism and scarred by partition, will eventually pass away and hybridity will be the defining character of a new structure of feeling" (223). The teleological substance of this belief is partly true for Yeats, in that his theory of the mask, as I explain in chapter two, has as its goal the attainment of Unity of Being, the creation of which occurs through the process of facing and incorporating into one's personality a series of opposites.

If we look more specifically into Yeats's cultural theories and practices around the turn of the century, however, we find that his views also have much in common with those of Kirkland, who finds fault with the celebratory treatment of an "awareness of the hybrid, the heterogeneous and the anomalous." For Kirkland, the problem lies not only in the theory's teleological leanings but in what he sees as its inherent ensnarement in and reinforcement of the "Orange/Green binarism by which Irish identity has been structured" (225–26). Instead, he suggests, awareness of these blind spots should provoke "a considered process of rereading to assess just how far the frames of representation themselves need to be re-evaluated" (226). Where does Yeats fall along this continuum? If we focus on his proto-cultural theory—specifically, in this case, his understanding of the effect that a few key players in education and publishing had on the battle over Irish self-definition during the 1890s—we find that Yeats's celebratory awareness of heterogeneity is not entirely dependent upon the Orange/Green binarism of Irish identity. Rather, the cultural theory Yeats elaborates around the turn of the century proffers an early call to reassess the bourgeois, materialistic, colonial frames of representation within which the binarisms find their genesis.

Well aware that, until the mid-1800s, "[i]t had not paid to praise things Irish, or write on Irish subjects" (*UPI* 88), Yeats began early in his career to advance the interests of Irish nationalism, not only in his own prose, poetry, and drama, but also by encouraging others to publish works on Irish subjects. For instance, under Yeats's influence, the *Bookman* printed numerous "notices of Irish books, Irish literary gossip, and profiles of Irish literary personalities" (*UPI* 32). His promotion of Irish art and the Irish voice was not, however, unqualified, for he had very specific ideas about what would and would not lead his country into a new and better existence. Encouraged by the Celtic Renaissance transpiring around him, Yeats deplored the many influential individuals who might, if they chose, help to encourage the writing, publication, and reading of Irish literature both at home and abroad—but who, in the end, were either uninterested in or overtly hostile toward the Irish arts. An especial target of Yeats's contempt was Yeats's former friend, Edward Dowden, Trinity College Professor of English who, in Yeats's opinion, embodied the indifference to, even hostility toward nationalist goals displayed by the leading Anglo-Irish College.[4] There can be little wonder that Yeats increasingly found Dowden's attitudes irksome when we hear what the Trinity professor had to say about the Irish. For instance, in an 1895 article for the *Dublin Daily Express*, Dowden maligns Irish writers with the naïve and imperious comment that "'there was no prejudice against Irishmen in England when they proved themselves worthy of being received'" (*UPI* 346)—a statement that exposes Dowden's West Briton taste for English literature.

It is only fair, at this point, to qualify Yeats's stated dislike for Dowden's academic politics by pointing out that, with one major and significant exception, the two men had similar literary tastes. Yeats's letters remind us that on several occasions Dowden publicly and privately recommended Yeats's work. Dowden particularly liked "The Wanderings of Oisin" and quoted from *John Sherman* in the November 1891 issue of *The Fortnightly Review* (*CLI* 129, 268). Moreover, Dowden played a role, along with Maud Gonne, in influencing Yeats to write the "poetic drama with a view to the stage" that became *The Countess Cathleen* (*CLI* 138). And Yeats returned the compliment of the attention Dowden paid to his writing career, as we know from a May 1901 letter to Lady Gregory in which Yeats praises Dowden as the best Shakespearean critic of the age (*CLII* 70).

In addition, both Dowden and Yeats regarded with disfavor the poetry of Thomas Davis, which Dowden, John P. Frayne tells us, considered "not of the first, second, or perhaps even third rank" (*UPI* 346). However, Yeats never conceded to Dowden's stance on Irish poetry as a whole, the "typical defects" of which Dowden described as an "'undue tendency to rhetoric . . . sentimentality, . . . and deficiency of technique'" (qtd. in *UPI* 346). Yeats was entirely more open to Irish poetry's future possibilities, even if he did not always find its past achievements acceptable. And in his response to Dowden's letter in the *Dublin Daily Express*, Yeats counters Dowden on two important points. First, he argues vehemently against Dowden's accusation that he had encouraged people "'to boycott English literature.'" This defensive stance speaks to Yeats's inclusivity, in that he insists on clarifying the fact that his support of Irish literature does not come at the expense of his support of English literature. Second, Yeats finds fault with Dowden's argument that a national Irish literature must find its sources in "Celtic legends" and "Celtic people," must "have the basis and inspiration of race and racial tradition," and must be "Catholic" in religious sentiment. Specifically, he thwarts Dowden's essentialist assessments of literature and race with the "obvious correction" that "Ireland is not wholly Celtic any more than England is wholly Protestant" (*UPI* 352).

Declan Kiberd's correspondent illustration of Dowden's exclusionary practices leads him to describe the Professor in terms that, interestingly, remind us of Yeats's doctrine of the mask:

> The provincial's inability to imagine a second self, to play instinctively before a mirror, to formulate an awareness of how he must appear to others, was a failure of the republican imagination, for which *style* was always a conscious relation between a past and a putative self. Edward Dowden, the Professor of English at Trinity College Dublin, was just such a provincial, unable to shape a metropolitan but none the less Irish style, for he employed on himself the received categories of English thought. (121)

Kiberd describes Dowden as a man who, in Yeatsian terms, is afraid to face his mask. Mired in a self-definition built of "received categories of English thought," Dowden will not "play instinctively" before the "mirror" of his Irish "second self" and, therefore, remains limited in perspective. That is, in refusing to face his opposite, he can neither escape binarism nor emerge as a unified, or in contemporary critical terms, syncretistically hybridized, being. That is, he is not able to synthesize elements from English and Irish (literary) cultures. Dowden's support of hierarchical dualisms such as English-versus-Irish literature thus appear static, even sterile. Moreover, his disapproval of endeavors that sought to incorporate the voice of the Irish other into the Trinity curriculum shows his support of a society in which, to paraphrase Yeats, consciousness is identified with scientific, rational knowledge and not with conflict, as it is in the doctrine of the mask.

Nor did the institution of Trinity College escape the condemnation of Yeats, who criticized the school for more than mere indifference to nationalist goals. Yeats perceived in its very essence as an establishment of higher education—or, more specifically, in its pedantic adherence to strict pedagogical and scholarly methodology—that Trinity College was less a cultivator of young, bright minds than it was an impediment to their growth.[5] He felt so strongly about this issue that he penned an article in 1892 for *United Ireland*, "Dublin Scholasticism and Trinity College," in which he wrote: "In England every clever boy had his hobby—literature, entomology, or what not. In Ireland every energy of the kind was discouraged and trampled upon, for the shadow of scholasticism was over all and the great god of examinations ruled supreme" (*UPI* 232–33). However, not only does he castigate the university for setting the precedent whereby the product of obedient, exam-mastering student is valued over the process of learning itself. In the following political analogy, Yeats also reveals his fear of the far-reaching consequences of the refusal, on the part of the ranking institute of higher education, to recognize the accomplishment and potential of Irish literature, nationalist and otherwise: "As Dublin Castle with the help of the police keeps Ireland for England, so Trinity College, in abject fear of the National enthusiasm which is at her gates, has shut itself off from every kind of ardour, from every kind of fiery and exultant life" (*UPI* 233). It was, no doubt, rhetoric of this sort that led Declan Kiberd to conclude: "Yeats believed passionately in education, which valued a child for its intrinsic sake, and he despised mere schooling, which concerned itself more with producing the kind of adult the child must eventually become" (111). And the sort of adult Trinity apparently hoped to create was just the mindlessly obedient sort Yeats regarded with unguarded contempt. He describes the type in *Explorations*: "Life, which in its essence is always surprising, always taking some new shape, always individualising, is nothing to [the social institutions that attempt] to move men in squads, to keep them in uniform, with their faces to the right enemy, and enough hate in their hearts to make the muskets go off" (120).[6]

The infamous battle over control of the New Irish Library series provides another revealing example of Yeats's discriminating taste, in this case regarding the forms employed by proponents of the Irish nationalist cause. Like Dowden, Yeats was unwilling to accept all genres—propaganda, for instance—as literature. Unlike Dowden, he had high hopes for the future of Irish literature. One of the earliest attempts to launch this future, to which Yeats lent his support, was the New Irish Library. In 1892, Yeats and T. W. Rolleston, in conjunction with the Irish Literary Society, decided to publish a new, inexpensive book series focusing on Irish subjects, to be edited by T. Fisher Unwin. When it came to his attention that Sir Charles Gavan Duffy, and not he, would have chief editorial control of the series, Yeats mourned the defeat of the project on political and artistic grounds before its first volume even appeared. For Duffy, co-founder with Thomas Davis of the Young Ireland publication, the *Nation*, represented the "old 'New Ireland'" (Alldritt 117) and therefore the "culturally separatist, essentially Anglo-phobic, and increasingly sectarian" sort of nationalism Yeats found suspect (Foster, *Modern Ireland* 313). Yeats's fears came to fruition when the series launched publications of the Davis and Moore school of verse he so despised, as well as their prose counterparts: In the words of Roy Foster, Yeats had been "tarred with the Fenian brush" (*W. B. Yeats* 122). In a *Bookman* review (of which he wrote several, not only to reveal the inadequacies of the works as literature, but for revenge purposes as well), Yeats provides an example of the type of verse printed in the New Irish Library series:

"Come, Liberty, come! We are ripe for thy coming;
Come, freshen the hearts where thy rival has trod;
Come, richest and rarest! Come, purest and fairest!
Come, *daughter of science*! Come, gift of the god!"

(qtd. in *UPI* 41, emphasis added)

Yeats felt assaulted by such poetry on many levels: in its repetitive diction and sing-song rhythm, its blatant propagandism, its sentimental treatment of Liberty, and, not least for Yeats, its equation of Liberty with science, one of the fathers of rationalistic progressivism, as savior. As I explain in chapter two, Yeats recognized scientific methodology's faith in categorization as one of the most powerful of nineteenth-century impetuses for the general social standardization that necessitated capitulation to the norm. Thus Yeats found fault with any prose or literature that attempted to canonize scientific and rationalist ways of thinking. Similarly, Yeats disagreed with the New Irish Library's advocacy of prose narrowly focused on political aims, such as a series of popular histories that, as Roy Foster explains, "stressed the romance of violent resistance to English oppression" (*Modern Ireland* 312) and, therefore, sent a message that would only serve to reinforce the English-versus-Irish dichotomy.

In defense of his own position, Yeats attempted to build a public appreciation of his personal dissatisfaction with the New Irish Library. His many reviews and editorial letters on the subject portrayed the series as a dangerous influence on the Irish. For example, in an 1894 letter in *United Ireland*, he contends: "Believing, as I do, that literature is almost the most profound influence that ever comes into a nation, I recognize with deep regret, and not a little anger, that the 'New Irish Library' is so far the most serious difficulty in the way of our movement" (*UPI* 340). Had Yeats achieved the editorship of the series, he would have, he maintains in the same letter, "require[d] books by competent men of letters upon subjects of living national interest, romances by writers of acknowledged power, anthologies selected from men like De Vere, and Allingham, and Fergusson [sic], and impartial picturesque lives of Emmet, Wolfe Tone, Mitchel, and perhaps O'Connell" (340). Here Yeats displays that he preferred impartiality and a focused attention to literary excellence—vague and biased as his definition of excellence may be—to flag-waving in any and every form.

Yeats's scathing critiques of the New Irish Library series and of Trinity College emerge, in part, from his belief that literature should encourage individualism and not, as it often did in the Victorian era, foster capitulation to the normative model. Yet all around him—in the New Irish Library series, on Irish, English, and American stages, and even in the halls of Ireland's leading university—the Irish man and woman were cast as types. Of course, the stage Irishman stereotype differs from its nationalist counterpart in character as well as in intent. The cheerful, foolish drunkard appeared in popular theater and prose as a figure of ridicule. To counteract the negative stereotype, nationalist writers fashioned the fearless, weapon-wielding, victim-no-more icon as "authentic" Irish hero. The two disparate depictions of the Irish nevertheless produced the same result: that is, both the anti-Irish and pro-Irish figures (to simplify the political interpretation of these figures for the moment) became stereotypes. Yeats believed that Trinity College aimed to typify the Irish along the comparably stereotypical lines of the English bourgeois ideal: self-controlled and good at external measurements of accomplishment like examinations, but entirely void of "ardour" and "life."

Yeats, however, discerned something that the propagandistic nationalists and Trinity College dons, in their perception of these Irish types as polar opposites, did not. Specifically, he recognized the apparent opposites as members of the selfsame order: the type. He argues specifically against stereotyping in all forms in the following passage: "A nation is injured by the picking out of a single type and setting that into print or upon the stage as a type of the whole nation. Ireland suffered for a century from that single whiskey-drinking, humorous type which seemed for a time the accepted type of all" (*Explorations* 191). Here Yeats might appear to side with the nationalists who believed the Irish should be represented as heroes and champions, brave and powerful and willing to fight for liberty from the shackles of English colonialism. However, this reading is challenged by Yeats's further argument that imaginative writers—that is, for Yeats, good writers—"will never impose a general type on the public mind, for genius differs from the newspapers in this, that the greater and more confident it is, the more is its delight in varieties and species" (*Explorations* 191).[7] Therefore, although Yeats, too, believed in "fill[ing] the popular imagination again with saints and heroes" (*Explorations* 79), in his early writings, he did not pursue the narrow-mindedness or jingoism of works that attempted to force individuals into one "general type," whatever that type might be.

Most importantly, Yeats's goals of reviving ancient Irish heroes and saints and of creating new ones provided the key component in his literary struggle to impress upon Ireland the value of diversification. But first he needed to make a break from conceptions of Ireland fostered under the rule of British colonialism and rationalist progressivism, which seemed to lock Ireland indefinitely into the role of lesser partner in the binary set of relationships in which England stood for all that is civilized and masculine, and Ireland represented savageness and/or effeminacy. As we see in the following passage from "The Celtic Element in Literature," Yeats began to define his anti-rationalist project early in his career. Analyzing the reasons behind the resurgent interest in Irish legends, he suggests that, along with "the symbolical movement" it "is certainly the only movement that is saying new things. The arts, by brooding upon their own intensity have become religious, and are seeking, as I think Verhaeren has said, to create a sacred book" (*EI* 187). The part of Yeats's understanding of Irish legends that assigns them specifically "Irish" entities—that is, as evincing the purity and strength of the Irish, as opposed to another, race—allies him with the ultimately limited position of reactionary traditionalism, in which, as Patrick Hogan explains, there is a "rigidification of indigenous tradition" (11). However, when viewed as part of a larger literary scheme including a more personal yet also universal symbolism, the primary value of the legends lies in their essential spirituality and a-materialism, neither of which Yeats believed to be solely Irish traits.

For evidence of this, we can look to the heterogeneous nature of Yeats's spiritual philosophies, particularly the doctrine of the mask and his theory of Unity of Being. Yeats worked within a binaristic system in which he hoped to balance materialism with spirituality and realism with symbolism. His reaction is a reaction *against* the establishment, specifically against rationalism and materialism. Yet his answer, in the form of spirituality and symbolism, allows for an escape from the binaristic system in which all possible alternatives are immobilized by rationalism and materialism, which, by virtue of their very nature, "would drill everyone into the same posture." As Yeats argues for Unity of Being, in which each person and nation progresses on an individual path toward a more heterogeneous personality, symbolists believe that unique, personal emotional responses can be conveyed to the public via symbols, thus fostering a cross-breeding of personal symbols within and between communities. Even more specifically, from Blake, Yeats understood symbolism as "a natural language by which the soul when entranced, or even in ordinary sleep, communes with God and with angels" (*EI* 368). Thus, the spiritual and symbolist systems that Yeats advocates encourage the enhancement of the individual along a unique, not homogeneous or typified, path. Both systems, furthermore, require the expression, and spiritual and aesthetic absorption, of diverse insights into self, spirit, and world.

But before Ireland could escape the "drill," Yeats knew its citizens would have to change their existing habits and prejudices. Although Yeats "would have Ireland re-create the ancient arts, the arts as they were understood in Judaea, in India, in Scandinavia, in Greece and Rome, in every ancient land" (*EI* 206), he perceived the difficulty of convincing a materialistic and realism-loving public to appreciate the arts as a spiritual entity. In 1901, the year Yeats published the essay in which this famous artist-as-priest proclamation appeared, Yeats had already experienced firsthand, through reviews of his plays, the public's negative reaction to the ousting of realism for more symbolic modes of communication.[8] Therefore, he understood that if Ireland were to get (or return) to the place when such legends "moved a whole people," he somehow would have to get beyond the historic moment in which he lived, when only "a few people who have grown up in a leisured class and made this understanding their business" studied the ancient arts (*EI* 206). Significantly, Yeats was convinced that this set of circumstances had much to do with the influence of the English on the Irish. Many an Irish man and woman, he maintained, had come to think like "[a]n Englishman, with his belief in progress, with his instinctive preference for the cosmopolitan literature of the last century," and such individuals, he knew, would and did define the ancient arts as "parochial" (*EI* 206). That is, if confidence in realism and materialism had replaced Ireland's faith in spiritual values and ancient art, as Yeats believed it had, this clearly could be explained, here in Timothy Webb's words, as the "power of the center express[ing] itself in insidious ways" (509).

In addition to his "dislike, his hatred even, of British materialism" (Webb 510), Yeats perceived the English as particularly narrow-minded, even xenophobic. Much of this feeling originated in the years of his youth and young adulthood; or, as Webb puts it, they "were proved upon the pulse or, if you prefer, existentially experienced" (512). Yeats received early training in anti-English bias from his parents. Brown points to his mother's distaste for the English (23), and Webb similarly references his parents' "propagation of racial stereotypes" (511). The young poet's growing recognition of his own status as a (racial or national and aesthetic) other played an especially important role in feeding this nascent bias.[9] Brown writes, for instance, that after Yeats moved with his family to London, his "developing sense of his own distinctiveness as an Irish son of an artist overcame him and anti-Englishness began to coalesce, indeed, into a distinct sense of the individual and his world" (23). Thus, although he lived *as an Irishman* for more than half of his life in London, he was not "one of those political or intellectual refugees, . . . the dislocated fathers of modernism," like T. S. Eliot or Joseph Conrad, who found "much to admire in the ancient stabilities, the historical resonances of English life" (Webb 525). Instead, as Brown explains, Yeats found Victorian London characterized by a "reactive fear" of the other that resulted, in many corners, in a cry for "the forced removal of unwanted people" (23). Such an atmosphere could only reinforce what Webb calls Yeats's "sense of alienation" (516). As an Anglo-Irishman, an Irishman living in London, and a writer charting new aesthetic territory in his attempt to establish new definitions of Irishness as an antidote to the political, spiritual, and psychological damage done to the Irish by English colonialism, Yeats could not help but understand the English-Irish relationship in an "antithetical context" (Webb 519).[10]

It was in this cultural context that Yeats formulated a metaphor of spiritual illness in which, as he saw it, the English idealization of aesthetic and social uniformity infected his fellow Irish citizens with the affiliated "belief in progress." He expresses his resentment about this condition in the "First Principles" essay in *Samhain* of 1908: "English provincialism shouts through the lips of Irish patriots who have no knowledge of other countries to give them a standard of comparison, and they, with the confidence of all who speak the opinions of others, labour to thwart everybody who would dig a well for Irish water to bubble in" (*Explorations* 232–33). The cure for the illness lay in the Irish Revivalists' well digging, a metaphorical taking of the waters, the origin of which Yeats credits to Samuel Ferguson's revision of the Irish mythic cycle decades before. Ferguson, Yeats avows, had "worn the pathway" so that "many others [could] follow, and bring thence living waters for the healing of our nation, helping us to live the larger life of the Spirit, and lifting our soul away from their selfish joys and sorrows to be the companions of those who lived greatly among the woods and hills when the world was young" (*UPI* 82).[11] As with the well imagery above,[12] Yeats again utilizes a water metaphor here, in this case to credit Irish literature as having the potential to perform the baptismal function of healing the wounds inflicted by English materialism and provincialism, via colonialism. Ferguson and the Irish Revivalists, Yeats implies, might yet save the Irish from becoming the sort of Englishmen he despised.

But it wasn't that he aimed to save the Irish from inheriting Englishness in and of itself so much as the English-influenced but more generally bourgeois habit of capitulation to the regularizing impulsion outlined by Habermas. As Foucault reminds us, both biology and economics encouraged nineteenth-century Western culture to view individuals and the world according to "average *norms*" and to act according to "a body of *rules*" (*The Order of Things* 357). Eric Hobsbawm explains, furthermore, that these norms and rules commonly attain during times "when a rapid transformation of society weakens and destroys the social patterns for which 'old' traditions and their institutional carriers and promulgators no longer prove sufficiently adaptable and flexible, or are otherwise eliminated" (4–5) and are frequently used for "establishing or legitimizing institutions, status or relations of authority" (9). In the Victorian era, the hierarchies of gender, race, and class that judged individuals by their relative adherence to strict codes of, for instance, manliness and Englishness, were strengthened by the ideological justification, formalization, and ritualization (Hobsbawm 3–4) of traditions "invented" for the purposes of retaining order and power in a world in which rationalism, materialism, and Christianity presided under the rule of British imperialism. Although, as I have discussed elsewhere, Yeats disliked the aforementioned institutional discourses for several reasons, one of the most important is their insistence on cultural homogeneity.

Yeats aimed to aid in the diversification of his country and his era by reinstating a bardic culture. Powerful spiritual and social as well as literary role models, ancient bards were "the most powerful influence in the land, and all manner of superstitious reverence environed them round." For bards and those who respected them, a "poem and an incantation were almost the same" (*UPI* 163–64). Yeats continues in this passage to explain the social and spiritual significance of the bard in Irish history, one he hoped his contemporaries would also ascertain—although, as I have shown in my discussion of *The King's Threshold*, his expectations for success were low. In this lengthy but useful excerpt from "Bardic Ireland," Yeats provides an allegorical depiction of the problems of, and a potential solution for, his times:

> Th[e] power of the bards was responsible, it may be, for one curious thing in ancient Celtic history: its self-consciousness. The warriors were not simply warriors, the kings simply kings, the smiths simply smiths: they all seem striving to bring something out of the world of thoughts into the world of deeds—a something that always eluded them. When the Fenian militia were established in the second century they were not mere defenders of coast-line or quellers of popular tumult. They wanted to revive the kind of life lived in old days when the Chiefs of the Red Branch gathered round Cuchulin [*sic*]. They found themselves in an age when men began to love rich draperies and well-wrought swords, to exult in dominion and the lordship of many flocks. They resolved to

live away from these things in the forest, cooking their food by burying it under a fire; and passing such laws as that none of their order should take a dowry with his wife, but marry her for love alone. Nor would they have among them any man who did not understand all the several kinds of poetry. (*UPI* 164)

Luke Gibbons's use of the term "allegory" in its "Irish context" is serviceable here (20). For, in this passage, Yeats would have allegory act as "a figural practice that infiltrates everyday experience, giving rise to the aesthetics of the actual" (20). In other words, attempting to *live* the allegory in both its actual and figural aspects, Yeats effectively erases the line between the symbolic and the real—a line, Gibbons notes, that traditionally has been seen as emptying allegory of its own materiality (20). By fusing allegory with actuality, Yeats posits an invented tradition of his own.

Like the Fenians of old, Yeats and his compatriots "found themselves in an age," the materialistic and colonial heyday of Victoria, "when men began to love rich draperies and well-wrought swords, to exult in dominion and the lordship of many flocks." Yeats, however, chose not to "live away from these things" but to do battle with them via literary and dramatic production. In fact, the battle—and the antithetical relationship (between England and Ireland, middle class values and Yeats's preferred values)—which inspires it is central to Yeats's line of progress. With this agenda, in Christopher T. Malone's words, Yeats "moves toward a form of cultural production that could engage and transform the public sphere, a form that depends on the antithetical fashioning of audience and poet in dialectical relationship with one another" (260). Malone goes so far as to credit Yeats's theory of the mask as "extend[ing] from the desire to recreate for himself the bardic role by imagining an autonomous imaginative space for persistent interrogation of self, a space that will in turn antithetically shape his audience" (260). More specifically, in the role of bard, Yeats created fictional worlds in which, as we have seen, his heroes, male and female both, refuse to capitulate to materialism and moralism and whose values, some of which are comparable to those of the Fenians, nonetheless consist of a broader range of acceptance than those typical of his historical contemporaries, which depend on socially-enforced type. From this perspective, the Yeatsian plan for progress depends on the combination of imagination and heterogeneity, not rationalism and moralism. Yeats thus found in his bardic capabilities a vehicle for philosophical inspiration. We see this when, against the common point of dissension toward Celtic literature that asks, "if it has come from so far off, what good can it do us moderns, with our complex life?", Yeats answers, "Assuredly it will not help you to make a fortune, or even live respectably that little life of yours. Great poetry does not teach us anything—it changes us" (*UPI* 84).

Yet even amongst fellow proponents of Celtic literature, the precise form the change would take was a matter of great importance to Yeats. The revivalist impulse, Yeats argued, too easily could be made to reinforce the very values of rationalism and moralism he hoped it would eradicate. For example, in his 1897 review of Charles Gavan Duffy's *Young Ireland*, a New Irish Library book, Yeats purports:

> The "Young Irelanders" . . . were too preoccupied with public conduct to attend to the persuasions of their own temperaments, and all good literature is made out of temperament. To be preoccupied with public conduct is to be preoccupied with the ideas and emotions which the average man understands or can be made to understand, and out of the ideas and emotions of the average man you can make no better thing than good rhetoric. (*UPII* 34)

It is tempting to dismiss this whole passage because of Yeats's use of the term "average," which makes manifest a certain amount of intellectual snobbery and classism. However, if we don't (as it were) throw the baby out with the bathwater, the passage provides an insightful example of Yeats's keen awareness of the problematic tendency for people concerned with "public conduct" or social mores to revert to the standard or obvious or stereotypical rather than attempt to move above and beyond them. The problem, as Yeats understood it, lay in the power invested in an institutionalized group of individuals by both the individual group itself and by society in general. Habermas explains one associated practice that, by Yeats's time, was well established.

> Wherever the public established itself institutionally as a stable group of discussants, it did not equate itself with *the* public but at most claimed to act as its mouthpiece, in its name, perhaps even as its educator—the new form of bourgeois representation. The public . . . was conscious of being part of a larger public. Potentially it was always also a publicist body, as its discussions did not need to remain internal to it but could be directed at the outside world. (37)

Yeats specifically saw that the Young Irelanders' preoccupation with public conduct prevented them from providing an alternative to the literary and political norm. Wilde similarly remarks about "Public Opinion" that, "bad and well-meaning as it is when it tries to control action, [it] is infamous and evil meaning when it tries to control Thought or Art" ("Soul" 34).

And of the school of realist folk-tale revivalists concerned with the accurate recording of the "facts" but not with atmosphere, tone, symbolism, or the other literary choices that Yeats felt did not limit the story to an historical evaluation of truth but rather enhanced it with a number of potentially revealing facets, Yeats writes:

> The man of science is too often a person who has exchanged his soul for a formula; and when he captures a folk-tale, nothing remains with him for all his trouble but a wretched lifeless thing with the down rubbed off and a pin thrust through its once all-living body. I object to the "honest folk-lorist" not because his versions are accurate, but because they are inaccurate, or rather incomplete. (*UPI* 174)

Whereas the Young Irelanders saw mythic revival as a mode of propaganda, and men of science looked for clues to the social and political history of Ireland among the tales of Ireland's mythic past, Yeats perceived in folklore the opportunity to recall the Irish to their pre-colonial roots—that is, before (English, bourgeois-identified) progress. C. L. Innes describes this type of anti-colonial activity in "Modernism, Ireland and Empire: Yeats, Joyce and their Implied Audiences":

> [The] emphasis on biographical and local detail serves not only as a means of asserting the authority of local readings of . . . texts and reversing the previous relationship between definer and defined, but such details allow Yeats . . . to create a different foundation from which to rebuild and reinvent a community outside of the categories imposed by the English colonizers. (148)

Yet Yeats's plan was not solely racial or nationalist in essence. As we have seen, for instance, his primary goal did not parallel that of the Young Irelanders, whom Roy Foster depicts as "attacking 'sullen Saxonism' and glorifying the racial virtues of the Celt" (*Modern Ireland* 313). However, we cannot ignore the fact that, at various points in his career, Yeats advocated the racial superiority of the Irish—and did so on the same scientistic grounds that he despised in English thought and imperialist political action. By doing so, Yeats opened himself up to the same criticism he directed at the invented British colonial tradition whereby the natives were semiotically barbarized and infantilized. Richard Rorty criticizes this trend in *Truth and Progress* when he writes that the

> exaltation of the non-Western and the oppressed seems to me just as dubious as the Western imperialists' assurance that all other forms of life are "childish" in comparison with that of modern Europe. The latter assurance depends on the idea that one's own power to suppress other forms of life is an indication of the value of one's own form. The former exaltation depends on a bad inference from the premise that what makes cultures valuable has nothing to do with power, to the conclusion that powerlessness, like poverty, is an index of worth, and indeed of something auratic, something like holiness. (190)

Yeats partakes most obviously in the Romantic championing of the glory of the Irish peasant early in his career, especially in *Crossways* (1889) and *The Rose* (1893), but this trend eventually loses out to his exaltation of other forms of socially legitimate power. Yeats's use, as I have shown, of Irish sagas as allegorical, sociopolitical mechanisms represents one of his most powerful attempts to build an Ireland empowered not only culturally but socially, politically, and economically as well. Past literary critical studies of Yeats have focused on his Revivalist attempt to authenticate Irishness and, therefore, frequently on the racist origins of his actions—which, as Marjorie Howes has rightly pointed out often puts Yeats in league with his perceived oppressors.[13] This focus shows itself to be limited, however, in its undervaluation of Yeats's attempts, even as he capitulated to some of the racist beliefs of his time, not to triumph over the English but to break the bonds—once and *for all*—of the rationalist and materialist definitions of progress that insist on conformity to type.

Yeats's version of progress, then, more closely resembles those of late twentieth-century philosopher-critics who continue to explore the problem of identity and the related issues of representation, authenticity, and hybridity. Beginning with a concern close to his heart, Irish identity, Yeats not only conceived of a world in which the Irish would be defined in more varying terms than not-English; by extension, he also aspired to a world that embraced the existence of "individual men and women and living virtues differing as one star differeth from another in glory" (*Explorations* 119). Here Yeats, like Rorty, celebrates the "ability to see more and more differences among people as morally irrelevant" (11). Although, later in life, he briefly supported dangerously hierarchical doctrines of difference such as eugenics and, to a lesser extent, fascism, the Yeats of the 1890s and early 1900s was different. The Yeats of this era made it clear that he disliked the moralism inherent in scientific rationalism, which, especially in the Victorian era, confined individuals to narrow roles in the social and moral hierarchies of gender and race. Yeats would credit Rorty's faith in the form of rationalism that consists of "the ability not to be overly disconcerted by differences from oneself, not to respond aggressively to such differences. This goes along with a willingness to alter one's own habits" (186–87). Unlike the Victorian bourgeois faith in a rationalism in which the recognition of difference "establishes an evaluative hierarchy" (Rorty 186), Yeats's doctrine of the mask, with its recognition of difference fosters, like Rorty's preferred brand of rationalism, a path to social and individual progress.

And it is this validation of difference that places Yeats half in and half beyond Richard Kirkland's "Cultural Traditions Group." If Yeats were to celebrate heterogeneity as the ideal form of social progress solely because of its opposition to institutional homogeneity, in Kirkland's estimation, he would be said to have failed in his attempts to "move beyond the final claims of the institution [he] seeks to displace and discredit" (216). Yeats's assertions do originate with an oppositional stance: he proposes to replace English colonial definitions of gender and race with definitions that began in early contemplations about Irish identity. Yet we must also attend to the fact that, in these early plays, Yeats goes beyond this type of binarism in the following way, as described by Stephanie Bachorz:

> by recognising the difference instead of denying it, the postcolonial citizen (and especially migrants and minorities) will be able to achieve a "double vision". This means they can actually accept the multiplicity of history, knowledge, and so on, by the very nature of their own existence, being brought up or living in-between two versions of history, culture, and knowledge. (10)

In other words, Yeats's theories fit Stephanie Bachorz's revised definition of postcolonialism in the Irish context, which she outlines in an essay that uses Theodor W. Adorno's *Negative Dialectics* "as a means to reconsider hybridity in terms of a dialectical process rather than a more or less 'stable' concept." This, she argues, helps lead to "a 'revised' postcolonial theory for Ireland, a notion of postcolonialism which does not depend on the exclusion of the 'Other,' but at the same time can account for the socio-political reality which created postcoloniality in the first place" (7). Arising out of this socio-political reality, Yeats's espousal of syncretistic hybridity, with its concomitant exposure of the morally legislated social construction of the other, helped direct attention to the need for and potential benefits of re-evaluating the institutional framework out of which Yeats hoped, eventually, to escape.

"[N]ICE LITTLE PLAYWRIGHTS, MAKING PRETTY LITTLE PLAYS"

Yeats's avowal of syncretistic hybridity, however, initially did not appear to influence the public in any significant way, if we use critical reviews of his plays as evidence. Reactions to Yeats's early plays were not nearly as riotous those infamously engendered by J. M. Synge in 1907. However, the plays Yeats wrote in the late nineteenth and early twentieth century nevertheless achieved a certain notoriety of their own. What most provoked or, actually, puzzled the press was Yeats's insistence on utilizing new theatrical forms for which the critical language of realism and its still popular forerunner melodrama was ill equipped. Yet, as with Synge, the collective response to Yeats's plays also reflected the public's concern with and investment in the theatrical depiction of the Irish and thus attended to the plays' language, costume, set and plot details. Like the *Playboy* crowds, which had never before been faced with that particular brand of Ireland, the critics, uncomfortable with the presence of difference, expressed their discomposure with vicious responses. I believe this sociological reading of the critical response only partly explains the dominantly inflammatory, racist remarks of the critics (and especially of English critics) about plays such as *The Countess Cathleen, Cathleen ni Houlihan, The Land of Heart's Desire, The Pot of Broth, The Shadowy Waters,* and especially *Where There Is Nothing.* Another more political reason is suggested by Luke Gibbons.

In explaining the "apparent ease with which colonial discourse establishes its legitimacy" (95), Gibbons exposes the otherness of the Irish as particularly disconcerting for the English because, as he explains, "it is clear that a native population which happened to be white . . . threw into disarray some of the constitutive categories of colonial discourse" (96). In the case of his early plays, which Yeats envisioned as changing both literary and social history, the mechanisms by which he breaks down the boundaries of dramatic form and of strict gender and race categorization allow him to break yet a third boundary, which has been described by Edward Said, borrowing from Frantz Fanon, as the "transformation of social consciousness beyond national consciousness" (83).

"[N]ice little playwrights, making pretty little plays" 145

To begin with, it is true that Yeats, in his involvement in the Irish dramatic movement at the turn of the century, encouraged the creation of a "social consciousness" that appears to hold fast to its "national" boundaries. For instance, one of the most important goals of the dramatic arm of the Irish Literary Renaissance, Yeats felt, was its ability to evoke a communal response from the Irish people. Again, as he noted in 1901, he hoped his recreation of the "ancient arts" would "mov[e] a whole people" (*EI* 206). Even more specifically, Yeats aspired to turn what he perceived, though not unequivocally, as a crazed crowd of political nationalists into a community of cultural nationalists. As he explains in an early press announcement for the Irish Literary Theatre:[14]

> Victor Hugo has said that in the theatre the mob became a people, and, though this could be perfectly true only of ancient times when the theatre was a part of the ceremonial of religion, I have some hope that, if we have enough success to go on from year to year, we may help to bring a little ideal thought into the common thought of our times. (*UPII* 141)

Disclosing elitist feelings and fears about the middle and lower classes' preferred form of Irish nationalism, here Yeats nonetheless reveals a desire to overcome the separation that divides "ideal" and "common" thought by organizing the "mob" into a "people." Marjorie Howes's study of Yeats's simultaneous fascination with and repulsion by crowds led her to similar conclusions about his initial involvement in the literary theater movement, namely that: "The theoretical and practical structures of Yeats's early Irish theatre embody his conflicted engagement with the idea of national politics as mass politics and his attempts to come to terms with the (potentially) mass character of Irish nationalism in a productive way" (67).

But it is important to note, if somewhat paradoxically, that Yeats's interest in the making of an Irish people and an Irish art was not constructed on a purely nationalist platform. His contemporaries' preference for realistic, social reformist, and problem plays led Yeats to the conclusion that "[t]he arts have failed; fewer people are interested in them every generation. The mere business of living, of making money, of amusing oneself, occupies people more and more, and makes them less and less capable of the difficult art of appreciation" (*EI* 203). The problem of gathering people into a community, therefore, had as much to do with overcoming the more universal philosophical or social barrier of materialism as it did with specific issues of national and ethnic identity. Yeats's attempts to fashion a bardic culture were meant to address both problems: "We who care deeply about the arts," he argues, "find ourselves the priesthood of an almost forgotten faith, and we must, I think, if we would win the people again, take upon ourselves the method and fervour of a priesthood. . . . We must baptize as well as preach" (*EI* 203). The "faith" he describes here is not only that in Irish community but in a generally more spiritual, less materialistic world for all.

If Yeats's plan as a playwright, as he notes in the 1906 issue of *Samhain*, was to produce a community interested in the discovery of literary subjects and forms imbued with both Ireland's past and "the thoughts of his own age," and who yet are able to "press into the future" (*Explorations* 209), we might next look into just what it was that united the journalistic critical community into two distinct—and distinctly adversarial—camps. Although some critics responded favorably to Yeats's efforts to create for his audience "new subject[s]" and "new technique[s]" (*Explorations* 209) in what he termed "not a theatre but the theatre's anti-self" (*Explorations* 257), the majority of English, American, and Irish newspaper reviews were at best skeptical of, and at worst downright nasty about those efforts, with insults frequently directed at the playwright but, interestingly, more often at the Irish.

Most critics did not, like President of the St. Louis Society of Pedagogy, E. D. Luckey, eulogize Yeats as "engaged in a great cause" and in "noble work, so disinterested and unselfish" (6 Jan. 1904). But Yeats did earn the esteem of individuals who, like him, appeared to have tired of realism and melodrama. For instance, a 1906 performance of the peasant farce, *The Pot of Broth*, earned the praise of the *Manchester Guardian* reviewer, C.E.M., for the pared-down acting style that went on to make the Irish National Theatre Company famous (or, in some cases, infamous, as the generally disapproving reviews excerpted here reveal). He explains, "Their movements or their stillness acquire to your sense, a curious value; they seem slower, graver, more controlled, more significant. . . . [Y]ou see [the characters] . . . devulgarised and a little transfigured" (25 Apr. 1906). The *Evening Citizen* critic similarly applauds the Irish National Theatre Society's (INTS's) production of *Kathleen ni Houlihan* for breaking away from "traditional Irish drama of the Boucicault type" ("Irish Plays at the Kings" 5 Jun. 1906). These readings are in line with Yeats's attempts to "de-vulgarise" the common stage depiction of the Irish as bloodthirsty, cunning and wily, or daft and drunk.

Yet, more often than not, his choice to break from popular theatrical trends merely earned Yeats, the INTS, and the Abbey Theatre the criticism of audience and professional critics alike. Early, pre-production reviews of *The Land of Heart's Desire* foreshadowed the typical audience response to his early plays. The *Daily Chronicle*, for instance, suggests, "he would do well to give his verse more dramatic movement" (24 Apr. 1894). The *Bookman* critic similarly notes, "Whether it could ever be successfully put on the stage is doubtful, but certainly only under conditions which do not exist on our stage today. The very simplest of our actors has a tradition of theatricality which is alien to the perfect simplicity here" ([?] Jun. 1894). The *[Bradford?] Observer* repeats this sentiment: "No actor, in fact, could be as simple as this play demands" ([?] Jun. 1894).

Reviewers also remarked on the responses of their fellow audience members who, likewise, seemed to have little interest in dramatic innovation. For example,

"*[N]ice little playwrights, making pretty little plays*" 147

the *Boston Herald* reported in a production review of *Cathleen ni Houlihan*, *The Land of Heart's Desire*, and *The Hour-Glass* that Yeats's "themes are not difficult only, to most people they have no reality" ([?] Feb. 1905). In a 1905 article, Oliver St. John Gogarty appears to take the side of Yeatsian innovation when he derides the audience for their "incapacity . . . to understand anything which may demand from them new standards and faculties of appreciation." Like Oscar Wilde, Gogarty here disparages the "public dislike" of "novelty" which, Wilde ascertains, arises out of fear ("Soul" 31). However, Gogarty goes on to unwittingly represent himself as sympathetic to this audience when he calls Yeats's plays "inartistic" because they are not "dramatic" (4 Mar. 1905). And a few final examples of the response to the 1904 London Stage Society production of *Where There Is Nothing* reinforce the previous critic's reading of the audience as less than interested. According to the *Daily Mirror*, the audience was "bored"; according to the *Pall Mall Gazette*, the audience was "bored"; and the *Standard* records the same observation a bit more playfully: "An amusing feature throughout the afternoon was the attitude of the audience, who evidently did not in the very least know what to make of it all" (28 Jun. 1904).

The *Manchester Guardian*, having recorded a comparable response, goes on to explain the popular and critical disdain for Yeats's plays not only in terms of the audience's predilection for realism but in a way that also illuminates the social and moral biases of Yeats's reviewers. More specifically, the critic argues that *Where There Is Nothing* could never be "popular" because "the idea which animates the hero, Paul Ruttledge, is essentially destructive and anarchic, whereas the great public in so far as it is accessible to ideas at all necessarily demands ideas of a positive, practical, constructive order" (29 Jun. 1904). With these last few words, a prescription for the "order[liness]" of realism and the "positive," "constructive" moralism of social reformist theater, the critic provides an example of the very force Yeats hoped to counter with his plays.

The irony here is that it is not Yeats but his contemporary audience whom we see demand over and again that art should not progress but remain within the narrow limits of the dramatic and social conventions of the time. Critics frequently singled out Yeats as being too progressive. As one representative reviewer from the *Birmingham Daily Mail* puts it, "Mr. Yeats is perfectly right in his idealistic ideas of dramatic presentation, but they are a half century in advance of the means at his command. If he should awaken public interest in the drama of Ireland and establish a dramatic literature of practical possibilities" he must please the public. "Far better," he continues,

> to deck the stage out in the tawdriest tinsel and play national plays with all the tricks and the glitter of modern melodrama, so that the first fundamental thing be assured—the awakening of the public interest. Refinement would follow as a natural process of evolution and the higher drama reached at last. ("Irish Drama in Birmingham" 29 May 1907)

For all this critic's optimism regarding the future of Irish nationalist theater, his aversion to change might be seen to represent the attitude typical of the colonialist viewing a ritual-theater performance by the colonized. As Helen Gilbert and Joanne Tompkins explain, the colonizer's criticism of ritualistic theater is "largely circumscribed by western critics' inability to comprehend—or, even in some cases, to be *willing* to comprehend—different sets of assumptions" (53). These alternative assumptions become manifest when the colonized insert traditional performance elements into contemporary plays, which make them able to "[stretch] colonial definitions of theatre to assert the validity (and the vitality) of other modes of representation" (54). In Yeats's case, traditional Irish subjects such as myth and peasant lore, increasingly combined with ritualized forms borrowed from other ancient cultures such as Greek verse drama and the Japanese Noh plays, not only stretch (Victorian bourgeois) English definitions of good/proper theater but assert the validity of his innovative, and also specifically (if not exclusively) Irish, modes of representation. Mainstream English critics' denial of the validity of these forms lies, at least in part, in the (colonizing) public's particular unwillingness or fear, at the turn of the century, to accept from the Irish what they essentially, though perhaps unconsciously, saw as an unauthorized trajectory of progress. From this perspective, it seems that the negative responses were meant to put the upstart Irish Yeats back into his place.

Gender bias, as applied in its racist form to the Irish via Arnold and Renan, was one of the major prejudices to infect the critical faculties of Yeats's reviewers. A 1906 debate that took place in response to an address Yeats made at the Abbey provides the typical use of such bias. After infantilizing the Irish dramatic movement with the complaint that "the spirit of Celtic tragedy need not be reduced to . . . the feeble and plaintive whining of a baby play," an unnamed *Morning Leader* critic challenges Yeats to find in all drama "a truer specimen of simple manhood, true nobility, staunch faith, or playful fancy than" the Stage Irish figures of the nineteenth century. Continuing with metaphors of masculinity, the critic argues, "till [Yeats] dominates more effectually; till he gives us plays fit to challenge comparison, long enough and strong enough to fight their way the world around," he and his cohorts will be stuck in the role of "nice little playwrights, making pretty little plays for good little amateurs" ("Mr. Yeats' Attack" [?] Jun. 1906). This rather defensive critic has clearly taken the gendered hierarchy of power, as depicted by the Victorians, to heart. His conviction that the current crop of Irish plays do not fulfill his dramatic ideal of creating characters who are "tru[e] specimens of simple manhood" reinforces the Anglocentric view of the Irish as feminine and thereby closes the door on the possibility of alternative views of gender and, more importantly, of the Irish.

When it came to his own dramatic theories, Yeats also did not escape the gendered essentialism of colonial discourse. For instance, in a 1901 essay, he discloses his hopes that the Irish dramatic movement will "give Ireland a hardy and shapely national character" (*Explorations* 75). By using the term "hardy," Yeats admits that he wants Ireland to be more masculine and, therefore, as hegemonic values went, more like England. In this sense, Yeats capitulates to the gendered, colonial shaping of English and Irish character. However, what is more important is that Yeats's plays, including *Where There Is Nothing*, *The Land of Heart's Desire*, and *On Baile's Strand*, are thematically denigratory of what Ashis Nandy designates as the English colonial values of materialism, control, and productivity. Thus, they represent Yeats's attempts to break the cycle of Irish inheritance of these values.

Even stronger than their predilection for gendered judgments, however, was the critics' apparent anxiety about the Irish Literary Renaissance's cultural nationalism, as seen in the collective demand that plays conform to what we now see as parochial (read: intolerant, not to mention colonial) definitions of morality, gender, and race. Examples of this contempt range from what Albert Memmi has called the "charitable racism" of the "paternalist" (76) to the pitilessly malevolent. A closer look at *Where There Is Nothing* will provide insight into this phenomenon, as well as reveal other prejudices typical of theater reviewers in the first decade of the twentieth century.[15]

Where There Is Nothing is the story of Paul Ruttledge, a member of the upper middle class who, at the opening of the play, is unsatisfied by his station in life. Longing for more than the conventional happiness of "a good house and a good property" (1069), Paul goes on a quest for freedom, the potential achievement of which he credits only to anarchy, to the complete destruction of church, state, and property. The play depicts Paul's successive transformations from bourgeois idler to tinker to monk to heretical preacher, all roles he uses to consciously upset the status quo. For instance, when he marries a tinker woman, Paul sponsors a week-and-a-half-long drinking party for the whole town, both for celebratory purposes and in order to bring a bit of the afterlife to his fellow, earth-bound sufferers, for Paul believes, "when we [are] all dead and in heaven it [will] be a sort of drunkenness, a sort of ecstasy" (1106). Similarly, after earning the reputation as the quickest-learning monk in the monastery, Paul disturbs the monastic order by engaging in and encouraging Eastern spiritual practices such as meditation—the divine knowledge of which he gains through mystical trance, a medium unfamiliar to his more conservatively Christian brothers. For Paul, the ultimate goal of these rebellious acts is to find the place "where there is nothing that is anything, and nobody that is anybody," (1091). "We must," he advises, "destroy the World; we must destroy everything that has Law and Number, for where there is nothing, there is God" (1140).[16] Here we see an early and rough version of Yeats's urge both to knock convention off its pillar of complacency and to replace materialism with passion. Or, as Paul exclaims, "I want the happiness of men who fight, who are hit and hit back" (1097), not of those who believe "you could be cheerful without ceasing to be a gentleman" (1082) or who "can't see why a man with property can't let well alone" (1083). That is, rather than fall into the bourgeois trappings of blind acceptance of the status quo, insistence on socially contrived and strictly delineated forms of middle-class respectability, and worship of material possessions as if they were sacred, Paul suggests simply, if in rather radical ways, that people should think for themselves. Through Paul's manipulation, the principles represented by the creation of "Law" and the counting of "Numbers"—symbols of the supposed evolution or progress made possible by science, society, and the Church—appear merely static and self-involved.

The two groups hit hardest by the play's anti-progressivist message are the Church and the bourgeoisie, the latter of which Yeats represents, as he so seldom does, with actual middle-class characters in the form of the Ruttledges, a family of country gentlemen and ladies, and magistrates (1064). A semi-autobiographical Yeats, the character of Paul repudiates the so-called social virtues of his neighbors, including "Dowler, who puts away thousands a year in Consols, . . . Algie who tells everybody all about it" (1066), and, more generally, those who value life experience only for monetary gain (1083). Paul further criticizes his middle-class cohorts when he argues that his bourgeois friends and family "think in flocks and roosts" (1070)—a phrase Yeats himself uses almost verbatim in an essay a few years later. In "The Controversy over *The Playboy of the Western World*" (1907), Yeats hones in on the particularly middle-class, "tyrann[ical]" entities, "clubs and leagues," and, echoing Paul, praises those who aim to achieve "individual sincerity, the eternal quest of truth, all that has been given up for so long that all might crouch upon the one roost and quack or cry in the one flock" (*Explorations* 228). But Paul does not stop there, and continues to complain of the social class into which he was born in overtly mocking terms: "When I hear these people talking I always hear some organized or vested interest chirp or quack, as it does in the newspapers" (1070). In other words, members of the bourgeoisie (not to mention the critics) are too busy building their bank accounts and bolstering the status quo to care about anything other than material, and materialistic, interests. George Mills Harper similarly explains about these characters that the "pursuit of wealth and comfort has spawned the mercantile middle class, who have established as truth a spurious code of ethics," which is "[d]esigned for the defense of property rather than the enjoyment of life" ("The Creator as Destroyer" 119).

Nor does Paul allow the Church any latitude, criticizing it for conceding to this bourgeois trend by helping to "build up the things that keep the soul from God" (1131). For instance, Paul questions the value of a religious organization that boasts, as its representative Father Jerome does,

> our school is increasing so much we are getting a grant for technical instruction. Some of the Fathers are learning handicrafts. Father Aloysius is going to study industries in France; but we are all busy. We are changing with the times, we are beginning to do useful things. (1068)

Rather than focus on building, progressing, changing with the times, and being useful—all words steeped in the values of progressivism—Paul suggests religion should be about "getting out of the body while still alive, getting away from law and number" (1131). Paul warns, as Jungians and Mircea Eliade would later, that, "[t]he Christian's business is not reformation but revelation, and the only labours he can put his hand to can never be accomplished in Time" (1139).[17] Rather than busy itself with worldly matters, Yeats's play suggests, the Church should encourage one to meditate in order to get "out of time into eternity, and [learn] the truth for itself" (1127).

Thus, Paul demonizes both the bourgeoisie and the Church for unquestioningly believing in historical progressivism, which, moreover, serves to foster the status quo that serves these groups. Yeats further encourages this interpretation by having both Paul's middle class neighbors and the Church frown upon even the smallest display of individuality. For instance, the neighbors pity Paul because he does not belong, as they all do, to an organization such as the militia, the Masonic Lodge, or the Horticultural Society (1078). "I wish he would join something," his brother laments, expressing his discomfort with Paul's refusal to ally himself with any organized society (1077). Similarly, Paul's sister-in-law describes his refusal to "be sociable" in ways approved by his peer group as Paul "always doing uncomfortable things" (1066, 1067). Later in the play, when Paul is a monk, a character identified simply but significantly as Superior repeats the plea for not only obedience but conformity when he insists on Paul's "entire submission" to, or else his dismissal from, the Church (1129).

This theme of conformity is significant, first, because it elucidates the pressures of the Victorian bourgeois ideal that one must literally and metaphorically "play the game." Imbued by the ideology of progressivism, "playing the game"—or, in terms of this play, being involved in and submissive to the social and religious circles in which Paul finds himself—would, if one assented to it, ideally propel one up the economic and social ladder and, in terms of gender, allow one to be considered a "man" (P. Anderson 54). Paul, however, quite obviously refuses to "play the game." In fact, he insists on playing his own game—a game without rules, without the security of "teams" like the Horticultural Society, and in which no one keeps score and, therefore, in which no one can win or lose. In the world of Victorian bourgeois and Christian progressivism, such a philosophy is unthinkable. Individuals like Paul, Cuchulain, Mary Bruin, or Seanchan who won't play the game not only make others uncomfortable; they are perceived as a threat to the social order. Thus, even before Paul becomes an anarchist in a literal sense, others view him as a metaphoric anarchist: that is, as a threat to the value of productivity. Yeats makes Paul's lack of traditional productivity quite clear from the opening scene, where he chooses to cut greenery into the shapes of farm animals rather than build relationships (or in twenty-first-century parlance, network) with his neighbors. Furthermore, Paul's personal enjoyment and preaching of the economically unproductive and liberating joys of drink, spiritual ecstasy, and life experience—the latter notably opposed to the Victorian bourgeois consecration of work and the Protestant work ethic—also allies him with those so-called good-for-nothings (the pauper, the drunken Irish peasant) who lack self-control. In fact, "How splendid is the cup of my drunkenness" (Paul's revision of "My cup runneth over") is one of his favorite refrains throughout the play.

A second significance of the play's critique of conformity is that the value systems that encourage such allegiance exist not only in the play itself, but also in the criticism of Yeats's early plays, including *Where There Is Nothing*. For instance, one insightful critic of the printed play noted that the work's:

> main interest is in the hero's logical working out of his mystic Nihilism, impeded at every step by the irresistible impulse in others to *organise, define, legislate, formalise*—to re-create, sometimes from the advancement of his own ideas as they conceive them—*the whole apparatus of regulation and convention*, which to him is a mere curtain interposed between the soul and the light. (*The Manchester Guardian* 11 Jun. 1903, emphasis added)

This critic recognizes Yeats's anti-progressivist stance and, in pointing out Paul's (and Yeats's) use of logic in the attempt to work out his social/spiritual conundrum, elucidates, even if unconsciously, one of the play's ironies. Despite the fact that Yeats argued, for example in a 1911 interview in the *Pall Mall Gazette*, that "I do not think that the play that displays argument is the best, nor the best that its writer can probably do. Logic in art should be hidden up as bones are hidden by flesh" ("The Irish National Theatre: A Chat with W. B. Yeats" 9 Jun. 1911), he chose this method to argue his point in *Where There Is Nothing*.

Yet, rather than use this apparent contradiction, as some have, as a reason to impugn the play's reliability as a source of Yeats's beliefs, we must see *Where There Is Nothing* as an important moment in Yeats's career as a dramatist. He goes on to say, in the passage quoted above, "But I look upon realistic drama as a phase in the evolution of nationalist drama in every country." Although he refers here to realists such as Lennox Robinson and St. John Ervine, I think we can also apply the statement to his own play as one of the few examples of Yeats's early logical "arguments" against progressivism—arguments that, later in his career, do not disappear but merely change shape. For, as I discuss in chapter two, in the years that follow *Where There Is Nothing*, Yeats came to rely on the verse dramatic form as a different and, as he came to believe, better form of corrective for society's progressivist ills. That is, with verse drama, Yeats attempted to offer his audiences an opportunity similar to that which Paul, as heretical monk, offers his followers: to "keep [the audience member's] mind on . . . one high thought" for at least a short duration so that he or she could get "out of time into eternity, and [learn] the truth for itself" (1127). However, even though its "logic" is not "hidden up as bones are hidden by flesh," *Where There Is Nothing* does not falter in its anti-progressivist stance. It merely argues in a different form, chosen specifically by Yeats because he thought it would appeal to audiences accustomed to realist plays.

In spite of Yeats's attempts to reach out to the general public in this way, many in the critical audience did not understand, or at least did not approve of, the message of *Where There Is Nothing*. Like Paul's bourgeois neighbors and Church cohorts, the play's reviews are full of progressivist language and beliefs. For instance, the *Manchester Guardian* critic censures Yeats for his refusal to kowtow to a public which, "in so far as it is accessible to ideas at all necessarily demands ideas of a positive, practical, constructive order" (29 Jun. 1904). Another critic's depiction of Paul as insane due to "the early isolation of his solitary life" reveals his own advocacy of the game-playing ideology by implying that, if Paul had socialized more, he would be more like the others, that is, normal. It is clear that these critics, like the play's villains, the bourgeoisie and the Church, are indoctrinated with progressivist notions of reform.

Not only are the critics unable to escape a clearly moralistic, progressivist slant; the language they use to review the play and its author, not surprisingly, betrays their racist and classist prejudices as well. Just a quick look at reviews of the London Stage Society performance reveals the following judgments: The *Daily Mail* reviewer calls Paul "a mystic of the customary incoherent Celtic variety" (28 Jun. 1904). The *Free Lance* critic similarly contends, "we propose to take the view that Paul has lost the balance of his mind, partly owing to the early isolation of his solitary life, and partly owing to that poetical Celtic temperament of his, which is so emotional as to prevent his viewing the facts of life in any true light" (1 Jul. 1904). Turning their attention to Paul's patronage of the tinker's life, the critics' comments flow in a more dastardly vein. The *Free Lance* critic continues, deriding Paul's "retrogression" to the "primitive" state of the tinkers as not only a condemnable idea but "a crime of madness" (1 Jul. 1904) on Paul's part—and assumedly on Yeat's part as well. Another reflects a theme popular with many of the critics when he describes Paul's untraditional—or as the critic would have it, "iconoclastic"—marriage to a tinker woman (the ceremony consists of jumping over a "budget") as a "kind of connubial union with . . . a dirty girl to whom he does not even teach the doctrine of soap or water" (*Westminster* 28 Jun. 04). And still another sarcastically observes, "it is difficult to imagine a search for godliness in connection with uncleanliness—but then the Irish may have other ideas on the subject of Pears and Sapolio than ourselves" (*Sunday Times* 3 July 1904).

The biases reflected in these passages make manifest that the critics perceive the Irish other in entirely negative terms. Moreover, the critics show themselves to be unwilling to entertain, even for the momentary duration of the play's performance, an alternative reading of what, from colonial and bourgeois perspectives, has been a traditionally disparaging view of, respectively, the Irish and the poor or working classes. This totalizing depiction of the Irish as savage tinkers and peasants denies the presence in the play—and in reality—of the existence of other types of Irish people. This serves to reinforce the group's identificatory principle, whereby all individuals of a group are made to bear the brunt of the same (negative) categories of description created by a (hostile) other. The public outcry against the themes, characters, and actions of *Where There Is Nothing* reflects the more general critical discomfort with the forms and themes of Yeats's other early plays as well as contempt, on the part of many English and Irish literary critics and a powerful contingent of the Irish educational establishment, for Irish literature. What this shows us is not that Yeats was misguided in his attempts to revise and revitalize Irish theater, but rather that he was, in fact, on to a significant social problem.

CONCLUSION

My examination of Yeats's early plays within their socio-historical and critical contexts emblematizes what Yeats was up against and what he was attempting to do with plays that spoke to both nationalist and general social concerns. That is, although he dabbled in propagandistic nationalism (most obviously with *Cathleen ni Houlihan*), Yeats saw his role as dramatist as, at least in part, one in which he could—and should—choose, like Paul Ruttledge, not to "play the game," in terms of the literary construction of his plays and the social construction of identity. Rather, his early plays expose certain complications of an unquestioning belief in conventional definitions of progress and, consequently, of identity.

And therein lies the important difference between the typical Victorian and Edwardian literary or theater critic and Yeats. Unlike Dowden or the critics, Yeats confronted the entrapments of colonial discourse with plays meant to "refute the misguided belief that colonised people do/did not have a history of their own, [by staging] aspects of pre-contact past in order to re-establish traditions, to lay claim to a heritage or territory, and to recuperate various forms of [Irish or not-English] cultural expression" (Gilbert and Tompkins 110). This is especially true of the peasant and mythological plays in which Yeats proclaims Irish history and custom as important and viable forms of cultural expression—though not, I would argue, only for the Irish.

My study of Yeats's plays, moreover, evinces, that they are capable of fulfilling the expectations of two different sorts of readers and spectators. Irish nationalists can find something to recommend in most of Yeats's early plays such as *Cathleen ni Houlihan*, *On Baile's Strand*, *The King's Threshold*, and *Deirdre*, which foster pride in an ancient, heroic, independent, and powerful Irish heritage.[18] But the early plays function on another level as well. Readers and spectators concerned not only with Irishness but also with more general social, economic, and political concerns might obtain insight, via these plays, into the fact that (and ways in which) their own gender, class, and ethnic identities were being socially constructed. By creating alternative depictions of the Irish on the stage, Yeats does refuse colonialist definitions of the Irish. Perhaps more importantly, however, his plays do more than just redefine, again in Luke Gibbons's terms, the "constitutive categories of colonial discourse" (96) with which the English were comfortable. By using alternative dramatic forms and by investing his plays with socio-critical critiques of materialism, moralism, philistinism, and other ideologies used to forward bourgeois and imperialist definitions of progress, Yeats works toward what Said calls "liberation": that is, with the plays written between 1892 and 1907, Yeats began to move above and beyond the narrowly-defined identities imagined under the English/Irish colonial experience.

Notes

NOTES TO THE INTRODUCTION

1. Ireland's status as a colonial or postcolonial nation, and Yeats's status as a postcolonial or anti-colonial writer, has been debated by many scholars. A selected list of the most recent work on these topics includes that by Stephanie Bachorz, C. L. Innes, Jahan Ramazani, and Rajeev S. Patke. Also see Vol. 7.1 of the *Journal of Commonwealth and Postcolonial Studies*, edited by Caitriona Moloney, Helen Thompson, and Frederick Sanders.

2. For more on this time period, see Warwick Gould's edited collection *Yeats and the Nineties*.

3. Roy Foster notes that Yeats was influenced early by Mangan's idea that "the artist of genius must wear a mask at will" (*W. B. Yeats* 90). Yeats's association with Wilde also suggests the influence of the elder writer's notion that "A mask tells us more than a face" and that "These disguises intensified . . . personality" ("Pen, Pencil and Poison" 72).

NOTES TO CHAPTER ONE

1. I am grateful to Marjorie Howes for this particular insight, as conveyed in her presentation, "Yeats, the Enlightenment, and the Postcolonial," at the 1999 American Conference for Irish Studies National Meeting.

2. For a specific instance of this derogatory attitude toward Africans in popular literature, see chapter two.

3. Yeats's belief in an elaborate system of reincarnation is outlined in great detail in *A Vision*. See especially "Book III: The Soul in Judgment."

4. Although Yeats does not begin to formally elaborate these theories until 1917, when he and Georgie Hyde-Lees Yeats began work on the Automatic Script that would become *A Vision*, the theories are nonetheless relevant to the earlier peri-

od to which I limit myself in this study. I will discuss the unique and significant relationship between Yeats's early plays and these theories in more detail in chapter two.

5. These ideas from *Per Amica Silentia Lunae* reveal the influence of Yeats's father on him, as described in *Autobiographies*. For instance, Yeats notes that his father "disliked the Victorian poetry of ideas, and Wordsworth but for certain passages or whole poems" (66). His father clearly instilled in him an antipathy toward conformity to social ideals, as the following passage reveals: When asked as a boy to write on topic of "'Men may rise on stepping-stones of their dead selves to higher things,'" his father responded by saying such topics make boys "'insincere and false to themselves. Ideals make the blood thin, and take the human nature out of people.'" Instead, his father told him to write on the Shakespearean theme, "'to thine own self be true.'" Yeats concludes this passage by noting, "All he said was, I now believe, right" (58). On the other hand, as I display in this study, Yeats was to react strongly to "his father's rationalism and positivism" (Brown 17), and the son's interest in spiritual matters "meant that he was seriously at odds with his father" (Brown 32).

6. See Elizabeth Butler Cullingford's *Yeats, Ireland and Fascism* and Joseph Chadwick's "Violence in Yeats's Later Politics and Poetry."

7. As with almost every other concept in Darwin's seminal work, *On the Origin of Species*, the presence or absence of a teleological bent has been both enthusiastically supported and denied. John Dewey, for instance, "eulogized Darwin for liberating science from the shackles of teleology by destroying the old idealistic notion of a species as a fixed form or final cause" (Himmelfarb 343). However, as Yeats was strongly influenced by the Social Darwinist Huxley, if in the negative, I will focus my discussion around the Darwinism evolved by Huxley and those of like mind.

8. This and following page citations are, respectively, from the first (1859) and last (1876) versions of *On the Origin of Species*, the latter of which includes Darwin's final changes. The original page numbers were noted by the editors of the New York University Press edition of *The Works of Charles Darwin*, edited by Barrett and Freeman in 1988. There were no significant changes from one version to the next in any of the passages I used.

9. Unless otherwise noted, all page references to Huxley are from the collection *The Essence of T. H. Huxley*, edited by Cyril Bibby. However, I provide original sources within the text for informational purposes.

10. The values that infuse R. S. S. Baden-Powell's *Scouting for Boys*, which appeared in 1908, and *Rovering to Success*, a sort of scouting manual for young men published in 1922, were extensions of related Victorian notions of masculinity and health, which I will explain in more detail later in this chapter.

11. Yeats himself was not immune to the craze of coupling science with sexuality, as his infamous late-in-life experimentation with medical procedures meant to increase sexual prowess evinces.

12. Although many of the nineteenth-century theorists who contribute to the development of my argument about Yeats's understanding and manipulation of ethnicity actually refer, most often, to the more limited, biologically essentialist concept of race, I have chosen to formulate my arguments around ethnicity because I believe, like Harold Abramson, that although "race is the most salient ethnic factor, it is still only one of the dimensions of the larger cultural and historical phenomenon of ethnicity" (175).

13. Because they have a special relationship to one another as well as to the coding of Irish as other in the nineteenth century, I have granted gender and ethnicity special attention in this chapter. I will discuss a third category of the other, class, in detail in chapter three, in which I focus specifically on Yeats's version of the peasant in his early plays.

14. For a more in-depth discussion of the history of the women-at-work debate in Ireland as well as influences of and its effects on the progressivist "science" of political economy, see T. P. Foley's "Public Sphere and Domestic Circle: Gender and Political Economy in Nineteenth-Century Ireland."

15. One example of Yeats's absorption of the newly popularized psychiatric and medical theories can be seen in *Per Amica Silentia Lunae*, in which he considers the theory that dreams are unfulfilled desire and are condemned by the conscience (*Mythologies* 341).

16. J. A. Mangan notes that although Kingsley originated the ideas behind "muscular Christianity," as it came to be popularly designated, he disliked the term, preferring instead "manly Christianity." Kingsley's preference, of course, reinforces my point that health reform was male-focused.

17. Marked Volume 40, the issue of *Leisure Hour* in which I found this piece was missing a specific date.

18. Elaine Showalter defines the New Woman of the 1890s as independent and, in the U.S., college-educated: a woman who "criticized society's insistence on marriage as woman's only option for a fulfilling life" (38).

19. See, for instance, "From Democracy to Authority" in Yeats's *Uncollected Prose II*.

20. It is interesting to note that, as George Watson points out in "Celticism and the Annulment of History," history preceded Arnold's and Renan's representation of Celticism and "change" as "antithetical categories" by at least a century, as evinced, for instance, in Samuel Johnson's *Journey to the Western Islands* (224–25).

21. Marjorie Howes refers to some of the more positive views of the hysteric, such as those applauded by Freud and Breuer in *Studies in Hysteria*, in which they commended the hysteric as "gifted, cultured, and morally sensitive" (21). While it is true that Arnold also found value in the so-called hysterical/feminine-coded characteristics of the Celt, nineteenth-century psychiatry overwhelmingly defined hysteria as an affliction, thus devaluing the positive effects of the condition.

22. See the first chapter of Howes for more on the connection between Arnold and Weininger.

23. For example, see Perry Curtis's *Anglo-Saxons and Celts: A Study of Anti-Irish Prejudice in Victorian England*.

24. See *Apes and Angels: The Irishman in Victorian Caricature* by Perry Curtis and *How the Irish Became White* by Noel Ignatiev.

25. Although Eagleton's Gael is a chronological predecessor of the Victorian Celt, and the terms "Gael" and "Celt" are not exact equivalents, for the purposes of my argument here, I will use them interchangeably.

26. See my discussion on Darwinism and Social Darwinism elsewhere in this chapter for some of the reasons why racial identity loomed large in the Victorian mind.

NOTES TO CHAPTER TWO

1. The first passage is from "The Literary Movement in Ireland" in *Uncollected Prose II* (193–94). The second is included in Yeats's essay, "Oscar Wilde's Last Book," in *Uncollected Prose I* (203).

2. I say fairly consistent because one must take into account Yeats's late-life fascination with eugenics, which represents a return to his earlier interest in scientific evaluations.

3. I discuss this in more detail in chapters five and four, respectively.

4. The term "syncretistic hybridity" is Patrick Colm Hogan's and will be discussed in more detail later in this chapter.

5. In *A Vision*, Yeats depicts the following philosophers as spiritual and cognitive muses: "Anaximander, a pre-Socratic philosopher, thought there were two infinities, one of co-existence where nothing ages, the other of succession and mortality, world coming after world and lasting always the same number of years. Empedocles and Heraclitus thought that the universe had first one form and then its opposite in perpetual alternation" (246). Yeats also credits Cicero's writings, in part, for his understanding of the Great Year and of the Eternal Return: "'By common consent men measure the year . . . by the return of the sun, or in other words by the revolution of one star. But when the whole of the constellations shall return to the positions from which they once set forth, thus after a long interval re-making the first map of the heavens, that may indeed be called the Great Year'" (245–46).

6. It is interesting to note that Toby Joyce credits the nineteenth-century Irish Republican Brotherhood (IRB) with a neo-chivalric code similar to that which permeated Victorian culture from London to the West of Ireland. According to Joyce, the IRB barred its members from joining the public riots in which poor laborers took part in the hopes of developing "discipline among their supporters, and [to] help make respectable the country" (76). In Ireland, as in England, the middle classes seemed eager to keep their distance from the lower classes, which they perceived

as having less self-control and therefore, according to Victorian precepts, lower moral standards.

7. Standish O'Grady's works include the trilogy, *The Coming of Cuculain* (1894), *In the Gates of the North* (1901), and *The Triumph and Passing of Cuculain* (1920), as well as *Finn and his Companions*, which was published in the T. Fisher Unwin's Children's series in 1892. Patrick Pearse wrote eight plays for children between 1909 and 1916. For a more in-depth survey of Irish mythological works written for Victorian and Edwardian children, see West.

8. See Stephen J. Brown, S. J.'s *Ireland in Fiction: A Guide to Irish Novels, Tales, Romances, and Folk-Lore* for a detailed list of literature about Ireland and by Irish writers that was written during this time period. His annotations tell us almost as much about the era's interest in morality as do the works themselves.

9. Although Alcott was an American writer, she was extremely popular with English girls as well (Mitchell *The New Girl* 143).

10. For a book that provides excellent insight into girls' reading culture during the late Victorian and Edwardian era, see *The New Girl: Girls' Culture in England, 1880–1915*, by Sally Mitchell.

11. The popular literature quoted in this chapter is merely a sampling of the many magazines and journals published for a general bourgeois audience in Victorian England and Ireland. As it would be impossible to convey every point of view, the examples are meant to represent the norm in a society obsessed with normalizing.

12. More recently, postcolonial theorists have discussed the problematic nature of the belief that, to quote Gerry Smyth paraphrasing David Lloyd, "the central paradox of Irishness [is] its inability to constitute itself as a final, fixed, finished identity" (244). See Smyth's "The Past, the Post, and the Utterly Changed: Intellectual Responsibility and Irish Cultural Criticism" for his insightful explication of the idea that "[i]dentitarian politics, in fact, are part of the problem for post-colonial criticism" (244). However, for the purposes of my argument, I merely want to note the similarities between Yeats's and the later critics' ideas, not to discuss their viability in postcolonial studies in general, which perhaps is a topic for another essay.

13. As with the passage about "beer, bible, and the seven deadly virtues," this is a paraphrase of a Wildean epigram. In "The Soul of Man Under Socialism, " Wilde writes, "To live is the rarest thing in the world. Most people exist, that is all" (24).

14. See Mary Trotter's *Ireland's National Theaters: Political Performance and the Origins of the Irish Dramatic Movement* for a discussion of the political elements of performance in Irish theatre of this time period.

15. Jahan Ramazani reads Yeats's poetry in a similar fashion, remarking that in his outward- and inward-looking style, Yeats anticipates the dual emphasis of many later postcolonial writers, eager at once to explore, expand, and promote the poetic resources of their own cultures, and at the same time to ransack the international lit-

erary trove of the *Spiritus Mundi*. (812) In doing so, Ramazani continues, "Yeats skillfully navigates between the Scylla of blinkered provincialism and the Charybdis of shallow internationalism" (813).

16. There is, however, no evidence that Yeats was aware specifically of Fuchs's theories.

17. I will return to a more in-depth exploration of Yeats's contemporary critics in chapter five, where I focus on the considerations of race and ethnicity as they relate to the critical response to Yeats's early plays.

NOTES TO CHAPTER THREE

1. The passages hail, respectively, from Williams's *Culture and Society 1780–1950* (xv), Hobsbawm's *The Invention of Tradition* (10), and George's *Progress and Poverty* (9).

2. Four excellent sources on Yeats and class are Elizabeth Butler Cullingford's *Yeats, Ireland and Fascism*, Marjorie Howes's *Yeats's Nations: Gender, Class and Irishness*, David L. Kubal's "Our Last Literary Gentlemen: The Bourgeois Imagination," and Peter Lecouras's "'Traditional Sanctity and Loveliness': Class and Gender in the Poetry of William Butler Yeats."

3. Although Yeats wrote other prose plays, as well as other plays in which the middle classes played a key role, I point to these two examples because, of all of his plays, they best exemplify Yeats's efforts to reach a popular audience using both a prose form and the middle class as subject matter, as was typical in the popular realist theater of the day.

4. As Daniel J. Murphy and others have pointed out, Yeats is indebted to Lady Gregory for, depending upon your point-of-view, her assistance with, co-authorship of, or authorship of his early plays. Although I do not deny Lady Gregory's presence, on some level, in the plays, I have chosen to follow the lead of the two authors involved, Gregory and Yeats, who themselves chose to leave the plays in posterity's hands under the authorship of Yeats. For more information on the topic, there are several sources available including: Murphy's "Lady Gregory, Co-author and Sometimes Author of the Plays of W. B. Yeats" and "Yeats and Lady Gregory: A Unique Dramatic Collaboration," James Pethica's "'Our Kathleen': Yeats's Collaboration with Lady Gregory in the Writing of *Cathleen ni Houlihan*," Henry Merritt's "'Dead Many Times': *Cathleen ni Houlihan*, Yeats, Two Old Women, and a Vampire," Mary Lou Stevenson's "Lady Gregory and Yeats: Symbiotic Creativity," and Katharine Worth's introduction to the 1987 re-publication of *Where There Is Nothing* and *The Unicorn from the Stars*.

5. The plays of Dion Boucicault's *The Colleen Bawn* (1860), *Arrah-na-Pogue* (1865), and *The Shaughran* (1874) typify the genre. For a more in-depth discussion of the Stage Irishman in the history of Irish theater, see Christopher Fitz-Simon's *The Irish Theatre*. Alternative sources include Micheál Ó hAodha's *Theatre in Ireland*

(1974), Micheál MacLiammhóir's *Theatre in Ireland* (1950), Peter's Kavanagh's *The Irish Theatre, Being a History of the Drama in Ireland from the Earliest Period up to the Present Day* (1946), and John P. Harrington's *The Irish Play on the New York Stage, 1874–1966*, which addresses the American perspective.

6. David Lloyd has written widely on this and related topics. See, for instance, *Nationalism and Minor Literatures: James Clarence Mangan and the Emergence of Irish Cultural Nationalism* and *Anomalous States: Irish Writing and the Post-Colonial Moment*. Also see the highly influential piece, "Can the Subaltern Speak?" by Gayatri Spivak.

7. Yeats's *The Pot of Broth* (1904) also falls under this category of "peasant" peasant plays. However, because it is an exception to the rule in terms of Yeats's peasant plays of this era—Yeats himself chose not to include the play "in Mr. Bullen's collected edition of [his] work as it seemed too slight a thing to perpetuate" (*VP* 254)—I will not discuss it in any detail.

8. J. M. Synge, whose peasant characters in *The Playboy of the Western World* reveal an acute awareness of the outside world and who tug at the harness of their limited, rural existence, reveals interests similar to those found in Yeats's class critique.

9. On this point, my opinion obviously differs somewhat from that of Deborah Fleming, who argues that, "in creating the peasant ideal, Revivalists . . . ignored common life of a great many peasants" (33). As I discuss later in this chapter, although it is true that the Revivalists—Yeats included—idealized the peasant, Yeats's peasant plays also partake in a social critique of the rural Irish which, as much as it stems from his idealization of traditional Irish life, also touches on some of the realities of the lifestyles of the late Victorian rural Irish. My arguments in this chapter will also redress, or at least complicate, the commonly held (and, I will add, for the most part, entirely valid) contention, here via Fleming, that Yeats valued peasants for, amongst other things, "their supposed lack of materialism" and "their being uncorrupted by the bourgeois mind of the urban centers" (51). Rather, I show Fleming's contention that actual peasants were molded by land reform into a "rural bourgeoisie striving to attain ultimately materialistic goals" (52) as a mainstay of Yeats's characterization in his early peasant plays.

10. They might also have had limited access to the upper-class, Anglo-Irish lifestyle in that some rural inhabitants were tenants of Big Houses and their landlords. However, the huge political and religious as well as socioeconomic divide between landlord and tenant would not have influenced many dreams of attaining creature comforts by that route. Moreover, with the passing of a series of land legislation acts, the Anglo-Irish gentry had lost much of their prestige and money by the end of the nineteenth century.

11. This, of course, includes Yeats, especially in these early years, as I discuss elsewhere in this study. Also see the first chapter of Howes, in which she theorizes Yeats's involvement in the Celtic movement.

12. For Victorian views on this topic as expressed in the popular journals of the day, see chapter two.

13. In this way, Yeats reflects Marxist beliefs about the middle class as a hungry machine that continues to eat its way through the proletariat, absorbing the underclass in its wake. As I discuss later in this chapter, however, any comparison between Yeats and Marx must necessarily be a limited one.

14. For more on *Souls for Gold* see Adrian Frazier, "The Making of Meaning: Yeats and *The Countess Cathleen*" and Joseph Leerssen's *Remembrance and Imagination*.

15. Among those critics who previously noted the significance of the anti-materialism message in *The Countess Cathleen* are David R. Clark (128), Andrew Parkin (71), John Rees Moore (60*ff*), Alex Zwerdling (76), and James W. Flannery (144). However, none of these authors focuses his interpretation on this issue.

16. Utilizing Jacques Ellul's classifications of propaganda, Frazier calls Yeats's *The Countess Cathleen* an example of "integration propaganda," which supports his interpretation of the play as an expression of the values of "tradition, noble manners, and the whole feudal way of life" as "universal truths"—and thus as an expression of the status quo (464). This reading of the play explains the Countess Cathleen's role as that of royal or Ascendancy savior, a theme that also appears in *Cathleen ni Houlihan*, in which the title figure has "the walk of a queen" (231). While I agree with his assessment, I also believe that, on at least one level, the play represents that which Frazier denies it to be, "agitation propaganda," in that its critique of middle class materialism is, I believe, part of Yeats's attempt to subvert the status quo. Moreover, Yeats's praise of "royalty" might be seen as another of Yeats's digs at the middle class whose moralism, materialism, and philistinism, would diminish, he thought, under the leadership of the more educated and encultured Ascendancy class.

17. Deborah Fleming also casts these characters in a negative light when she writes, "These peasants are [neither] interesting . . . nor are they wise"; instead, they are "fearful, suspicious, and opportunistic" (95).

18. Yeats's veiled reference to Souperism has been observed by other critics, including Peter Alderson Smith in "'Grown to Heaven like a tree': The Scenery of *The Countess Cathleen*" and Adrian Frazier in "The Making of Meaning: Yeats and *The Countess Cathleen*." For a related reading of the play as an indictment of the Catholic Church, with Shemus and Teigue representing the "Church at its typical worst" (78), see Smith.

19. Zwerdling remarks that *Cathleen ni Houlihan* marks Yeats's last use of the "Victorian ideal of the social savior" (21). As I show, however, the play was not

Yeats's last attempt at social criticism, in itself a form of optimism, as Carlos Fuentes has argued.

20. Many have credited the realistic character of the dialogue of *Cathleen ni Houlihan*, and sometimes much more, to Lady Gregory. This does not, however, weaken my argument about the significance of the realist elements of the play. Rather, the fact that Yeats went out of his way to obtain the help of the (relatively) master dialectician displays his dedication to the realist format of an essentially mythic play, the original idea for which was suggested to Yeats by a dream (Brown 134).

21. As elaborated in his 1902 work, *The Protestant Ethic and the Spirit of Capitalism*, Max Weber elaborated a theory of the Protestant work ethic that emerged from the historical influence of Calvinism. More specifically, Weber argued that "the protestant ethic broke the hold of tradition while it encouraged men to apply themselves rationally to their work." As influenced by the Calvinist faith, wealth was taken as a sign of (spiritual and religious as well as economic) success. "The protestant ethic therefore provided religious sanctions that fostered a spirit of rigorous discipline, encouraging men to apply themselves rationally to acquire wealth" ("The Protestant Ethic").

22. It also, of course, reveals an inherent philistinism, another negative quality with which Yeats especially identifies bourgeois thought. However, I will defer a detailed discussion of this topic for the fourth chapter, in which I discuss philistinism in the context of *The King's Threshold*, where it plays a central role.

23. The most obvious examples of this phenomenon, of course, are Marx's *Capital* and Carlyle's *Past and Present*.

24. An insightful correlation also might be made here between the disvaluing of Mary's intellectual activity (or non-activity, depending on who is doing the defining) and Marx's rendering of private versus social labor. That is, within the microcosmic context of the family circle, in which the family represents capitalist society and every member of the group is expected to contribute his or her share of labor, Mary's activity of reading constitutes the type of labor that, because it is "expended privately" and is not "devoted to the production of commodities actually exchanged" (in Mary's case, she's expected to help produce a tidy house, clean clothes, meals, and eventually children), does not "produce value and does not enter directly into the complex social division of labor sustained by the exchange of commodities" (D. Foley 16).

25. This line in particular induces one to consider the play as Yeats's plea to Maud Gonne, who Yeats famously would have liked to tame in the same manner the Bruins hope Shawn will domesticate Mary. In this way, the play can easily be seen to reflect Yeats's ambivalence toward Gonne: he desires her as mate yet respects what her refusal to be tamed allows her to do in the public arena. This biographical point requires mention, I believe, because, as my discussion later in this chapter shows,

both Mary and Gonne attempted to obtain a life in which "quiet hearths" exist alongside of the "bewilderment of light and freedom" (193).

26. Andrew Parkin explains Maurteen's welcoming invitation as "motivated by Christian charity and a desire to establish a mood of happiness in the quarrelsome household" (57). While I won't deny Maurteen his soft side, I believe his behavior here and elsewhere reveal his motives in this instance to be guided more by his desire for domestic peace and what's *expected* of him as Christian patriarch than by any real Christian desire to help the destitute. His motions toward domestic peace and charity reflect the Victorian social hierarchy of gender and class roles of which, as bourgeois-motivated male, Maurteen here attempts to gain control using the same tools, Christianity and patriarchy, that help mold the more general social construction of class and gender.

27. Yeats's belief that the aristocrats should provide the gentle hand of guidance for the middle and lower classes, thus leading the Irish into a better and brighter future, complicates this interpretation somewhat. If you were to shift the class structure in *The Countess Cathleen* down one notch, for instance, you could imaginatively transplant Maurteen into a role similar to the one the Countess Cathleen plays in her town and in the play that bears her name, thus making Maurteen's attempts to help those less fortunate than him a less self-interested act of charity, like the Countess's. He is, after all, a peasant and therefore a member of the class that, in Yeats's view, is most like the aristocrats. But my arguments, in this particular instance and in the remainder of my discussion of *Land*, show that Maurteen too clearly resembles the middle classes—or a bourgeois peasant, to be exact—to support the argument I suggest here.

28. In this way, Andrew Parkin points out, she might remind us of Ibsen's characters, Nora or Hedda Gabler (58).

29. For an interesting pseudo-historical depiction of Mary's feelings about her own lack of agency, see Yeats's poem, "The Mother of God." (

30. See chapter one.

31. For more on this topic, see chapter two.

32. For evidence of how seriously this threat was taken by the rural Irish in the nineteenth and early twentieth century, see Angela Bourke's *The Burning of Bridget Cleary*, a study of just one actual instance in which the belief in fairy abduction led to tragic consequences for one woman.

33. See Michael Walsh's "Reading the Real in the Seminar on the Psychoses" for an interesting discussion of the relationship between madness and the Other in Lacanian terms.

34. For more on the contemporary critical response to *Land*, see chapter five.

NOTES TO CHAPTER FOUR

1. The opening passages are taken, respectively, from Mary Daly's *Beyond God the Father: Toward a Philosophy of Women's Liberation* (15), Judith Butler's *Gender Trouble: Feminism and the Subversion of Identity* (10), and Donna Haraway's *Simians, Cyborgs, and Women* (149).

2. This is not to say that Yeats overlooked the material well being of Ireland. For instance, in "Home Rule and Religion," he lectured about the need for Anglo-Irish leadership to fight cultural and political "intolerance" in order to help lead Ireland toward a "fruitful" material and intellectual existence" (9).

3. For additional insight into Yeats's sex/gender identification, see Elizabeth Butler Cullingford's *Gender and History in Yeats's Love Poetry*. In this groundbreaking work, Cullingford explores Yeats's treatment of women in his poetry in the context of his own gender identification she sees as changing greatly after the Treaty of 1922, when "his identification between woman and Ireland was ruptured" (8). Also see Janis Tedesco Haswell's perceptive *Pressed Against Divinity: W. B. Yeats's Feminine Masks*. On a related topic, see Jason Edwards's "'The Generation of the Green Carnation': Sexual Degeneration, the Representation of Male Homosexuality and the Limits of Yeats's Sympathy."

4. Haswell's convincing emphasis on the influence of the automatic writings (of 1917 and following) on Yeats's mature gender theories (and poetry) supports my contention here that, during the time period that he was working on *The King's Threshold*, *On Baile's Strand*, and *Deirdre*, he was, in fact, just beginning to work out these same theories—a fact that would explain the hesitancy or lack of confidence I see represented in the changes in the letter.

5. The same cannot be said of the later Yeats who was, for better or for worse, influenced by theorists who fostered belief in biological determinist actions like ethnic cleansing. The Yeats of many of the late poems, including the "Crazy Jane" poems—in which a woman finds power in her very existence as a biologically sexed woman—similarly reflect deterministic beliefs about gender, though, obviously, in a more positive form.

6. I must point out that the focus of the article from which I take the preceding quotations is on Lady Gregory's book, not Yeats's play. Nonetheless, I remain in disagreement with her and with A. S. Knowland, whom she quotes as calling Yeats's Deirdre "'dependent on Naoise for strength'" (37).

7. For instance, see Barbara Charlesworth Gelpi's "The Politics of Androgyny" and Daniel A. Harris's "Androgyny: The Sexist Myth in Disguise."

8. I discuss the relationship between Yeats's celebratory treatment of the intermingling of gender differences as it relates to his theories on racial hybridity in chapter five.

9. Susan C. Harris makes a similar observation in "Blow the Witches Out: Gender Construction and the Subversion of Nationalism in Yeats's *Cathleen ni Houlihan* and *On Baile's Strand*" (475).

10. See S. B. Bushrui's "*The King's Threshold*: A Defence of Poetry" and Barton R. Friedman's "Under a Leprous Moon: Action and Image in *The King's Threshold*."

11. Yeats's play speaks to the complicated history of hunger striking in Ireland, which helped to make suffering a widely used ploy of political protest. See Cullingford, "'Thinking of Her...'" (16–17).

12. James W. Flannery elsewhere points to the importance of irony in terms of the Yeatsian hero. He sees characters such as the Mayor as important to the "development" in *The King's Threshold* "of an ironic counterpoint to his concept of the heroic ideal" (90).

13. To be fair to the Mayor, he is in a tight situation and, as in any political situation, must work the system in which he is, after all, only a cog. The grazing lands he tries to protect are much in need, his town "being so pinched that our mowers mow with knives between the stones" (272). The king, he implies, has a ready answer to his problem, but will not oblige the town with his graces; Kinvara, it seems, is to suffer for its townsman Seanchan's doings. This oblique reference to famine times, though less heavy-handed than in *The Countess Cathleen*, thus places another stone around the neck of the King, whose reputation sinks continually deeper under Yeats's direction.

14. When Fedelm's selfless concern for Seanchan's life nevertheless fails to work its magic, she surrenders to his will. His mother, intuitively recognizing that they "'cannot change'" her son (275) similarly concedes to Seanchan's martyrdom. These women, who are intuitive, reasonable, and emotionally strong as well, provide yet another example of the ways in which individuals of either sex have or can develop traits traditionally associated with the both genders.

15. Susan C. Harris similarly argues that *On Baile's Strand* dramatizes the "dependence on dangerously simple conceptions of femininity, masculinity, and identity" (475). However, her focus on the female figures of Aoife and the witches and on the otherworldly elements of the play lead her to examine the issue in a different light.

16. It is important to note that Yeats's choice to include feminine elements in Cuchulain's personality differs from many versions of this myth. Lady Gregory, for instance, depicts virility as his dominant attribute: He is the "brave champion of Ireland" with "flames of the hero-light . . . shin[ing] about his head" (238–39).

17. Many critics provide comparisons between Yeats's Cuchulain and that of other versions, but see especially Reg Skene's *The Cuchulain Plays of W. B. Yeats: A Study* and Patrick McCarthy's "Talent and Tradition in Yeats' *On Baile's Strand*."

18. Susan C. Harris provides another, related interpretation of witchcraft, as a metaphor for that which breaks down boundaries (485).

19. Harris also sees the Young Man, with the body of a man and a head like a woman (i.e., his mother's), as androgynous and, therefore, as "a possible solution" to the separation of the material and spiritual worlds, "a way to bring what Aoife represents within the boundaries of the kingdom without destroying it" (484). This assessment works to support my argument in this chapter that the play's characterization helps elucidate the theme of the bringing together of all sorts of worlds—masculine and feminine, Conchubar's and Aoife's kingdoms, logic and intuition.

20. The significance of the play's linguistic elements has also been recognized, though for different reasons, by Adrienne Gardner and Gordon M. Wickstrom. Gardner reads Yeats's use of "the kind of sustained use of imagery that one is accustomed to look for in poetry" (35) as an element of its status as Greek tragedy. Her recognition of the depth and intensity of poetic images in the play reinforces my contention that "reading" is an important thematic element. In discussing Yeats's theatrical use of the legend of Lugaidh Redstripe and his Queen, Wickstrom likewise comments on the way in which, through Deirdre's linguistic articulations, "poetry becomes theatre" (470).

NOTES TO CHAPTER FIVE

1. Wilde's arguments on the importance of individualism as expressed in this essay are relevent here, as they clearly influenced Yeats's own ideas on the subject. That Yeats read the essay when it appeared in *The Fortnightly Review* seems likely. Not only does he mention reading the journal several times in his letters during the late 1880s and early 1890s; he quotes almost directly from "Soul" in a review written seven months after the appearance of Wilde's essay. Moreover, Yeats would have come to know about Wilde's ideas through his alliance with Wilde in William Morris's group of young London socialists, which met regularly in the late 1880s.

2. See, for instance, Homi Bhabha's edited collection *Nation and Narration*, Luke Gibbons's *Transformations in Irish Culture*, Declan Kiberd's *Inventing Ireland*, and Sean Moore's "'Anglo-Irish' Hybridity: Problems in Miscegenation, Representation, and Postcolonialism in Irish Studies." For an overview of recent theorizations on the topics of authenticity and hybridity, *Ireland and Cultural Theory: The Mechanics of Authenticity*, edited by Colin Graham and Richard Kirkland, has several insightful essays, as does the "Nationalism and Post-Nationalism" section of *Reviewing Ireland: Essays and Interviews from* Irish Studies Review, edited by Sarah Briggs, Paul Hyland, and Neil Sammells.

3. The original statement, as expressed by Said in his seminal essay on Yeats as postcolonial writer, "Yeats and Decolonization," associates Yeats with the provision of "historical alternatives to the nativist impasse" (85).

4. As Terence Brown explains, "when his own personal identity as the distinctive kind of Irishman he became, was more secure," Yeats "was to indict the professor and family friend as the chief representative of an intellectual Unionism which

in Victorian Dublin had betrayed Irish possibility" (27). Moreover, Yeats was not the only person disappointed with Dowden's public disparagement of Irish literature. As Yeats, at any rate, tells us, for his "scorn for the Irish Lit movement & Irish Lit generally" Dowden "ha[d] been catching it from all the Dublin papers" (*CLI* 427).

5. Most critics and biographers, including Terence Brown, agree that biography—that is, Yeats's own inability to perform well in the traditional classroom—had at least some influence on his later political and philosophical dislike for "measur[ing] the worth of . . . pupils solely by examination prowess" (26).

6. Yeats's ambivalence about military violence has been well documented. We need only to turn to his famous poem "The Second Coming" for an example from a primary source: "The best lack all conviction, while the worst / Are full of passionate intensity." However, for the purposes of my argument, what I think is important about this passage is its distinction between individualistic passion, which Yeats favors, and that which he despises: the type of moralistic fury which convinces men and women of the righteousness of their (squad-driven, uniform-clad) homogeneous front against a common enemy.

7. Yeats's use of the terms "varieties" and "species" seems to here reflect the influence not only of the passage from Oscar Wilde's "The Soul of Man Under Socialism" that I quoted at the opening of this chapter, but also of Charles Darwin, who maintained that the ability to adjust to one's environment and the cohabitants of one's community in most cases ensures the propagation and improvement of the species. In both we see the backbone of an argument for hybridity—though both Darwin and Yeats have been used for arguments of a contrary nature (see, for instance, Gertrude Himmelfarb).

8. I will explore this subject in detail later in this chapter in ways that will reveal that Yeats's contemporary critics surely recognized, though they did not necessarily appreciate, his attempts to provide an alternative to realistic theater.

9. The powerful yet marginal position of Anglo-Irishness, of course, plays a large part in Yeats's identity crisis. See Robert Tracy's *The Unappeasable Host: Studies in Irish Identities* for a helpful study of "the Anglo-Irish writer's struggle to define his or her own identity" (3).

10. David Pierce remarks on the typicality of these views for the time period when he comments, "Yeats's view of Englishness is bound up with his sense of Irishness; his sense of Irishness is bound up with his view of Englishness, and in this he was no different from his contemporaries" (650).

11. Yeats similarly idealizes this life in "Who Goes with Fergus?" and speaks of the attainment of such an existence as the time when Irish men and women will "brood on hopes and fears no more."

12ß.The well was an important image for Yeats, as he explains in a letter quoted by Richard Ellmann in *The Identity of Yeats:* "'My main symbols are sun and moon (in all phases), Tower, Mask, Tree (Tree with mask hanging on the trunk), Well"

(170). Mine provides just one explanation for the significance of the well in Yeats's symbolic system.

13. See especially the first chapter of Howes.

14. For an insightful discussion of the Irish Literary Theatre's publicity as it affected the public's perception of their goals, see Brian Cliff's "'As Assiduously Advertised': Publicizing the 1899 Irish Literary Theatre Season."

15. The fact that *Where There Is Nothing* is not entirely Yeats's play in conception (it came from an idea he discussed with George Moore, and its first draft was written by Yeats, Douglas Hyde, and Lady Gregory together) or language (Lady Gregory helped with the dialogue) has not only been well-documented by Yeats himself (see the accompanying materials in *VP*) but has been explored by numerous critics. See, for instance, David S. Thatcher, Daniel J. Murphy, and especially Katharine Worth for more information on this topic. I have chosen to include it in my study of Yeats's plays and the critical response to them for many reasons, the three primary reasons being: 1) both Yeats and Lady Gregory saw fit to leave the play to posterity as a Yeats creation (while *Unicorn from the Stars*, the revision of *Where There Is Nothing*, is widely known to be more Gregory's than Yeats's), 2) the critics reviewing the play saw it as a Yeats play, and 3) I am less concerned with the play's language and characterization than with its themes, which, as I show here, clearly reflect Yeatsian interests.

16. As many critics have explained, the title of this play comes from a particularly Nietzschean sentiment. For more information on this topic, see the essays by George Mills Harper and by Patricia McFate and William E. Doherty.

17. For more on Jung and Eliade in this context, see chapter two.

18. Of course, this is not to say that all of Yeats's early plays appealed equally to a nationalist audience. As I discussed in chapter three, what many perceive to be the anti-Catholic nature of *The Countess Cathleen* insulted many members of the early audiences.

Bibliography

Abramson, Harold J. *Ethnic Diversity in Catholic America.* New York and London: John Wiley, 1973.

Alldritt, Keith. *W. B. Yeats: The Man and the Milieu.* New York: Clarkson Potter, 1997.

Anderson, Benedict. *Imagined Communities. Reflections on the Origin and Spread of Nationalism.* 1983. Rev. Ed. London: Verso, 1991.

Anderson, Patricia. *When Passion Reigned: Sex and the Victorians.* New York: Basic Books, 1995.

Arnold, Matthew. "On the Study of Celtic Literature." *On the Study of Celtic Literature and On Translating Homer.* New York: MacMillan and Co., 1883. 1–137.

Ashcroft, Bill, Gareth Griffiths, and Helen Tiffen. *The Empire Writes Back: Theory and Practice in Post-colonial Literatures.* London and New York: Routledge, 1989.

Bachorz, Stephanie. "Postcolonial Theory and Ireland: Revising Postcolonialism." *Critical Ireland: New Essays in Literature and Culture.* Ed. Alan A. Gillis and Aaron Kelly. Dublin: Four Courts Press, 2001. 6–13.

Bannerji, Himani, Shahrzad Mojab, and Judith Whitehead, eds. *Of Property and Propriety: The Role of Gender and Class in Imperialism and Nationalism.* Toronto: U of Toronto P, 2001.

Bazin, Nancy Topping and Alma Freeman. "The Androgynous Vision." *Women's Studies* 2.2 (1974): 185–215.

Bery, Ashok and Patricia Murray, eds. *Comparing Postcolonial Literatures: Dislocations.* New York: Macmillan, 2000.

Bhabha, Homi K. "Dissemination: Time, Narrative, and the Margins of the Modern Nation." *Nation and Narration.* Ed. Homi K. Bhabha. London: Routledge, 1990. 291–322.

Blake, William. *The Complete Poems.* Second ed. Ed. W. H. Stevenson. London: Longman, 1989.
"Bourgeois Society." *Encylopedia of Marxism.* 9 Jan. 2003. <http://www.marxists.org/glossary/frame.htm>.
Bourke, Angela. *The Burning of Bridget Cleary.* London: Pimlico, 1999.
Bratton, J. S. "Of England, Home and Duty: The Image of England in Victorian and Edwardian Juvenile Fiction." *Imperialism and Popular Culture.* Ed. and Intro. John M. MacKenzie. Manchester: Manchester UP, 1986. 73–93.
Briggs, Sarah, Paul Hyland, and Neil Sammells, eds. *Reviewing Ireland: Essays and Interviews from* Irish Studies Review. Bath: Sulis Press, 1998.
Brown, Stephen J., S. J. *Ireland in Fiction: A Guide to Irish Novels, Tales, Romances, and Folk-Lore.* Dublin and London: Maunsel, 1919.
Brown, Terence. *The Life of W. B. Yeats: A Critical Biography.* Oxford and Malden, MA: Blackwell, 1999.
Bushrui, S. B. "*The King's Threshold*: A Defence of Poetry." *A Review of English Literature* 4.3 (1963): 81–94.
———. *Yeats's Verse-Plays: The Revisions 1900–1910.* Oxford: Clarendon Press, 1965.
Butler, George F. "The Hero's Metamorphosis in Lady Gregory's *Cuchulain of Muirthemne*: Scholarship and Popularization." *Eire-Ireland: A Journal of Irish Studies* 22.4 (Winter 1987): 36–46.
Butler, Judith. *Gender Trouble: Feminism and the Subversion of Identity.* 1990. New York and London: Routledge, 1999.
Cairns, David and Shaun Richards. "What Ish My Nation?" *Writing Ireland: Colonialism, Nationalism and Culture.* Manchester: Manchester UP, 1988.
"The Caves of Kildoran." *Every Week: Journal of Entertaining Literature.* (25 Jun.1884): 9ff.
C. E. M. "Midland Theatre: The Irish National Theatre Company." Rev. of *A Pot of Broth, The Building Fund,* and *Riders to the Sea. Manchester Guardian* 25 April 1906: Abbey Theatre Cuttings 7271. National Library, Ireland.
Césaire, Aimé. *Discourse on Colonialism.* 1955. Trans. Joan Pinkham. Intro. Jean-Paul Sartre. New York and London: Monthly Review Press, 1972.
Chadwick, Joseph. "Violence in Yeats's Later Politics and Poetry." *ELH* 55.4 (Winter 1988): 869–93.
Checkland, Olive. *Philanthropy in Victorian Scotland: Social Welfare and the Voluntary Principle.* Edinburgh: J. Donald, 1980.
Clark, David R. *W. B. Yeats and the Theatre of Desolate Reality.* 1965. Washington, DC: Catholic UP, 1993.
Cliff, Brian. "'As Assiduously Advertised': Publicizing the 1899 Irish Literary Theatre Season." *Critical Ireland: New Essays in Literature and Culture.* Ed. Alan A. Gillis and Aaron Kelly. Dublin: Four Courts Press, 2001. 30–36.
Cribb, J. J. Ll. "Yeats, Blake and *The Countess Kathleen.*" *Irish University Review* 11.2 (Autumn 1981): 165–78.

Bibliography

Cullen, L. M. *An Economic History of Ireland Since 1660.* London: B. T. Batsford Ltd., 1972.

Cullingford, Elizabeth Butler. *Gender and History in Yeats's Love Poetry.* Syracuse: Syracuse UP, 1996.

———. "'Thinking of Her . . . as . . . Ireland': Yeats, Pearse and Heaney." *Textual Practice* 4.1 (Spring 1990): 1–21.

———. *Yeats, Ireland and Fascism.* London: Macmillan, 1981.

Curtis, L. Perry, Jr. *Anglo-Saxons and Celts: A Study of Anti-Irish Prejudice in Victorian England.* Bridgeport, CT: Conference on British Studies, 1968.

———. *Apes and Angels: The Irishman in Victorian Caricature.* Washington, DC: Smithsonian Institution Press, 1971.

Daly, Mary. *Beyond God the Father: Toward a Philosophy of Women's Liberation.* Boston: Beacon Press, 1973.

Darwin, Charles. *Life and Letters.* Ed. Francis Darwin. 3 vols. London: John Murray, 1888.

———. *On the Origin of Species by Means of Natural Selection, or the Preservation of Favoured Races in the Struggle for Life.* 1859. *The Works of Charles Darwin.* Ed. Paul H. Barrett & R. B. Freeman. Vol. 15. New York: New York UP, 1988.

Deane, Seamus. *Celtic Revivals: Essays in Modern Irish Literature, 1880–1980.* London and Boston: Faber and Faber, 1985.

———. *Strange Country: Modernity and Nationhood in Irish Writing since 1790.* Oxford: Clarendon, 1997.

Digby, Anne. "Women's Biological Straitjacket." *Sexuality and Subordination: Interdisciplinary Studies of Gender in the Nineteenth Century.* Ed. Susan Mendus and Jane Rendall. London & New York: Routledge, 1989. 192–220.

Donohue, Denis. *We Irish: Essays on Irish Literature and Society.* New York: Alfred A. Knopf, 1986.

Dorn, Karen. *Players and Painted Stage: The Theatre of W. B. Yeats.* Totowa, NJ: Barnes and Noble, 1984.

Dunbar, Robert. "Rarely Pure and Never Simple: The World of Irish Children's Literature." *The Lion and the Unicorn* 21.3 (1997): 309–21.

Eagleton, Terry. *Crazy John and the Bishop and Other Essays on Irish Culture.* Notre Dame: U of Notre Dame P, 1998.

———. *The Eagleton Reader.* Ed. Stephen Regan. Oxford: Blackwell Publishers, 1998.

Early, Gerald. "Performance and Reality: Race, Sports and the Modern World." *The Nation* 10–17 Aug. 1998: 11–20.

Edwards, Jason. "'The Generation of the Green Carnation': Sexual Degeneration, the Representation of Male Homosexuality and the Limits of Yeats's Sympathy." *Modernist Sexualities.* Ed. Hugh Stevens and Caroline Howlett. Manchester: Manchester UP, 2000. 41–55.

Eliade, Mircea. *The Myth of the Eternal Return; or Cosmos and History.* Trans. Willard R. Trask. Princeton: Princeton UP, 1971.

Ellmann, Richard. *The Identity of Yeats*. London: Faber, 1964.

Fackler, Herbert V. *That Tragic Queen: The Deirdre Legend in Anglo-Irish Literature*. Salzburg: Institut fur Englische Sprache und Literatur, Universitat Salzburg, 1978.

Fischer-Lichte, Erika. *The Show and the Gaze of Theatre: A European Perspective*. Iowa City: U of Iowa P, 1997.

Fitz-Simon, Christopher. *The Irish Theatre*. London: Thames and Hudson, 1983.

Flannery, James W. *W. B. Yeats and the Idea of a Theatre: The Early Abbey Theatre in Theory and Practice*. New Haven: Yale UP, 1976.

Fleming, Deborah. *"A man who does not exist": The Irish Peasant in the Work of W. B. Yeats and J. M. Synge*. Ann Arbor: U of Michigan P, 1995.

———, ed.. *Yeats and Postcolonialism*. West Cornwall, CT: Locust Hill Press, 2001.

Foley, Duncan K. *Understanding Capital: Marx's Economic Theory*. Cambridge: Harvard UP, 1986.

Foley, T. P. "Public Sphere and Domestic Circle: Gender and Political Economy in Nineteenth-Century Ireland." Kelleher and Murphy 21–35.

Foster, John Wilson. "Natural History in Modern Irish Culture." *Science and Society in Ireland: The Social Context of Science and Technology in Ireland, 1800–1950*. Ed. Peter J. Bowler and Nicholas Whyte. Belfast: The Institute of Irish Studies, The Queen's University of Belfast, 1997.

Foster, R. F. *Modern Ireland 1600–1972*. New York: Penguin, 1988.

———. *W. B. Yeats: A Life. I: The Apprentice Mage 1865–1914*. Oxford: Oxford UP, 1997.

Foucault, Michel. *The History of Sexuality. Volume 1: An Introduction*. 1976. Trans. Robert Hurley. New York: Vintage, 1990.

———. *The Order of Things: An Archaeology of the Human Sciences*. 1966. Trans. Alan Sheridan-Smith. New York: Pantheon Books, 1970.

Frazier, Adrian. "The Making of Meaning and *The Countess Cathleen*." *Sewanee Review* 95.3 (Summer 1987): 451–69.

Friedman, Barton R. "Under a Leprous Moon: Action and Image in *The King's Threshold*." *Arizona Quarterly* 26 (1970): 39–53.

Gardner, Adrienne. "*Deirdre*: Yeats's Other Greek Tragedy." *Yeats, Joyce and Beckett: New Light on Three Modern Irish Writers*. Ed. Cathleen McCrory and John Unterecker. Lewisburg, PA: Bucknell UP, 1976. 35–38.

Gelpi, Barbara Charlesworth. "The Politics of Androgyny." *Women's Studies* 2.2 (1974): 151–60.

———. "Sex as Performance with All the World a Stage." *Mosaic: A Journal for the Interdisciplinary Study of Literature* 30.3 (1997): 185–95.

George, Henry. *Progress and Poverty: An Inquiry into the Cause of Industrial Depressions and of Increase of Want with Increase of Wealth; the Remedy*. New York: Robert Schalkenbach Foundation, 1940.

Gibbons, Luke. *Transformations in Irish Culture*. Notre Dame: U of Notre Dame P, 1996.

Gilbert, Helen and Joanne Tompkins. *Post-Colonial Drama: Theory, Practice, Politics.* London and New York: Routledge, 1996.

Gilman, Charlotte Perkins. *"The Yellow Wallpaper" and Other Stories.* Mineola, NY: Dover, 1997.

Gogarty, Oliver St. John. "The Irish Literary Revival: Present Poetry and Drama in Dublin." Rev. of *The Shadowy Waters,* by W. B. Yeats. [?] 4 Mar. 1905: Abbey Theatre Cuttings 7271. National Library, Ireland.

Gould, Warwick, ed. *Yeats and the Nineties.* Houndmills, England: Palgrave, 2001.

Graham, Colin. "'. . . maybe that's just Blarney': Irish Culture and the Persistence of Authenticity." Graham and Kirkland 7–28.

—— and Richard Kirkland, eds. *Ireland and Cultural Theory: The Mechanics of Authenticity.* Intro. Colin Graham and Richard Kirkland. New York: St. Martin's, 1999.

Gramsci, Antonio. *A Gramsci Reader: Selected Writings 1916–1935.* Ed. David Forgacs. London: Lawrence and Wishart, 1988.

Gregory, Lady. *Cuchulain of Muirthemne.* 1902. Gerards Cross: Colin Smythe, 1993.

——. *Our Irish Theatre.* Intro. Daniel J. Murphy. New York: Capricorn, 1965.

Habermas, Jürgen. *The Structural Transformation of the Public Sphere: An Inquiry into a Category of Bourgeois Society.* 1962. Trans. Thomas Burger with Frederick Lawrence. Cambridge, MA: The MIT Press, 1993.

Haraway, Donna. *Simians, Cyborgs and Women: The Reinvention of Nature.* New York: Routledge, 1991.

Harper, George Mills. "The Creator as Destroyer: Nietzschean Morality in Yeats's *Where There Is Nothing.*" *Colby Library Quarterly* 15 (1972): 114–25.

——. *The Mingling of Heaven and Earth: Yeats's Theory of Theatre.* Dublin: Dolmen Press, 1975.

Harrington, John P. *The Irish Play on the New York Stage, 1874–1966.* Lexington: U of Kentucky P, 1997.

Harris, Daniel A. "Androgyny: The Sexist Myth in Disguise." *Women's Studies* 2.2 (1974): 171–84.

Harris, Susan C. "Blow the Witches Out: Gender Construction and the Subversion of Nationalism in Yeats's *Cathleen ni Houlihan* and *On Baile's Strand.*" *Modern Drama* 39.3 (Fall 1996): 475–89.

Haswell, Janis Tedesco. *Pressed Against Divinity: W. B. Yeats's Feminine Masks.* DeKalb: Northern Illinois UP, 1997.

Heilbrun, Carolyn. "Further Notes Toward a Recognition of Androgyny." *Women's Studies* 2.2 (1974): 143–49.

——. *Toward a Recognition of Androgyny.* 1964. New York: W. W. Norton, 1973.

Himmelfarb, Gertrude. *Darwin and the Darwinian Revolution.* Chicago: Elephant Paperbacks, 1962.

Hinz, Evelyn J. "Introduction: All that Glitters." *Mosaic: A Journal for the Interdisciplinary Study of Literature* 30.3 (1997): vii-viii.

Hobsbawm, Eric and Terence Ranger, eds. *The Invention of Tradition*. 1983. Cambridge: Cambridge UP: 1992.

Hogan, Patrick Colm. *Colonialism and Cultural Identity: Crises of Tradition in the Anglophone Literatures of India, Africa, and the Caribbean*. Albany: State U of New York P, 2000.

Hogan, Robert and James Kilroy. *The Abbey Theatre: The Years of Synge 1905–1909*. Atlantic Highlands, NJ: The Dolmen Press, 1978.

Howes, Marjorie. *Yeats's Nations: Gender, Class, and Irishness*. Cambridge: Cambridge UP, 1996.

Hughes, Thomas. *Tom Brown's Schooldays*. 1857. Ed. and Intro. Andrew Sanders. Oxford and New York: Oxford UP, 1989.

Hutchinson, John. *The Dynamics of Cultural Nationalism: The Gaelic Revival and the Creation of the Irish Nation State*. London: Allen and Unwin, 1987.

Huxley, T. H. *The Essence of T. H. Huxley*. Ed. Cyril Bibby. New York: St. Martin's Press, 1967.

———. *Life and Letters*. Ed. Leonard Huxley. 3 vols. New York: D. Appleton, 1900.

Hyde, Douglas. *Selected Plays of Douglas Hyde*. Intro. Gareth W. Dunleavy and Janet Egleson Dunleavy. Irish Drama Selections 7. Gerrards Cross: Colin Smythe, 1991.

Ignatiev, Noel. *How the Irish Became White*. London: Routledge, 1995.

Innes, C. L. "Modernism, Ireland and Empire: Yeats, Joyce, and Their Implied Audiences." *Modernism and Empire*. Ed. Howard J. Booth and Nigel Rigby. Manchester, England: Manchester UP, 2000. 137–55.

———. "Postcolonial Studies and Ireland." Bery and Murray 21–30.

"Irish Drama in Birmingham: Last Night's Production." Rev. of *A Pot of Broth* and *On Baile's Strand*, by W. B. Yeats. Midland Institute, Birmingham. *Birmingham Daily Mail* 29 May 1907: Abbey Theatre Cuttings 7271. National Library, Ireland.

"The Irish National Theatre: A Chat with Mr. W. B. Yeats." *Pall Mall Gazette* 9 Jun. 1911: Abbey Theatre Cuttings POS 7273. National Library, Ireland.

"Irish Plays at the Kings." Rev. of *Kathleen ni Houlihan*. *Evening Citizen* 5 Jun. 1906: Abbey Theatre Cuttings 7271. National Library, Ireland.

Jeffares, A. Norman. *W. B. Yeats. A New Biography*. New York: Farrar Straus Giroux, 1988.

Joyce, Toby. "'Ireland's Trained and Marshalled Manhood': The Fenians in the Mid-1860s." Kelleher and Murphy 70–80.

Jung, C. G. "Foreword to Abegg: Ostasien Denkt Anders." *The Collected Works of C. G. Jung*. Vol. 18. Trans. R. E. C. Hull. Bollingen Series 20. Princeton, Princeton UP, 1974. 654–55.

———. "The Spiritual Problem of Modern Man." *Modern Man in Search of a Soul*. Trans. Cary F. Baynes and W. S. Dell. New York: Harcourt Brace, 1934. 226–54.

Kavanagh, Peter. *The Irish Theatre, Being a History of the Drama in Ireland from the Earliest Period up to the Present Day.* Tralee: The Kerryman Ltd., 1946.

Kelleher, Margaret and James H. Murphy, eds. *Gender Perspectives in Nineteenth-Century Ireland.* Intro. Margaret Kelleher. Dublin: Irish Academic Press, 1997.

Kiberd, Declan. "From Nationalism to Liberation." Sailer 17–28.

———. *Inventing Ireland.* Cambridge: Harvard UP, 1995.

Kidd, Alan. *State, Society, and the Poor in Nineteenth-Century England.* New York: St. Martin's, 1999.

Kirkland, Richard. "Questioning the Frame: Hybridity, Ireland and the Institution." Graham and Kirkland 210–28.

Kubal, David L. "Our Last Literary Gentlemen: The Bourgeois Imagination." *Bucknell Review* 22.2 (1976): 27–49.

Lamont-Stewart, Linda. "Androgyny as Resistance to Authoritarianism in Two Postmodern Canadian Novels." *Mosaic: A Journal for the Interdisciplinary Study of Literature* 30.3 (1997): 115–30.

Lecouras, Peter. "'Traditional Sanctity and Loveliness': Class and Gender in the Poetry of William Butler Yeats." *Yeats-Eliot Review: A Journal of Criticism and Scholarship* 16.3 (Spring 2000): 20–30.

Leerssen, Joseph Th. *Mere Irish & Fíor-Ghael: Studies in the Idea of Irish Nationality, Its Development, and Literary Expression Prior to the Nineteenth Century.* Amsterdam and Philadelphia: John Benjamins, 1986.

———. *Remembrance and Imagination: Patterns in the Historical and Literary Representation of Ireland in the Nineteenth Century.* Notre Dame: U of Notre Dame P, 1997.

Lewes, George. Rev. of *Shirley*. *The Brontës: The Critical Heritage.* Ed. Miriam Allott. London and Boston: Routledge and Kegan Paul, 1974. 160–70.

Lloyd, David. *Anomalous States: Irish Writing and the Post-Colonial Moment.* Durham: Duke UP, 1993.

———. *Nationalism and Minor Literatures: James Clarence Mangan and the Emergence of Irish Cultural Nationalism.* Berkeley: U of California P, 1987.

Logan, John. "The Dimensions of Gender in Nineteenth-Century Schooling." Kelleher and Murphy 36–49.

Luckey, E. D. Letter to W. B. Yeats. 6 Jan. 1904. Abbey Theatre Papers 12,145. National Library, Ireland.

MacKenzie, John M. "The Imperial Pioneer and Hunter and the British Masculine Stereotype in Late Victorian and Edwardian Times." Mangan and Walvin 176–98.

MacLiammhóir, Micheál. *Theatre in Ireland.* Dublin: Colm Ó Lochlainn, 1950.

Malone, Christopher T. "Modernist Ethos in the Postcolonial Moment: Yeats's Theory of Masks." Fleming 253–76

Mangan, J. A. and James Walvin, eds. *Manliness and Morality: Middle-Class Masculinity in Britain and America 1800–1940.* New York: St. Martin's Press, 1987.

Mangan, J. A. "Social Darwinism and Upper-Class Education in Late Victorian and Edwardian England." Mangan and Walvin 135–59.

Marx, Karl and Freidrich Engels. *The Marx-Engels Reader.* Ed. Robert C. Tucker. New York: Norton, 1972.

McCarthy, Patrick. "Talent and Tradition in Yeats' *On Baile's Strand.*" *Eire-Ireland: A Journal of Irish Studies* 11.1 (1976): 45–62.

McCurry, Jacqueline. "From Domestic Warrior to 'Some mild modern housewife': Lady Gregory's Transformation of the Deirdre Story." *Colby Quarterly* 28.1 (March 1992): 34–38.

McFate, Patricia and William E. Doherty. "W. B. Yeats's *Where There Is Nothing*: Theme and Symbolism." *Irish University Review: A Journal of Irish Studies* 2.2 (1972): 149–63.

Memmi, Albert. *The Colonizer and the Colonized.* 1957. Expanded ed. Trans. Howard Greenfeld. Intro. Jean-Paul Sartre. Afterword Susan Gilson Miller. Boston: Beacon Press, 1991.

Merritt, Henry. "'Dead Many Times': *Cathleen ni Houlihan*, Yeats, Two Old Women, and a Vampire." *Modern Language Review* 96.3 (July 2001): 644–53.

Mitchell, Sally. "Girls' Culture: At Work." Nelson and Vallone 243–258.

———. *The New Girl: Girls' Culture in England 1880–1915.* New York: Columbia UP, 1995.

Moloney, Caitriona, Helen Thompson, and Frederick Sanders, ed. "Ireland as Postcolonial." *Journal of Commonwealth and Postcolonial Studies* 7.1 (Spring 2000). 1–168.

Moore, John Rees. *Masks of Love and Death: Yeats as Dramatist.* Ithaca and London: Cornell UP, 1971.

Moore, Sean. "'Anglo-Irish' Hybridity: Problems in Miscegenation, Representation, and Postcolonialism in Irish Studies." *Journal of Commonwealth and Postcolonial Studies* 7.1 (Spring 2000): 75–110.

"Mr. Yeats' Attack on Irish Actors: A 'Distressed Allen's' Reply." [*Morning Leader?*] [? 1906]: Abbey Theatre Cuttings 7271. National Library, Ireland.

Murphy, Daniel J. "Lady Gregory, Co-author and Sometimes Author of the Plays of W. B. Yeats." *Modern Irish Literature: Essays in Honor of William York Tindall.* Ed. Raymond J. Porter and James D. Brophy. New York: Iona College Press and Twayne, 1972.

———. "Yeats and Lady Gregory: A Unique Dramatic Collaboration." *Modern Drama* 7 (1964): 322–28.

Murray, Alice Effie. *A History of the Commercial and Financial Relations Between England and Ireland from the Period of the Restoration.* New York: Books for Libraries Press, 1970.

Nandy, Ashis. *The Intimate Enemy. Loss and Recovery of Self Under Colonialism.* Delhi: Oxford UP, 1983.
Nelson, Claudia and Lynne Vallone, eds. *The Girl's Own: Cultural Histories of the Anglo-American Girl, 1830–1915.* Athens and London: U of Georgia P, 1994.
O'Gorman, Kathleen. "The Performativity of Utterance in *Deirdre* and *The Player Queen.*" *Yeats and Postmodernism.* Ed. Leonard Orr. Syracuse: Syracuse UP, 1991. 90–104.
O'Grady, Standish. *Finn and His Companions.* Ilustr. J. B. Yeats. London: T. Fisher Unwin, 1892.
Ó hAodha, Micheál. *Theatre in Ireland.* Totowa, NJ: Rowman and Littlefield, 1974.
O'Shea, Edward. *A Descriptive Catalog of W. B. Yeats's Library.* New York and London: Garland, 1985.
Park, Roberta J. "Biological Thought, Athletics and the Formation of a 'man of character': 1830–1900." Mangan and Walvin 7–34.
Parkin, Andrew. *The Dramatic Image of W. B. Yeats.* New York: Barnes and Noble, 1978.
Patke, Rajeev. "Postcolonial Yeats." *W. B. Yeats: Critical Assessments.* Vol. IV. Ed. David Pierce. East Sussex: Helm Information, 2000. 814–26.
Pethica, James. "'Our Kathleen': Yeats's Collaboration with Lady Gregory in the Writing of *Cathleen ni Houlihan.*" Toomey 205–22.
Pierce, David. "Yeats and Sligo." *Yeats's Worlds: Ireland, England and the Poetic Imagination.* New Haven: Yale UP, 1995. 1–2, 4–6. Rpt. in *W. B. Yeats: Critical Assessments.* Vol. IV. Ed. David Pierce. East Sussex: Helm Information, 2000. 646–52.
"The Protestant Ethic." The Max Weber Page. 11 Jan. 2003. <http://www.hewett.norfolk.sch.uk/curric/soc/WEBER/protest.htm>
Ramazani, Jahan. "Is Yeats a Postcolonial Poet?" *Raritan* 17.3 (Winter 1998): 64–89.
Renan, Ernest. *The Poetry of the Celtic Races, and other Studies.* Trans. William G. Hutchison. London: Walter Scott, Ltd., 1893.
Rev. of *Cathleen ni Houlihan, The Land of Heart's Desire,* and *The Hour-Glass,* by W. B. Yeats. Chickering Hall, Boston, MA. *Boston Herald* [?] Feb. 1905: Abbey Theatre Papers 12,145. National Library, Ireland.
Rev. of *The Land of Heart's Desire,* by W. B. Yeats. *The* [*Bradford*?] *Observer* [?] Jun. 1894: Abbey Theatre Papers 12,145. National Library, Ireland.
———. *Bookman* [?] Jun. 1894: Abbey Theatre Papers 12,145. National Library, Ireland.
———. *Daily Chronicle* 24 Apr. 1894: Abbey Theatre Papers 12,145. National Library, Ireland.
Rev. of *Where There Is Nothing,* by W. B. Yeats. London Stage Society, Royal Court Theatre, London (26 - 28 June 1904). *Daily Mail* 28 Jun. 1904: Abbey Theatre Papers 12,145. National Library, Ireland.

———. *Daily Mirror* 28 Jun. 1904: Abbey Theatre Papers 12,145. National Library, Ireland.

———. *Free Lance* 1 Jul. 1904: Abbey Theatre Papers 12,145. National Library, Ireland.

———. *Manchester Guardian* 29 Jun. 1904: Abbey Theatre Papers 12,145. National Library, Ireland.

———. *Pall Mall Gazette* 28 Jun. 1904: Abbey Theatre Papers 12,145. National Library, Ireland.

———. *The Standard.* 28 Jun. 1904. Abbey Theatre Papers 12,145. National Library, Ireland.

———. *Sunday Times* 3 Jul. 1904: Abbey Theatre Papers 12,145. National Library, Ireland.

———. *Westminster* 28 Jun. 1904: Abbey Theatre Papers 12,145. National Library, Ireland.

Rev. of *Where There Is Nothing*, by W. B. Yeats. *Manchester Guardian* 11 Jun. 1903: Abbey Theatre Papers 12,145. National Library, Ireland.

Rickaby, Joseph, SJ. "What Has the Church to Do with Science?" *The Dublin Review* 49 (October 1885): 243–53.

Rickard, John. "Studying a New Science: Yeats, Irishness, and the East." Sailer 94–112.

Rorty, Richard. *Truth and Progress. Philosophical Papers, Volume 3.* Cambridge: Cambridge UP, 1998.

Said, Edward. "Yeats and Decolonization." *Nationalism, Colonialism, and Literature.* Ed. Terry Eagleton, Fredric Jameson, and Edward Said. Intro. Seamus Deane. Minneapolis: U of Minnesota P, 1990. 69–95.

Sailer, Susan Shaw, ed. *Representing Ireland: Gender, Class, Nationality.* Gainesville: U of Florida P, 1997.

Salway, Lance. *A Peculiar Gift: Nineteenth-Century Writings on Books for Children.* Hammondsworth: Kestrel Books, 1976.

Scott, Bonnie Kime, ed. *The Gender of Modernism: A Critical Anthology.* Intro. Bonnie Kime Scott. Bloomington and Indianapolis: Indiana UP, 1990.

Secor, Cynthia. "Androgyny: An Early Appraisal." *Women's Studies* 2.2 (1974): 161–69.

Showalter, Elaine. *Sexual Anarchy: Gender and Culture at the Fin de Siècle.* New York: Viking, 1990.

Skene, Reg. *The Cuchulain Plays of W. B. Yeats: A Study.* New York: Columbia UP, 1974.

Smith, Peter Alderson. "'Grown to heaven like a tree': The Scenery of *The Countess Cathleen.*" *Eire-Ireland: A Journal of Irish Studies* 14.3 (1979): 65–82.

Smyth, Gerry. "Decolonization and Criticism: Towards a Theory of Irish Critical Discourse." Graham and Kirkland 29–49.

———. "The Past, the Post, and the Utterly Changed." Intellectual Responsibility and Irish Cultural Criticism." Briggs, Hyland, and Sammells 240–49.

"Some Women's Manners and Ways." *The Leisure Hour* Vol. 40 [1890?]: 256–91.
Spivak, Gayatri. "Can the Subaltern Speak?" *Marxism and the Interpretation of Culture.* Ed. Cary Nelson and Lawrence Grossberg. Urbana and Chicago: U of Illinois P, 1988. 271–313.
Stephens, James. *Irish Fairy Tales.* Illustr. Arthur Rackham. New York: Macmillan, 1920.
Stevenson, Mary Lou. "Lady Gregory and Yeats: Symbiotic Creativity." *Journal of the Rutgers University Libraries* 40 (1978): 63–77.
Toomey, Deirdre, ed. *Yeats and Women.* Intro. Deirdre Toomey. London: Macmillan, 1997.
Tracy, Robert. *The Unappeasable Host: Studies in Irish Identities.* Dublin: U College Dublin P, 1998.
Trebilcot, Joyce. "Two Forms of Androgynism." *"Femininity," "Masculinity," and "Androgynism": A Modern Philosophical Discussion.* Ed. Mary Vetterling-Braggin. Totowa, NJ: Littlefield, Adams and Co., 1982.
Trotter, Mary. *Ireland's National Theaters: Political Performance and the Origins of the Irish Dramatic Movement.* Syracuse: Syracuse UP, 2001.
Tyndall, John. "On the Scientific Use of the Imagination." *Half Hours with Modern Scientists.* Intro. Noah Porter, D.D., LL.D. New Haven: Charles C. Chatfield & Co., 1872. 247–88.
"Varieties." *The Leisure Hour* No. 1257 (29 Jan. 1876): 80.
"Varieties." *The Leisure Hour* No. 1266 (1 Apr. 1876): 224.
"Varieties." *The Leisure Hour* Vol. 40 [1890?]: 285.
Vicinus, Martha. "Models for Public Life: Biographies of 'Noble Women' for Girls." Nelson and Vallone 52–70.
Walsh, Michael. "Reading the Real in the Seminar on the Psychoses." *Criticism and Lacan: Essays and Dialogue on Language, Structure, and the Unconscious.* Ed. Patrick Colm Hogan and Lalita Pandit. Athens and London: U of Georgia P, 1990. 64–83.
Walsh, Oonagh. "'A Lightness of Mind': Gender and Insanity in Nineteenth-Century Ireland." Kelleher and Murphy 159–67.
Warren, Allen. "Popular Manliness: Baden-Powell, Scouting, and the Development of Manly Character." Mangan and Walvin 199–219.
Watson, George. "Celticism and the Annulment of History." Briggs, Hyland and Sammells 223–33.
Webb, Timothy. "Yeats and the English." *The Internationalism of Irish Literature and Drama.* Ed. Joseph McGinn, Anne McMaster, and Angela Welch. Savage, MA: Barnes and Noble, 1992. 232–51. Rpt. in *W. B. Yeats: Critical Assessments.* Vol. IV. Ed. David Pierce. East Sussex: Helm Information, 2000. 506–26.
Weil, Kari. *Androgyny and the Denial of Difference.* Charlottesville and London: UP of Virginia, 1992.
Weininger, Otto. *Sex and Character.* London: William Heineman, 1906.

West, Máire. "Kings, Heroes and Warriors: Aspects of Children's Literature in Ireland in the Era of Emergent Nationalism." *Bulletin of the John Rylands University Library of Manchester* 76.3 (Autumn 1994): 165–84.

Wharton, Edith. *The Age of Innocence*. New York: Collier, 1986.

Wickstrom, Gordon. "Legend Focusing on Legend in Yeats's *Deirdre*." *Educational Theatre Journal* 30 (1978): 466–74.

Wilde, Oscar. "Pen, Pencil and Poison." *The Complete Works of Oscar Wilde*. Vol. 5. Ed. Edgar Saltus. Garden City, NY: Doubleday, Page, and Co., 1923. 67–103.

———. "The Soul of Man Under Socialism." *Plays, Prose Writings and Poems*. 1930. Ed. Anthony Fothergill. London: Everyman, 1996. 15–47.

Williams, Raymond. *The Sociology of Culture*. 1981. Chicago: U of Chicago P, 1995.

Yeats, William Butler. *Autobiographies*. London: Macmillan, 1956.

———. *The Collected Letters of W. B. Yeats, Vol. I, 1865–1895*. Ed. John Kelly and Eric Domville. Oxford: Clarendon Press, 1986.

———. *The Collected Letters of W. B. Yeats, Vol. III, 1901–1904*. Ed. John Kelly and Ronald Schuchard. Oxford: Clarendon Press, 1994.

———. *The Collected Poems of W. B. Yeats*. Ed. Richard J. Finneran. New York: Collier, 1989.

———. *Deirdre*. Ts. POS 7491. National Library, Ireland.

———. *Essays and Introductions*. New York: Macmillan, 1961.

———. *Explorations*. New York: Collier, 1962.

———. "Home Rule and Religion." *The Irish Times*. 25 Jan. 1913: 9.

———. *The Land of Heart's Desire: Manuscript Materials*. Ed. Jared Curtis. Ithaca: Cornell UP, 2002.

———. Letter to George Russell. Ts. POS 15,600. National Library, Ireland.

———. *The Letters of W. B. Yeats*. Ed. Allen Wade. New York: Macmillan, 1955.

———. Notebooks. Ms. 13,574. National Library, Ireland.

———. *The Oxford Book of Modern Verse, 1892–1935*. New York: Oxford UP, 1936.

———. *Uncollected Prose I: First Reviews and Articles, 1886–1896*. Coll. and Ed. John P. Frayne. New York: Columbia UP, 1970.

———. *Uncollected Prose II: Reviews, Articles, and Other Miscellaneous Prose 1897–1939*. Coll. and Ed. John P. Frayne and Colton Johnson. New York: Columbia UP, 1976.

———. *Variorum Edition of the Plays of W. B. Yeats*. Ed. Russell K. Alspach. New York: Macmillan, 1966.

———. *A Vision*. New York: Macmillan, 1937.

———. *Where There Is Nothing* [and] *The Unicorn from the Stars*. Ed. and Intro. Katharine Worth. Washington, DC: The Catholic U of America P, 1987.

——— and Edwin Ellis, eds. *The Works of William Blake: Poetic, Symbolic, and Critical*. London: B. Quartich, 1893.

Zabriskie, Paul. "America as the 'New World.'" *Quadrant* 21.1 (1988): 57–70.

Zipes, Jack. "The Changing Shape of the Fairy Tale." *The Lion and the Unicorn: A Critical Journal of Children's Literature* 12.2 (Dec. 1988): 7–31.

Zwerdling, Alex. *Yeats and the Heroic Ideal.* New York: New York UP, 1965.

Index

Adorno, Theodor W., 144
Alcott, Louisa May, 42
Anderson, Benedict, 65
Arnold, Matthew, xx, 11, 19, 21, 22–26, 49, 64, 65, 73

Baden-Powell, Robert, 16, 66
Ballantyne, R. M., 38
    Blake, William, xvi, 23, 31, 51, 52, 77
    The Marriage of Heaven and Hell, xvi
    "The Sick Rose," 77
Brown, Terence, xvii, 34, 38, 52, 138
Browning, Robert, 37

Carlyle, Thomas, 79
Cavey, Rosa, 42
Césaire, Aimé, 19, 23, 27
Chatterji, Mohini, 73
Clarke, Edwin H., 14
Craig, Gordon, 54
Crop, Hilda, 54
Cullingford, Elizabeth Butler, 74, 113

Darwin, Charles, xx, 3, 5–6, 20–21, 30, 45–46, 47, 48
Davis, Thomas, 132, 134
Deane, Seamus, 24, 28, 40
de Vere, Aubrey, 127
Dowden, Edward, 132–33, 134
Duffy, Sir Charles Gavan, 134, 141

Eagleton, Terry, 26–27, 64, 65

Eliade, Mircea, 35, 151
Ellis, Edwin, 77
Ellis, Havelock, 14
Ervine, St. John, 152

Farr, Florence, xvii, 12
Ferguson, Sir Samuel, 127
Fleming, Deborah, 61, 74, 78
Foster, R. F., 53, 70, 134, 135, 142
Foucault, Michel, 10, 11, 12, 30, 68–69, 139
Fuchs, Georg, 53, 54
Gaelic League, 39
Gibbons, Luke, 36, 48, 59, 131, 140, 144, 155
Gilbert, Helen, 148, 154
Goethe, Johann Wolfgang von, 50
Gogarty, Oliver St. John, 147
Gonne, Maud, xvii, 12
Gramsci, Antonio, 64, 68
Gregory, Lady (Isabella) Augusta Persse, xvii, 12, 39, 40, 54, 55, 58, 60, 61, 96, 116, 127, 132
Griffin, Gerald, 44

Habermas, Jürgen, 49, 69, 130, 139
Hancock, William Neilson, 12
Harper, George Mills, 150
Haswell, Janice Tedesco, 34, 92, 93
health reform, 9–10, 15–16
Heaney, Seamus, 41
Hobsbawm, Eric, 57, 58, 59–61, 65, 139

187

Hogan, Patrick Colm, xx, 34, 100, 103, 136
Holloway, Joseph, 54, 55
Houston, Arthur, 12
Howes, Marjorie, 12, 26, 75, 91–92, 94, 95, 99, 142, 144
Hughes, Thomas, 67
　Tom Brown's School Days, 39, 40, 66–68
Huxley, Thomas, xx, 3,5,6–7,10, 21, 43, 45, 105
　Address on Behalf of the National Association for the Promotion of Technical Education, 10
　Controverted Question, 6
　Joseph Priestley, 6, 7
　A Liberal Education; and Where to Find It, 6
　On Some Fixed Points of British Ethnology, 22
　On the Advisableness of Improving Natural Knowledge, 6
　On the Study of Biology, 6
Hyde, Douglas, 58, 61

Ibsen, Henrik, 57
Innes, C. L., 142

Joyce, P. W., 127
Joyce, R. D., 127
Jung, Carl, 35, 151

Kershentsev, Platon, 53
Kiberd, Declan, 30–31, 36, 48, 50, 131, 133
Kickham, Charles J., 44
Kingsley, Charles, 9, 12, 16, 66
Kingston, W. H. G., 38
Kipling, Rudyard, 38, 67
Kirkland, Richard, 131, 143

Lacan, Jacques, 87–88
Leerssen, Joep, 61, 103
Leisure Hour, 8, 17, 46–47, 85
Lewes, George H., 14
Lloyd, David, 40
Locke, John, 3

Marinetti, Filippo Tommaso, 53
Martyn, Edward, xvii, 58

Marx, Karl, 35, 75, 79, 81
　Capital, 81
　Communist Manifesto, 75
Maudsley, Henry, 14
Memmi, Albert, 19, 23, 26, 27, 64, 149
Meyerhold, Vsevolod, 53
Mill, John Stuart, 13, 25, 30
Moore, George, 58

Nandy, Ashis, 18, 19, 108
Nast, Thomas, 65
national school, Irish, 8–9
New Irish Library, 134–35, 141
New Woman, 12, 17

O'Grady, Standish James, 39, 40–42, 96
O'Leary, John, xvii, 69

Pearse, Patrick, 39, 40
Purohit, Shri, 73

Reid, Captain Mayne, 38
Reinhardt, Max, 54
Renan, Ernest, xx, 11, 22, 24, 25, 26, 48, 73
Rhys, Ernest, 30
Robinson, Lennox, 152
Rolleston, T. W., 127, 134
Rorty, Richard, 130, 142, 143
Rossetti, Dante Gabriel, 37
Royal Society, 13, 25
Russell, George (AE), 15, 58, 94, 127

Said, Edward, 19, 130, 155
Sartre, Jean-Paul, 27, 113
Shakespear, Olivia, xvii
Sharp, William, 127
Shaw, George, Bernard, 57
Shelley, Percy Bysshe, 37
Showalter, Elaine, 120, 122, 124
Spencer, Herbert, 14
Stephens, James, 40–42
Swinburne, Algernon Charles, 37
Symons, Arthur, xvii, 38
Synge, John Millington, 53, 54, 58, 61, 99
　The Playboy of the Western World, 53, 54, 59, 61, 99, 144

Tagore, Rabindranath, 73

Index

Tennyson, Alfred, Lord, 37
Tompkins, Joanne, 148, 154
Trench, Herbert, 127
Trinity College (Dublin), 133–34, 135, 136
Tyndall, John, 3, 5, 7

Unity of Being, 4, 32–34, 92, 97, 131, 137
Unwin, T. Fisher, 134

Weininger, Otto, 25
Wharton, Edith, 66, 68
Wilde, Oscar, 11, 29, 50, 57, 120, 129, 141, 147
Williams, Raymond, 57, 66, 68
Wordsworth, William, 5

Yeats, George Hyde-Lees, 32
Yeats, John Butler, xvii, 30, 38
Yeats, William Butler (works)
   "Apologia Addressed to Ireland in the Coming Days," 69
   At the Hawk's Well, 54
   Autobiographies, xvii, 3, 8, 37, 38
   "The Autumn of the Body," 49
   "Bardic Ireland," 139
   Cathleen ni Houlihan, xx, 53, 58, 69, 74–76, 87, 88, 91, 100, 129, 144, 146, 147, 154
   "The Celtic Element in Literature," 39, 73, 94–95, 136
   "Certain Noble Plays of Japan," 32
   "The Controversy over *The Playboy of the Western World*," 150
   The Countess Cathleen, xviii, xx, 58, 62, 69–74, 78, 84, 85, 86, 91, 100, 129, 132, 144
   Crossways, 142
   Deirdre, xx, 32, 53, 55, 56, 89, 92, 93, 94, 96, 97, 119–28, 154
   "Dublin Scholasticism and Trinity College," 133
   "Ego Dominus Tuus," 49
   Fairy and Folk Tales of Ireland, 71
   The Hour-Glass, 147
   "If I Were Four and Twenty," 34
   John Sherman, 132
   The King's Threshold, xx, 32, 54, 56, 89, 92, 93, 94, 96, 97, 100–10, 112, 119, 120, 139, 154
   The Land of Heart's Desire, xx, 53, 56, 58, 62, 69, 76–89, 91, 100, 129, 144, 146, 147, 149
   "The Literary Movement in Ireland," 37
   "The Man and the Echo," 74
   On Baile's Strand, xx, 32, 56, 89, 92, 93, 94, 96, 97, 106, 110–19, 121, 149, 154
   Oxford Book of Modern Verse, 38
   Per Amica Silentia Lunae, 5, 49, 100
   "Plans and Methods," 70
   The Player Queen, 54
   Plays for Dancers, xviii
   The Pot of Broth, 144, 146
   preface to *Cuchulain of Muirthemne*, 39, 96
   Purgatory, 69
   The Rose, 142
   "The Second Coming," 36
   The Shadowy Waters, 144
   "The Theatre, the Pulpit, and the Newspapers," 5
   "To Ireland in the Coming Times," 69–70
   "The Wanderings of Oisin," 132
   Where There Is Nothing, xx, 32, 58, 69, 144, 147, 149–54
   "William Blake and the Imagination," 23
   The Words ipon the Window-Pane, 5, 69
   A Vision, xv, xvii, xviii, 4, 32
The Yellow Book of Lecan, 96, 116
Yonge, Charlotte, 42

DATE DUE

DEC 29 2003		
DEC 01 2003		

GAYLORD — PRINTED IN U.S.A.

PR 5908 .D7 S84 2003

Suess, Barbara Ann.

Progress and identity in the plays of W.B. Yeats, 1892-